Yitzhak Rabin

To Joe and Connie,

In hope of peace,

David Horovitz

YITZHAK RABIN

SOLDIER OF PEACE

The Jerusalem Report Staff

EDITED BY DAVID HOROVITZ

PETER HALBAN
LONDON

FIRST PUBLISHED IN GREAT BRITAIN BY
PETER HALBAN PUBLISHERS LTD
42 South Molton Street
London W1Y 1HB
1996

British Library Cataloguing in Publication Data

A catalogue record for this book is available from the British Library.

ISBN 1 870015 62 2

All illustrations courtesy of the Israel Government Press Office
except for the 'Memorial Poster of Yitzhak Rabin'
(courtesy of Esteban Alterman, *The Jerusalem Report*)

Typeset by Computape (Pickering) Ltd, North Yorkshire
Printed in Great Britain by
WBC Print, Bridgend

Contents

Acknowledgements

THIS BIOGRAPHY IS the product of a team effort by the writers and editors of *The Jerusalem Report* newsmagazine, Israel's leading English-language publication. The prologue was written in the immediate, shocked aftermath of Yitzhak Rabin's assassination, by The Report's editor-in-chief Hirsh Goodman, whose insights also enhance the rest of the book. The main writing was shared by Calev Ben-David, Gershom Gorenberg, David B. Green, Peter Hirschberg, Avi Hoffmann, Isabel Kershner, Margo Lipschitz Sugarman, Tom Sawicki, Stuart Schoffman, Hanan Sher, Eric Silver, Leslie Susser and myself. Ronnie Hope, along with Gershom Gorenberg, oversaw the copy-editing and enriched the content. Sharon Ashley ensured overall continuity. Hilary Cemel slaved through the page proofs. Esteban Alterman took some of the photographs and arranged for the supply of the rest. Crucial research was done by Karen Finklestone, Freda Covitz, Daniel Grynberg, Gregory Lewis, Yuval Lion and Janine Zacharia. Others who provided much appreciated contributions include Michael Elkins, Yossi Klein Halevi, Ze'ev Schiff, Natan Sharansky and Ehud Ya'ari. And Teodor Welt kept the computers alive.

For giving so generously of their time and knowledge, the writers would also like to thank Yehuda Avner, Mordechai Bar-On, Avi Becker, Oded Ben-Ami, Gad Ben-Ari, Ohad Ben-Efrat, Yehuda Ben-Meir, Paul Berger, Lenny Davis, Uri Dromi, Rafi Edri, Amos Eiran, Yuval Elitzur, Leonard Fein, Max Fisher, Ilan Flatto, Jacob Frenkel, Jean Frydman, Yeshayahu Gavish, Kalman Gayer, Mordechai Gazit, Micha Goldman, Dov Goldstein, Eitan Haber, Elyakim Haetzni, Yisrael Harel, Micha Harish, Amir Hayek, Ruhama Hermon, Avital Inbar, Avi Katzman, Niva Lanir, Dov Lautman, Orna Lebel, Moshe Levi, Ya'acov Levy, Amram Mitzna, Abie Moses, Alfred Moses, Uzi Narkiss, Yossi Nitzani, Sari Nusseibeh, Dan Pattir, Abe Pollin, Dan Propper, Rachel Rabin, Aviezer Ravitzky, Seymour Reich, Louis Schoffman, Nachman Shai, Neal

Sher, Shimon Sheves, Avraham Shochat, Dan Shomron, Joseph Sisco, Ehud Sprinzak, Israel Tal, Shabtai Teveth, Harry Wall, Raphy Weiner, Haim Yisraeli and other sources who prefer to remain anonymous. Israel's daily Hebrew newspapers were invaluable, and the staff at the *Ma'ariv* archives provided essential help. Particular reference was also made to Rabin's own memoirs (Weidenfeld and Nicolson, 1979) and to Robert Slater's *Rabin of Israel: Warrior for Peace* (Robson Books, 1977 and 1996).

And special thanks, of course, to Deborah Harris and Beth Elon, who suggested we do the book in the first place.

DAVID HOROVITZ
Jerusalem
January 1996

Prologue

5 November 1995, Jerusalem

THE USUALLY TRAFFIC-CLOGGED street beneath my office window is eerily silent for rush hour, the cafés and restaurants virtually empty. Yitzhak Rabin lies in state and Israel files by the coffin, all of Israel; an endless, silent, unbelieving line.

It's Sunday morning. Yesterday at this time, Yitzhak Rabin was still alive. Tomorrow at noon, together with David Horovitz, our managing editor, I was to interview the Prime Minister for the next cover story of *The Jerusalem Report*. Rabin's relationship with diaspora Jewry had been acrimonious of late. We, and he, thought it important the record be set straight before he addressed the Council of Jewish Federations' General Assembly in Boston later in November.

Instead, at noon tomorrow, Rabin's funeral entourage will leave for Mount Herzl, his message, like so much else, to be taken to the grave with him.

I knew Yitzhak Rabin for 28 years, from 1967 when I was a young paratrooper in the Six Day War, assigned as a bodyguard to the then-Chief of Staff as he toured the still smouldering battlefields of Sinai. I had been in the country for just over two years and the man – his intense inner quiet; rugged face; sabra Hebrew; slow, studious voice that resonated with authority and leadership – became my instant hero. He was Israel, that new generation of Jew, all that I aspired to be. And thus he remained, remains and will remain forever.

I cannot claim friendship with Yitzhak Rabin. He had few friends. But I knew the man as I knew few others. As it was my lot to ostensibly protect him as he toured Sinai, it later became my job to cover him as a journalist. Our first professional meeting was in Washington while he was ambassador there. Already he was at odds with the Jews. He felt they were overly intrusive in Israel's international affairs, that the Jewish lobby mistakenly thought it was, if not the Israeli government, at least the Israeli foreign ministry. He resented being lectured on security issues by people who had never worn uniforms, and no matter how hard he tried, he never felt comfortable at either diplomatic receptions or Jewish functions, particularly fundraisers – traits that were to remain with him to his final days.

Rabin was an iconoclast, a soldier who became a statesman but never shed his uniform. His diplomatic thinking was strategic, his political manoeuvring tactical. He had the vision to see beyond the obvious, and the lack of tact to say so. He was totally pragmatic, but understood that sometimes deals, like Oslo, are spun by dreamers who, once their job is done, have to be brought down to earth. He believed deeply that peace, not conquest, was an extension of victory, but never hesitated to use force if it was necessary for Israel's interests. He had no time for those who could not understand him, nor those who disagreed with his thinking. Though impatient with people he considered fools or opportunists – and they were many – and harsh to the point of contemptuous rudeness with those who opposed him, he seldom raised his voice or lost his temper. He held politicians and politics in disdain, considering them a means toward an end, just as he saw weapons as a means toward an end, using them against his will to achieve his will.

When Yitzhak Rabin spoke, he spoke the thoughts of many. Painfully inept at small talk, he would often lose a sense of time when speaking in public or in private on subjects he had on his mind. In interviews he was always the same, always counting off points on his fingers as he systematically worked through his arguments. Often he would say "and finally" about six or seven times, or say that he wanted to make three points and go on to make 30. His thoughts were always interlinked, part of a mosaic that usually only he could see with clarity; always analytical.

But while he had an uncanny ability to see weaknesses in the positions of others, he had a problem recognising the flaws in his own thinking and did not like being told about them. I was with him in Washington on the morning the Intifada broke out. I remember with clarity his disdain as reports of rioting and unrest throughout the occupied territories came in, and his increasing impatience with aides who were telling him Israel had a major problem on its hands, that this was not just another one-time splutter of protest, but the beginnings of a national struggle that could consume what others called Greater Israel from within.

I remember the same lack of patience several years earlier, when he decided to free hundreds of Palestinian prisoners, many of them terrorists, in return for the release of Israeli servicemen captured during the Lebanon war, and the step came up for discussion in private before it was publicly announced. He was immovable, unprepared to hear. It was the same when he decided to expel over 400 Islamic fundamentalist activists to Lebanon in an act of fury after a policeman was kidnapped and murdered in Lod in December 1992. His security advisers predicted exactly what would happen if he went ahead; he refused to listen. They were right. He was wrong.

But Rabin was not wrong often, and his mistakes are paltry when compared to his achievements, something even his most vociferous enemies reluctantly concede. He was accused of having collapsed from nervous tension on the eve of the Six Day War. But he masterminded and won that war. There are those who remember that he had to resign "in shame" in 1977 after he and his wife, Leah, were found to have had an illegal US bank account. But the Israel whose leadership he left in 1977 compared to that he inherited in 1974, after the catastrophe of the Yom Kippur War, was a different country, its armed forces judged by the brilliance of the Entebbe rescue, not the débâcle that saw Israel attacked on two fronts simultaneously by enemies it hardly judged worthy of a fight.

When he returned as Defence Minister in 1984, he played a major role in pulling Israeli troops out of Lebanon, a quagmire where previous government indecision had led to more men being killed after the war had ended than during the war itself.

While banished to the opposition benches for the first two years of this decade, he used his tiny Knesset office to lead the fight within his party to bring primaries into Israeli politics. At one stroke, he rejuvenated democracy in the country while setting the stage for his own political comeback with the legitimacy of the people behind him, not the sanction of kingmakers in the smoke-filled rooms he despised.

And at last came these three-and-a-half years during which he delivered peace with Jordan and a conciliation package with the Palestinians, during which the infrastructure of Israel leaped into the twentieth century and its economy grew at a pace even Rabin did not expect; during which hundreds of thousands of Jews from the former Soviet Union were brought to a safe haven, fed, housed and, but for a small proportion, integrated as best as can be expected into Israeli society.

Had he been allowed to run in the next election, he would have won hands down. He was a lion, slaughtered like a sheep because, despite all the evidence to the contrary, he refused to believe that a Jew would actually kill another Jew, no matter how deep the gulf of disagreement. Again, he was wrong. This time, however, fatally so.

Yitzhak Rabin was the right man for Israel at the right time. The Intifada had died out; the Soviet Union, supporter of Israel's most implacable enemies, had disappeared; Iraq was removed as a threat as a result of the Gulf War. As a general he knew that his forces had won, but unlike other leaders in Israel's not-too-distant past, he knew that victory was hollow unless it was translated into a better future for the country and surrounding region through the nego- tiation of peace, achieved not through weakness, but through strength.

He was a man who thought in terms of goals and knew that peace could not be reached overnight, that to achieve it he would first have to convince his people that peace was possible and, only after that, make it happen. For this reason he dictated that the Oslo process be phased, the implementation of each stage dependent on the successful implementation of the stage before. It was also the reason that he warned, from the outset, that timetables were not holy or carved in stone. He understood that there would be those, particularly in the Palestinian camp, who would resort to outrages and terror to try to derail the process, and he knew he had to fight them. And he did.

But what he did not know, or would not believe, was that terror and murder were not the exclusive domain of the Palestinians, and that the bumper stickers calling him a traitor and a murderer, which he dismissed with a wave of his hand, were not just words but marching orders for those who worship land more than they worship life.

Yitzhak Rabin was a giant of a man. A painfully shy and introverted giant who pretended that the hurtful slogans and vitriol heaped on him by right-wing demonstrators did not matter to him. They did. He claimed not to care whether he was loved by the people. He did. He once explained that as a general one has to send people into battle. In peace, he added, as in war, those you lead will not always fully understand what they are being asked to do. Peace, like war, will have its casualties, and no transition is achieved without cost. The price of unpopularity is something generals know they are going to have to bear, just as statesmen know that not all they do will be popular because not all the facts can be shared. But there is one more thing that Rabin knew. That the majority, the vast majority, even those who doubted what he was doing, trusted him. And it was on the basis of that trust that he moved forward to change this region forever.

I will miss Yitzhak Rabin, the calm, calculated, proud voice of Israel, now lying in state as over a million people, one out of five Israelis, file past his bier. I will miss his gruffness and directness, his leadership and vision. I will miss a leader with a steady hand at the helm, and the character and self-confidence to know that he was navigating this country to safe shores.

How tragic that it took Yitzhak Rabin's death for the love this people felt for him to surface, for the absolute majority who supported his policies to step forward. And how ironic, that it took this act of a Jew killing a Jew to make Rabin's last message, that this country cannot afford fratricide, finally ring true.

With bowed head I stand in silence, in tribute to a man like no other I have met: a son of Israel and the father of its future.

HIRSH GOODMAN

1

From Triumph to Tragedy

YITZHAK RABIN NEVER really felt enthusiastic about that final, fateful rally – the last night of triumph, which turned to disaster. When the idea of a pro-peace demonstration was first proposed in early October 1995, his initial response was pessimistic – a reflection of his sense of isolation, engendered by the increasingly vitriolic protests organised by the Israeli right wing. To his long-term friend and confidante, the journalist Niva Lanir, he confided his deepest fear: "What if people don't come?" To the organisers of the rally, former Tel Aviv mayor Shlomo (Chich) Lahat and Jean Frydman, a wealthy French industrialist and close friend of Shimon Peres, he gave a more diplomatic objection. "He said the 4th of November wasn't convenient," Frydman recalls. "He had some appointments, a dinner that he didn't want to postpone."

What changed Rabin's mind was an apparently minor incident on 10 October. As he strolled through the crowds at a day-long fair for Israelis from English-speaking countries at the Wingate sports institute, just outside the coastal town of Netanyah, a white-shirted, bearded figure darted out at him. Allegedly bent on physically attacking the Prime Minister, the man got past all but the last bodyguard before he was blocked and hustled away. He turned out to be Natan Ophir, rabbi of the Hebrew University and a resident of the West Bank settlement of Ma'aleh Adumim. Soon afterwards, when Rabin rose to address the 15,000 people present, a chorus of boos and jeers forced him back from the microphone. The heckling continued for more than 10 minutes; even when the Prime Minister finally began his speech, it was frequently interrupted. "You should be ashamed of yourselves," he shouted, red-faced and badly rattled. "Rabin, resign," the hecklers responded.

The disturbance at Wingate was no isolated incident, no one-time explosion of violent opposition to his government's peace accords with the Palestinians. Demonstrations, some of them riotous, had been going on for more than two years, but over the previous few months protests had taken a particularly menacing turn. Crude posters showing Rabin in Nazi uniform had been distributed at one rally; placards showing his features overlaid with the cross-hairs of a rifle sight were now commonly brandished – an unmistakable incitement to murder; a West Bank settler had tried to run left-wing Environment Minister Yossi Sarid's car off the main Jerusalem–Tel Aviv highway; Police Minister Moshe Shahal and the army's Chief of Staff Amnon Lipkin-Shahak had both been narrowly extricated from baying mobs at the scene of a Palestinian bus bombing; and a crowd of angry protesters had damaged Housing Minister Binyamin Ben-Eliezer's car, and tried to attack the minister himself, on 5 October, the night that the Knesset narrowly approved the Oslo II accord, expanding Palestinian self-rule in the West Bank.

Previously, Rabin had argued that right-wing demonstrations did more harm than good to the opposition cause, and that it would be foolish for supporters of the government's policies to be drawn into a series of tit-for-tat protests. He tended to dismiss most expressions of incitement as being "not serious". Take the case of Gil Sharon, for instance. On 31 October 1994, Social Affairs Minister Ora Namir walked into an Israeli cabinet meeting carrying a car bumper sticker. "Rabin must be killed" it read. Someone had given it to her during a visit to the town of Or Akiva. The Chief of Police, sitting in on the cabinet session, offered to trace the sticker's origins. Within hours, Sharon, an extreme right-wing activist and aspiring local politician, had been arrested. Acknowledging authorship, he was sentenced to three months' community service and given a small fine. In the summer of 1995, Rabin himself visited Or Akiva. Gil Sharon came up to him, identified himself, and offered an apology. Rabin, unhesitatingly, shook hands. "Forgive you?" the Prime Minister said with a smile. "It's already in the past. So many Arabs have tried and failed to kill me that what you did is nothing."

After Wingate, however, Rabin gave his tentative approval to the idea of a massive gathering in Tel Aviv. Originally conceived as a pro-peace rally, its theme was expanded to pro-peace and anti-violence. And it was the anti-violence message that won over Rabin. The need to moderate the hysterical tone of political debate in Israel, he decided, would be the centre-piece of his speech for that evening.

As the fateful date drew nearer, the organisers themselves caught the whiff of Rabin's apprehension: that the event would be a flop, that attracting the 50,000 people needed to fill the Kings of Israel Square would be beyond them. Publicity was hard to generate. Jean Frydman believes that state television and radio received orders from on-high not to be seen to be promoting a pro-government event. "And we didn't get much access to the commercial Channel Two either," he says. "The billboards were poor. Only the newspapers were providing coverage."

But still, they thought, they had one trump card: Barbra Streisand. Early in the planning stages, Moshe Theumim, a leading light in Israeli advertising, who was serving as a public relations consultant to the organisers, advised them that a spectacular star like Streisand could be the key to their success. Get Barbra, he said, and you'll fill the Square. Without her, you're in trouble. So Rabin, who travelled to New York in late October for the UN's 50th anniversary celebrations, was given the task of contacting the singer. Not surprisingly, though, amid the hectic bustle of the four-day trip, during which Rabin held up to 16 separate meetings a day with Heads of State and other international dignitaries, the call to Streisand was forgotten. So barely 10 days before the rally, Peres was asked to make the contact. Two days later, he reported back to Lahat and Frydman: Barbra can't come.

Together with some of the reserve army generals who had participated in previous, far smaller, pro-government rallies, Lahat and Frydman held a crisis meeting at Lahat's home in the Tel Aviv suburb of Afekah. There was even talk of cancelling the rally altogether. "I asked, 'Are you mad?',," Frydman remembers. "I said, 'Do you think that the only person who can save the peace is Barbra Streisand? That without Barbra Streisand we are lost? That 10 days before a demonstration the whole country knows about, we should cancel because we are afraid, because Barbra Streisand is not coming?'" Disappointed, but still determined, the organisers worked on.

Streisand wasn't the only artist to turn them down. Several Israeli performers, apparently concerned that an appearance might damage their popularity among right-wing album-buyers, also cried off. But, somehow, in the last few days, the crisis mood began to lift. Much of the change stemmed directly from Rabin, who seemed to have discovered a new sense of inner calm, and whose confidence in the viability of the Palestinian autonomy process had evidently reached new heights. Final preparations were proceeding smoothly for the military withdrawal from Jenin, the northernmost Palestinian city in the West Bank and the first to be handed over to the Palestinians under the Oslo II accord. Work on the network of bypass roads designed to enable settlers to reach their homes without entering Palestinian controlled territory was continuing apace. And, most crucially to his own and the national mood, Islamic extremist suicide bombers had not struck inside Israel for more than two months.

On Sunday, 29 October, Rabin was warmly received at the Middle East economic summit in Amman – a conference attended by delegates from all over the Arab world, including the Gulf states, that underlined Israel's blossoming relations with formerly hostile near-neighbours. The following Tuesday, he received a tumultuous welcome when he arrived at Tel Aviv's Mann Auditorium for the Israeli "Oscars" ceremony. The audience gave him a standing ovation, and Rabin himself had to get up, smile that trademark, half-embarrassed smile, and motion them down again. He made a speech later in the evening, apologising that he would have to leave early. "Some American is waiting for me," he said lightly – referring to Dennis Ross, the US peace talks co-ordinator, who had flown in that day to discuss ways of restarting negotiations with Syria.

On 1 November, grilled on Israel Television's flagship "Moked" interview programme by a panel of three top journalists, Rabin was generally relaxed and upbeat, highlighting Israel's improved international image, proudly assessing the successes of the peace process, and genially playing down suggestions that he might be too old to contemplate another term in office. More sombrely, though, he also bitterly castigated Likud opposition leader Benjamin (Bibi) Netanyahu for failing to take a stand against right-wing extremism, and said he would not accept an offer from Netanyahu to meet and discuss the escalating tensions on the streets because he thought Netanyahu was being "hypocritical". He said, sadly, that he did anticipate more "unruly instigation, verbal violence, violence in the street". He repeated this concern in a French magazine interview that week. But for all the threats of political violence, he insisted, "I don't believe a Jew will kill a Jew."

On 26 October, Fathi Shkaki, the founder and head of the fanatical Islamic Jihad Palestinian terror group, had been assassinated outside a hotel in Malta by two men who subsequently disappeared. Israel did not even bother to deny responsibility for the killing; it merely registered the hysterical threats of revenge from Shkaki's loyalists in the Gaza Strip, and braced itself for the worst. But attempts on Thursday, 2 November, to blow up two school buses between settlements in the Gaza Strip failed, and the only fatalities were the two suicide bombers themselves. As Israel's military analysts predicted soberly in the next day's newspapers, the bombers were bound to try and strike again. But at least their initial revenge effort had been frustrated. And so, despite the presence outside his apartment building of several dozen right-wing demonstrators, chanting "Rabin is a traitor," and "Rabin, resign," it was an upbeat, cheerful Prime Minister who said his weekend farewells that Friday afternoon to Yehezkel Sharabi, his veteran driver.

Most Friday nights, he and Leah had dinner with their daughter, Dalia Pelossof, and her family. But this Friday, it was just the two of them, relaxing in their penthouse apartment together – watching television and leafing through the Friday newspapers and supplements. Next day, the final day, he and Leah drove to the Ramat Aviv Country Club for their regular Saturday morning tennis doubles, Rabin partnering Zionah Leshem, a Tel Aviv architect, against Leah and Raphy Weiner, general manager of Jerusalem's Sheraton Plaza Hotel. Rabin was in good cheer, determined to play although he was suffering from tennis elbow. At the end of the match, he reminded Weiner to bring his racket to Boston the following week, where they were both due to attend the annual General Assembly of the Council of Jewish Federations.

Back at home after the game, Rabin took a phone call from Niva Lanir. "What if they don't come tonight?" he wondered again, but his tone was lighter now than the last time he'd asked her. "I said, 'Yitzhak, the Square will be full,'" Lanir remembers. "I told him, 'You take care of the peace, we'll take care of the people. Everyone I know is going.'" Anyway, she reassured him cheerfully, if the worse comes to the worst, and the people stay away in droves, "'We'll announce that the Prime Minister has a sore throat, and can't speak.'"

At lunchtime, the Rabins drove to opulent Herzliyah Pituah, celebrating the 50th birthday of a friend, Ronnie Katzin, with a meal on the lawn. The weight-conscious Rabin ate little, remarking that "I've had to work hard to lose five kilos. And I want to stay this way." Also there was Dr Ephraim Sneh, who had headed the Israeli army's governing Civil Administration in the West Bank in the mid-1980s, when Rabin was Defence Minister, and who was now the Minister of Health. "Tonight I'll speak mainly about the need to

5

uproot violence," the Prime Minister told him, launching into another mini-diatribe against Netanyahu. How dare the Likud leader try to distance himself from the fanatics screaming vicious anti-Rabin slogans at right-wing demonstrations, Rabin fumed. "Those people who stand outside my house, and shout to Leah, 'Next year we'll string you up,' they are Likud people. Likud activists."

Rabin returned to the theme in another conversation, with Herzliyah's Mayor Eli Landau, an old rival-cum-friend who was planning to run for a Likud Knesset seat in the next elections. "This verbal violence is also focused on Leah," he told Landau. "I'm amazed by the intensity of the hatred." Still, he was perky enough, at the end of their chat, to whisper into the Likud candidate's ear, "We're going to beat you."

At about 2.30 p.m., the Rabins went home for a Saturday afternoon siesta. As darkness fell, Haim Ramon, the leader of Israel's Histadrut labour federation and a firm political ally, paid a call. Rabin, in his slippers, was clearly feeling at ease with the world, discussing everything from family matters to Ramon's work at the Histadrut, his possible future return to the cabinet and the prospects for peace with Syria. Before they knew it, the clock had ticked past 7.30 p.m. Time to be making a move.

Rabin's relief driver, Menahem Damti, was waiting outside. As they drove to the rally, a warning came through from the security services: there was a very real threat, it ran, that Islamic Jihad activists might try to use the occasion to stage a suicide bombing or other attack – a revenge strike for the killing of their leader.

In Herzliyah, a short drive from where Rabin had nibbled at his lunch, but in a markedly less affluent neighbourhood, Yigal Amir, a 25-year-old law student at Tel Aviv's Bar-Ilan University, had also enjoyed a relaxing Sabbath. Weekends for Amir were often hectic affairs, as he grappled with the organisational tangles of transporting dozens – sometimes hundreds – of fellow university students to one or other West Bank settlement, there to spend an authentic Jewish Shabbat on the authentic Jewish soil that the iniquitous Rabin was now bent on handing over to Yasser Arafat. The settler Sabbaths were hard work for Amir and his small band of fellow activists. But it was worth it; simply by exposing so many people to the pioneering spirit of the dedicated settlers of historic Hebron in the West Bank, or isolated little Netzarim in the Gaza Strip, he felt he was winning over hearts and minds, helping to bolster opposition to Rabin's policies.

But Amir had given himself this weekend off. He had other plans. A more dramatic scenario for bringing a halt to the ungodly Rabin–Peres land handover. In the morning, he walked to the local Yemenite synagogue, Tiferet Tse'irim, with his father, Shlomo, and brother Hagai, hearing the Torah reading from *Lekh Lekhah* – the weekly portion preceding the episode in which God orders his servant Abraham to prove his faith by sacrificing his beloved son Isaac – Yitzhak – but then spares him. Amir ate a midday meal with the family, and returned to synagogue for evening prayers. After darkness had fallen, at about 8.30 p.m., he closed the white-panelled front door of 56 Borochov Street, walked the 10 minutes to the local bus station, and boarded Egged bus No. 274 for central Tel Aviv.

Some people say they saw him with some of his friends, leading a small but raucous right-wing counter-demonstration to the main rally in a side street just off the Kings of Israel Square. Others say they recall him trying to get on to the main stage at the rally, before Rabin had arrived, and being pushed back by the security guards. But whatever he may have done on first arriving at the Square, Amir soon found his way to a dimly lit parking area, accessed by a staircase at the back left of the stage, where Rabin's car was waiting to collect him and Leah when the rally ended.

Amir shouldn't have been allowed in there, of course. But he looked so harmless. Small, slight and curly-haired. In a nondescript blue shirt and beige trousers. Obviously a Jew, not an Arab. And he had even put his black skullcap into his pocket, just to be sure no one would take him for a settler or right-wing sympathiser and challenge him. At one point, Amir leaned casually on a black van, property of Israel Television; he perched on a concrete planter; he even exchanged small talk with some of the young policemen who had been hurriedly dispatched by their superiors to bolster security in the parking area. "He was there when I got there," one policeman, Motti Serchi, said later. "They placed me next to the stairs, by the public phones, to block the crowds coming through." When the evening's star musical performer, the shaggy-haired teen idol Aviv Geffen, arrived in his car, Amir remarked disparagingly to the young policeman, "How could they bring someone like that here?" "You're right," responded Serchi.

On the dais above them, all Rabin's fears were being proved groundless. He had arrived at about 8 o'clock, and Frydman immediately escorted him to the front of the stage. When he looked out at the sheer mass of people – an estimated 250,000 or more –

7

filling the Square and overflowing into the side streets as far as the eye could see, Frydman says he heard Rabin catch his breath in awe. He turned to Frydman: "So you were right," he said. And then, the rally organiser continues, "The people saw him and started shouting, 'Rabin, Rabin, Rabin.' He was in heaven. He'd never seen a crowd like it." Later on, Rabin caught Niva Lanir's eye. "He saw me and gave me the thumbs up. It really took a burden from him."

And then Rabin spoke. A fierce, emotional address before a crowd that at last he knew endorsed his policies and lovingly appreciated his leadership. Having endured so many months of vitriol, seen his portrait torched at right-wing demonstrations, heard the poisonous chants of "Rabin is a murderer," here his general's bark boomed out across hundreds of thousands of upturned, supportive faces. As he had promised, he spoke of the pressing need to confront the escalating undercurrent of violence. But he said much more as well, issuing a ringing declaration of his commitment to the peace process, his passionate conviction that it represented the only way to guarantee Israel's security into the future. But first of all he said thank you. Thank you to the people whose own commitment he had doubted, and whose presence now gave him such obvious reassurance.

"Permit me to say that I, too, am moved," he began. "I want to thank each one of you who has come here to make a stand against violence and for peace.

"I was a soldier for 27 years," he continued. "I fought as long as there was no prospect for peace. I believe that now there is a chance for peace. A great chance. Which must be seized." Left hand on the podium, right hand scything the warm Tel Aviv air for emphasis, he moved on to his theme. "Violence is undermining the foundations of Israeli democracy," he boomed. "It must be rejected and condemned, and it must be contained. It is not the way of the State of Israel. Democracy is our way. There may be differences, but they will be resolved in democratic elections as they were in 1992, when we were given a mandate to do what we are doing and what we will continue to do."

He spoke of his delight at seeing diplomatic envoys from Egypt, Jordan and Morocco in the front seats before him – "representatives here of countries with which we live in peace." He praised the PLO – "a partner in peace among the Palestinians ... which was an enemy and has now forsaken terrorism". And he stressed the likely obstacles on the road ahead. "There is no painless way forward for

Israel," he said, "but the way of peace is preferable to the way of war. And I am speaking as a military man, as a Minister of Defence, who sees the pain of the families of the soldiers of the Israel Defence Forces. It is for their sake, for the sake of our children and grand-children, that I want this government to exhaust every tiny possibi-lity to move ahead and reach a comprehensive peace." This rally, he concluded, "must send a message to the Israeli public, to the Jews of the world, to the multitudes in the Arab lands, and to the world at large: that the nation of Israel wants peace, supports peace. And for this, I thank you."

The response was extraordinary – no screaming, no pushing, just a vast rolling wave of clapping and cheering, applause that seemed to unite Rabin with his audience, an almost tangible bonding between the Prime Minister and his electorate. So moved, so euphoric was Rabin, that he, the crusty ex-general never given to public displays of emotion, embraced the Foreign Minister, Shimon Peres, right up there on stage, in full view of the cheering Square. It was the sealing of a partnership that in the joint pursuit of peace had come to transcend long years of rivalry, of mutual contempt. When a reporter expressed amazement at the unprecedented sight, Rabin professed indifference. "We've done it before," he said. But they hadn't. Not like this.

And now Rabin did something scarcely less extraordinary. Vocal-ist Miri Aloni had taken centre stage to sing "Song for Peace", a song denounced as defeatist when it first appeared in the late 1960s but which has since become an anthem of the peace movement. Affecting reluctance, Rabin nevertheless accepted a lyric sheet from Frydman and consented to stand to the singer's left, with Peres at her right, and join in. Rabin had no illusions about his singing ability, and he seemed to will the microphone away whenever Aloni pushed it under his nose. But he persevered, struggling valiantly to follow the words:

> Let the sun rise, and give the morning light
> The purest prayer will not bring back
> He whose candle was snuffed out . . .
> So sing only a song for peace
> Do not whisper a prayer
> Better sing a song for peace
> With a great shout.

When the song was over, Rabin, in his precise, methodical way, carefully folded the lyric sheet into four, and slipped it into his inside jacket pocket. Now Aviv Geffen came out to perform "To Cry for You", a song he dedicated "to all those people who won't be fortunate enough to see peace dawn". "I'm going to cry for you," ran the lyric. "Be strong up there." Aloni, listening at the side, turned to Leah Rabin and said, "Leah, watch over him." The Prime Minister's wife smiled and said, "I'm doing the best I can." When the last aching notes had faded away Geffen, who had once referred in a song to Rabin as a drunkard, and who took public delight in having obtained a medical release from military service, walked arms outstretched towards the Prime Minister. Rabin enfolded the waifish singer in his arms. "Your song was wonderful," he said.

Frydman, euphoric at the success of the evening, had suggested a departure from the pre-arranged script – a Rabin–Peres walkabout in the crowd. Gaby Last, the Tel Aviv police chief, had raised objections, fearing for their security, but then consented. In the end, though, when the national anthem, "Hatikvah" (The Hope), had brought the rally to a formal end, Rabin and Peres began making their way toward the back staircase, down to the parking area where their drivers were waiting. They stopped for a few moments to speak to Gidi Gov, a well-liked rock star turned talk-show host, and his wife and children. "I said 'Shalom' to Peres, to Rabin. I told Rabin we admired him, supported him," said Gov, "and that he should continue the peace process. He had studied with my father at the Kadoorie Agricultural School. They were friends, and Rabin chatted a bit about my father. He was very happy and very moved by the rally. He said he had a good feeling. Then he said 'Shalom' and walked on."

Rabin and Peres went down the first few stairs to the car park together, and then stopped. Rabin turned back, wanting to say a few words of thanks to Lahat and Frydman. "We embraced," said Lahat. "He told me it was one of the happiest days of his life." Then Rabin and Leah remembered they had a party to go to, at the home of Ido Dissenchik, former editor of the *Ma'ariv* daily, to honour Israel's newly appointed ambassador to France, Avi Pazner. They exchanged a last round of farewells.

Peres and his bodyguards had gone on without Rabin. In the shadows to the left of the stairwell, Yigal Amir, hands in pockets, half-hidden in the weak lighting, watched the Foreign Minister pass directly in front of him. Rabin's driver Damti was waiting by the Prime Minister's car. "Suddenly, I saw the Foreign Minister coming toward me," he said later. "He asked me when the Prime Minister was coming down. I said they'd told me on the walkie-talkie that he'd be down any minute. Peres said that, okay, he'd wait a few seconds. But then he said, 'You know what, I'll go.'"

Up above, Gaby Last and one of the Shin Bet security chiefs, relieved that the Islamic radicals had failed to strike, were congratulating themselves on a difficult operation successfully completed. "We did it," said the secret serviceman as the two shook hands.

Now Rabin's group had reached the stairs again. At the top, Rabin looked over to his right, toward Ibn Gvirol Street, where hundreds of people, mainly teenagers, were shouting, "Peace, peace," and "We're with you." Rabin waved, and headed down the 26 stairs – four bodyguards around him, one more walking ahead of him. Behind his right shoulder, Yoram Rubin, head of the bodyguard squad, anxiously scanned the teeming crowds. A few paces further behind, Leah was descending at a slightly slower pace. As Rabin took the final few paces towards the open door of his car, Amir was standing to his left, no more than three paces away.

As Rabin reached the car, and prepared to climb in, Amir darted up to his unprotected back. He produced a pistol from inside his trousers, and shot once, twice, three times, from point-blank range. According to Damti and some of the policemen nearby, Amir screamed simultaneously, "It's nothing. They're not real bullets. They're blanks. It's not real." The killer denied this, saying later that the shout came from elsewhere. Hit by two of the bullets, Rabin half-turned toward his assailant, then fell forward, collapsing on to his left side. Bleeding himself from the shoulder, where the third bullet had struck, Rabin's bodyguard, Rubin, forced the Prime Minister into the Cadillac, and sprang in after him. Damti scrambled to the wheel, and sped away with a squeal of burning rubber. Behind them Amir was forced to the ground and then marched by a group of police officers back against a wall. One policeman had his left arm firmly across Amir's throat. In the next day's papers, amid the dazed, panicked expressions caught by the photographers, only one man seemed utterly unfazed. Yigal Amir.

Damti says he really wanted to believe the shouts he'd heard, that the bullets were blanks, that Rabin was unharmed. Once out of the car park, he called out to his passenger, "Prime Minister, are you hurt?" Rabin groaned, and murmured, "Yes, yes." "Where does it hurt you?" the driver asked, when the horror of Rabin's response had sunk in. "In my back," Rabin groaned. "It's not so bad."

Those were his last words. Rabin lost consciousness, and his head slumped forward. While Rubin attempted to provide some kind of first aid to the dying Prime Minister, Damti, who, contrary to standard procedure, had not been briefed as to the best escape routes, set off for nearby Ichilov Hospital, forced by the crowds leaving the rally to forsake the most direct route – a mere 700 metres – and instead to make a circuitous journey, covering about 1.7 kilometres which, he said, took him 90 seconds. Trying to make a final right turn toward Ichilov, he ran into a police roadblock, stopped the car, and screamed out frantically to a policeman to get in and help escort them through. The hospital had not been alerted. As Damti pulled up, there was only one man in sight, a security guard. "I shouted at him to fetch a stretcher, quick." When the hospital guard returned, he, Rubin and Damti lifted Rabin out of the car and on to the stretcher, and carried him into the building. Still, there were no medical staff to be seen. "The Prime Minister is hurt," Damti called out desperately. "Come and take care of him." Only then did the doctors come running.

Back at the Square, utter confusion reigned. Nobody was really sure whether Rabin had been hit. Some policemen were saying that the bullets were blanks; but one, bending down in the car park to pick up the spent shells, insisted they were real. Against her will, Leah had been whisked away to a Shin Bet security facility in Ramat Aviv, and Peres's car was also rerouted there – routine emergency procedure. Along the route, Leah frantically scanned the traffic behind, wondering why her husband's car was not following hers. "They told me, 'It's not real,'" said Leah later. Someone spoke of a toy gun. "And they pushed me into another car and rushed me out of there, with sirens and horns blaring, speeding through red lights, until we got to the Shin Bet headquarters. And I was asking all the time, 'Where's Yitzhak? If it's not real, where's Yitzhak?' And they were saying, 'We don't know. When we know, we'll tell you.' And that's the way it was for a long time. I'm sitting alone in a room. So I called my daughter. I told her, 'Daddy's been shot.' I'd already begun to realise that it wasn't 'not real'. I'd begun to realise that something terrible had happened. But just how terrible, I hadn't yet grasped."

Amir had been taken away by the police for initial questioning, formally – and utterly indifferently – acknowledging on the way that, yes, he had pulled the trigger. "I did it to save the state," he said. "He who endangers the Jewish people, his end is death. He deserved to die, and I did the job for the Jewish people." Amir added that he hadn't expected to survive the assassination himself. "I came to the scene fully recognising that I would have to give up my life for the success of the holy mission," he said. "I had made no escape plans."

Aliza Goren, Rabin's spokeswoman, was frantically dialling every possible Rabin contact number on her mobile phone, and getting no answer anywhere. Most people had left the Square, to the strains of dance music playing over the loudspeakers, blissfully unaware that anything was awry.

Outside Ichilov, the crowd was swelling as radio and television spread the news. A handful of Kach members – among the most vicious right-wing opponents of the government – crowed repulsively, "Rabin is dead."

Eitan Haber, the director of Rabin's bureau, his speechwriter and right-hand man, had been watching the rally with Haim Ramon and left before the end for the same party that Rabin was scheduled to attend. "I hadn't even sat down," he recalled, "when the phone rang." Professor Gabi Barabash, the Ichilov Hospital director, was calling with the news that Rabin had been shot. "I drove like a maniac, running red lights. I was at the hospital in minutes, running to the operating room. On the way, I found things of his soaked in blood." Crying, Haber picked them up.

Finally released from their Shin Bet protective captivity, Leah and Peres arrived, to be joined by most of the government ministers, President Ezer Weizman, the army's Chief of Staff, and other dignitaries. US ambassador Martin Indyk had been one of the first to arrive, contacted by Haber.

"Until I got there," said Leah, "I still didn't know anything. But I could already see from the faces that it was really grave. They explained to me that he was badly hurt, but that there was hope. That hope evaporated very quickly. Three-quarters of an hour passed, and during that three-quarters of an hour, we realised that his life was slipping away, moment by moment." Haber remembers, "Our hopes were raised a little when a doctor said the blood pressure had gone up to 90. We hoped it wasn't critical, but I knew in my heart there was no chance."

There was a media scrimmage at the hospital entrance, journalists fighting to get the latest word on the Prime Minister's condition. Every local television and radio station had a contradictory assessment: the Prime Minister was badly hurt, but not critical; the Prime

Minister was in stable condition; the Prime Minister had been in critical condition, but had now stabilised. Inside, the doctors battled to save Rabin – to save a man whose lungs had been penetrated by dumdum bullets, adapted to inflict maximum injury. In the emergency room, Dr Motti Gutman and his team inserted a tracheal tube, respirated Rabin, inserted a chest drain and administered various drugs. For a brief period, a weak pulse was restored, and Rabin was rushed to the operating room, but the pulse died away.

"In other trauma cases," said Dr Yoram Kugler, the head of the trauma unit, afterwards, "I look at the victim, and think to myself, What will happen to the family if he dies on me on the operating table? This time I looked at the operating table and saw the leader I had admired for so many years, and I thought, What will happen to the state, to the people of Israel, if he dies? Then I pushed that kind of thought out of my mind, and listened to the updates on his condition.

"Rabin was critically wounded. I knew right away that the chances of saving him were slight." Still, for 50 minutes, "We massaged Rabin's heart in an effort to get the pulse back, simultaneously giving him 22 units of blood and other treatment. Those were 50 long minutes. We had the burden of the state on our shoulders." But, as Gabi Barabash said afterwards, the heart had already pumped air rather than blood to the brain, causing brain damage. And although the team tried every possible means of resuscitation, Rabin was actually dead within nine minutes of arriving.

At 11.10, Barabash left the operating room and went next door, where Leah and the family were waiting. He gave her the news, and she started sobbing heavily. "I asked to see him," Leah said the next day. "And they said to me that it wouldn't be easy, but that they would do it for me. And although it wasn't easy, I'm grateful. That they let me touch him one more time, and give him a kiss." Peres, too, went in with the family, kissed Rabin tenderly on the forehead, and hugged Leah.

By now, the rumours had begun to circulate outside. Haber emerged from the hospital, his right hand holding a note he had hurriedly scribbled, and was swallowed by the throng. For long moments he tried to call for quiet, to stop the shoving and heaving of the media pack all around him, to no avail. Finally, barking out the words with a kind of defiant desperation, he confirmed the awful, irreversible truth, the news that Yitzhak Rabin, the soldier who had engineered Israel's most famous victories, the peacemaker who had brought it to the brink of comprehensive peace, had been shot dead by one of his own citizens: "With horror, great sorrow and deep grief," said Haber, "the government of Israel announces the death of Prime Minister and Defence Minister Yitzhak Rabin, murdered by an assassin." From around Haber, from around the country, came a wail of despair.

2

Schooled in Battle

YITZHAK RABIN WAS born in Jerusalem in 1922, into the Labour Zionist aristocracy – an aristocracy not of wealth or property, but a pioneering élite of service and sacrifice.

While he was growing up in Tel Aviv in the '20s and '30s, his mother Rosa was an activist who outranked Golda Meir in the Zionist hierarchy, and not only there – Rabin once mentioned to Meir that in the early years his mother had worked as a cashier for a construction company owned by the Histadrut trade union federation. "No," Israel's only woman Prime Minister corrected him. "I was the cashier. Your mother was the accountant."

His father, Nehemiah, though less active in public affairs, was just as devoted to the cause as Rosa. David Ben-Gurion once told Rabin: "I recruited your father for the Jewish Legion. That's why you were born in Palestine." The World War I Legion mobilised Jewish soldiers from Britain and the United States to help drive the Turks out of the Middle East. Nehemiah was one of the American legionnaires who stayed on in Palestine and added a professional touch to the nascent Jewish self-defence effort.

Nehemiah Rubitzov was born in Smidovich near Kiev in the Ukraine in 1886. His father died when he was an infant, and Nehemiah went to work in a flour mill at the age of 10 to help his mother feed the family. He sailed for the United States eight years later, settling in Chicago, where he found work as a tailor, joined the Poalei Zion (Workers of Zion) movement and took night classes at the University of Chicago.

"I was brought up on my father's stories about the United States," Yitzhak Rabin told Robert Slater, author of a biography first published in 1977. "He always used to say it was the country in which he had learned the meaning of freedom and where he had seen the taste for education, and where organisations existed to fight for workers' rights." Yitzhak, who served for five years as Israel's ambassador in Washington after he retired from the army in 1968, grew to echo that admiration. Nehemiah lived in the United States for 12 years, but by the time he sailed for Palestine in 1917 he was determined to make his home in the Promised Land. He had changed his name to Rabin in 1917, after his first application to join the Jewish Legion was turned down on medical grounds. Under his new name, he was accepted by a different recruiting office.

Nehemiah's future wife was born Rosa Cohen in Russia in 1890. Her father was a rabbi, forestry manager and anti-Zionist. Rosa, who continued to use her maiden name until her death in 1937, initially shared his distaste for the new secular religion. But her education in a Christian high school opened up a world beyond the ghetto, and she was soon immersed in the social ferment that preceded the 1917 Russian Revolution – nursing Jewish victims of a pogrom in Homel, preaching a better future to Russian workers. When the revolution came, Rosa was too much of an individualist to accept its dictates and quickly fell foul of the Communists. In 1919 she resolved to get out and fled to Odessa, one jump ahead of the secret police.

Her choice of Zion was almost casual. The only ship in port was bound for Palestine, and she joined a band of aspiring pioneers. Infected by their enthusiasm, she followed them to drain swamps for a settlement on the shores of the Sea of Galilee, but after a bout of malaria she took a doctor's advice and went to stay in Jerusalem with her well-to-do Zionist uncle, Mordechai Ben-Hillel Hacohen, a businessman and writer.

Yitzhak Rabin's parents met unpropitiously in the Old City of Jerusalem during Arab nationalist riots in the spring of 1920. Both had donned disguises – Nehemiah as a hospital orderly, Rosa as a nurse – to evade a British curfew. According to family tradition, Nehemiah, an underground member of the Jewish defence committee while still serving as a British soldier, spotted Rosa and demanded to know what a Jewish girl thought she was doing out on her own. "What's it to you?" she snapped back, and the pair began to rant at each other in Yiddish. She tried to grab his gun; he resisted. Eventually, British soldiers separated the combatants.

They met again the following year in Haifa, where Rosa had started her job as a construction company accountant and Nehemiah, by then out of uniform, had joined a collective group of Jewish workers installing new telephone lines for the British, who were now ruling Palestine under a League of Nations mandate. The couple married a few months later. When their first child was due, Rosa returned to her uncle's home in Jerusalem, where Yitzhak was born in Shaare Zedek Hospital on 1 March 1922. Although he was always proud of being a native Jerusalemite, it was not until he became Prime Minister for the first time in 1974 that he ever lived there – in the official Prime Minister's Residence – and even then his family home remained in Tel Aviv.

Rosa took the baby back to Haifa, where she was appointed head of the Haganah defence organisation's unit charged with defending the port city's Jewish community. Nehemiah was hired by the Palestine Electric Corporation, a Zionist enterprise that had been granted a British concession to build a hydro-electric plant at Naharayim on the River Jordan. In 1923 he was transferred to a blue-collar job in a new power station near Tel Aviv and the family moved to the vibrant, young, all-Jewish city. Rosa found work in a bank. The Rabins' second and only other child, Rachel, was born in 1925.

While continuing in full-time employment, both parents flung themselves into voluntary work in Jewish defence and workers organisations. By 1929, Rosa had been appointed, still unpaid, to the national headquarters of the Haganah. Later, she was elected to the Tel Aviv City Council. As a matter of socialist principle, Nehemiah, a gentle pipe-smoker, rejected offers of promotion or office work. "He wanted to be a Jewish worker," explains Rachel, now a retired teacher, at her home in Menarah, an isolated kibbutz she helped found in 1943 high above the Hulah Valley on the turbulent Lebanese border. Her father also turned down jobs as a full-time labour organiser. "He valued his independence," Rachel says.

Instead, Nehemiah became a lay leader of his local union branch. The committee met in the Rabin family's three rooms in an apartment it shared with another family on Hamagid Street, a quiet road off Rothschild Boulevard. Rosa's political and defence committees met there too. "There was no private life and public life," recalls Shabtai Teveth, an author and journalist who went to elementary school with Yitzhak; "there was no home and office."

Although she was often away from the home and always busy with her job and public activities, Rosa was the dominant influence in shaping her children's personalities. "I seem to have inherited my character from her," Rabin wrote in his memoirs published in 1979. Elsewhere, he remembered her as "a very austere, extreme person, who stuck to what she believed in." Rachel labels her "authoritarian". "There was no fun around her," says Shabtai Teveth. "She was quite humourless. She was a very committed person, 24 hours a day. She wasn't a good mother in the conventional sense. But who was in those days? My parents went to work at 6.30 in the morning. I had to look after myself. So did Yitzhak."

Rachel insists that both their parents were very strong. "My father was warm and soft, but also very brave," she says. "He came to live with us in Menarah in 1968. When Katyusha rockets fell, he would never go into the shelter. It wasn't important what other people thought. When he was living alone in Tel Aviv, we had to fight with him to get a telephone in the house. He said, 'I don't need it for my work.' He always said what he thought was right, and did what he thought was right. That was typical of Yitzhak too."

Rabin also inherited Nehemiah's reticence. "Like my father," says Rachel, "Yitzhak often looked as if he was distant from people, or didn't care. Most of it was shyness. Yitzhak was modest. He didn't want to bother people. He thought that people had to solve their own problems. They must not be too dependent on others. So, many people kept their distance from him. They didn't know how he would respond. Yet he could be very warm with his children and grandchildren, his family and friends. He spent a lot of time with families who lost sons or husbands in wars."

Rachel remembers the apartment on Hamagid Street, where they lived until Rosa died in November 1937, as "very puritanical", with little furniture and no carpets. "We never went short of anything, but our parents never cared about material things. Your personal achievement was more important. My father respected people who worked. He respected human beings as human beings, regardless of whether they were rich or poor, wise or stupid." For the children, the spartan flat had its advantages. "Our home was very open," says Rachel, "so our friends liked to come and play there. Nobody was around to tell them where they could go and where they couldn't."

When German Jewish refugees were fleeing to Palestine in the '30s after the rise of Hitler, the Rabins gave up one room to new immigrants and made do with two. They also shared the kitchen with them. After Rosa died, the Rabins kept just one room for themselves. But by then Yitzhak had left home, and was boarding at the Kadoorie school, near the Biblical Mount Tabor in Lower Galilee.

Rabin's first school, Beit Hinuch, like Kadoorie, aimed to instil a love of the soil among urban Jews and produce farmers for the collective and co-operative Jewish settlements. Beit Hinuch (literally, the House of Education) was founded by Tel Aviv workers' organisations in 1924, and situated on Tchernichowsky Street, next to a downtown park where the pupils could grow vegetables. It offered the added appeal of hot lunches for the children of working parents. Rabin went there in 1928, when he was six, and stayed for seven rapturous years, during which he developed a passion for table tennis and soccer. At Beit Hinuch, according to his sister, he played goalie, advancing to centre forward when he graduated to Kadoorie. He captained the school team there.

"Today I am certain," Rabin wrote in the *Ha'aretz* daily newspaper in 1965, "that during those childhood years I developed the feeling of responsibility toward a job, and my love of landscape and the earth, and a feeling for comradeship."

Shabtai Teveth, four years younger than Rabin, fills in the details: "We didn't learn much at Beit Hinuch. Before we could qualify for high school, all of us had to stay another year in the top class. The primary object was not academic. What was important was responsibility, commitment, mutual aid, manual work. We had vegetable gardens, we planted trees. We each had to work two days a week in the kitchen. The older pupils had to do everything with the younger ones. It was called '*hevrat hayeladim*', the community of children. Everything had to be done together. Tasks had to be divided equally."

Rabin was in charge of the school donkey. "He was very devoted to her," Teveth recalls. "The donkey was always well fed and very clean." Rabin once hitched the donkey to its cart and took a boy of his own age and Teveth to buy produce in the market. "We loaded everything on to the cart," says Teveth. "The two bigger boys were sitting at the front, holding the reins. I was at the back, bouncing among the vegetables and cans. Yitzhak looked back and told the other boy to change places. He let me hold the reins. Some people say Rabin was cold. I know otherwise. He had warmth of heart, but he never showed it. The most awkward moment for him was to be thanked."

When Rosa died at the age of 47, of a combination of heart trouble and cancer, Rabin was already away at the Kadoorie school. He was summoned home to find his mother in a coma, unable to respond when he tried to say goodbye. He wrote later that he had never cried so much in his life. Yet he suppressed his grief in public.

Tel Aviv gave Rosa a civic funeral, which was attended by more than a thousand mourners. Teveth marched behind her coffin with a column of pupils from Beit Hinuch, where Rachel was still a student. "As we passed Rachel and Yitzhak with their father," he recollects, "Rachel was crying. Yitzhak's eyes were completely dry. It was as if nothing had happened. It was not so much self-control. He internalised his emotions."

If the earliest influences moulding Rabin's personality were home and school, the Palmah, the nucleus of a professional Jewish army, completed the process. Despite his parents' involvement in defence efforts, he had no ambitions to be a soldier. In more peaceful circumstances, he might well have taken the same kibbutz route as his sister, though he grumbled at the constrictions of communal living. At Kadoorie, which shared Beit Hinuch's aims but was more disciplined and more academic, he excelled in science. He hoped to study water engineering. The University of California at Berkeley offered him a scholarship. But in the shadow of Mount Tabor, Rabin became a soldier, whether he liked it or not. In the late '30s, Kadoorie was surrounded by hostile Arab villages, which constantly harassed the school. It had to take care of its own defence. Rabin's education was disrupted by training and guard duty.

His instructor was Yigal Allon, a Kadoorie graduate and son of the Galilee, four years older than Rabin. More than half a century later, Allon's portrait was one of the few pictures on the wall of Rabin's Prime Ministerial office. Allon, who was to become commander of the Palmah and later Foreign Minister in Rabin's first government, always claimed to have discovered the young Rabin's gifts as a commander: analysis, decision and execution. When the British closed Kadoorie for six months during the Arab riots of 1938, Allon invited his star pupil to undergo intensive training at Kibbutz Ginossar, on the shore of the Sea of Galilee. Although Rabin returned to Kadoorie, the demands of the Haganah, the pre-state military underground, began to eclipse his studies. A world war broke out in Europe and quickly spread towards the Middle East. Berkeley receded.

In 1941, with the threat of German invasion hanging over Palestine, the Haganah established the Palmah. Its commander was Yitzhak Sadeh, with Yigal Allon and Moshe Dayan as his aides and protégés. By then, Rabin had left Kadoorie and joined a group preparing to set up a new kibbutz. It was training at Kibbutz Ramat Yohanan, just east of Haifa. One evening in the dining hall, a local

Haganah commander invited Rabin to join the Palmah. "I did so without hesitation," Rabin wrote in his memoirs. "I will never know what prompted him to approach me, but the fact of the matter remains that the invitation to join the Palmah changed the course of my life."

Dayan soon recruited him for his first taste of war, a reconnaissance mission across the Lebanese border for Britain's Australian allies. Lebanon, controlled by Hitler's Vichy French puppets, was enemy territory. The British were planning an invasion to stop the Germans from using Syria and Lebanon as a springboard for attacking Palestine. Rabin and his comrades were warned that since they were not regular soldiers they would not be covered by the Geneva Convention on prisoners of war. But, their briefing officer comforted them, that shouldn't worry them. The sector was manned by French colonial troops from Senegal, who didn't take prisoners anyway.

In the event, Rabin's squad never encountered the enemy. It slipped across the border under cover of darkness and marched 30 miles to its target, where Rabin, as the youngest soldier, shinnied up a couple of utility poles and cut the telephone wires to prevent the garrison from calling reinforcements. Mission accomplished. "The story of the Haganah's participation in the invasion of Syria," Rabin conceded, "might never have been remembered had it not been for the fact that on that same night, in a clash with a Vichy French force, Moshe Dayan lost his eye."

Once World War II was over and it became clear that Britain was not going to deliver a Jewish state, the Haganah swung from cooperation to resistance. Rabin gradually scaled the ranks of the Palmah, from platoon to battalion and eventually to brigade command. In Israel's 1948 War of Independence – fought against Palestinian irregulars and five invading Arab armies – he served as deputy chief of the Palmah under his old mentor, Yigal Allon.

In October 1945, while still a junior officer, Rabin led an assault force that rescued about 200 "illegal" immigrants, Jewish survivors of the Holocaust, from a British prison camp at Atlit on the Mediterranean coast. His next target, in June 1946, was a British police station in Jenin, but he never got there. While reconnoitring on a motorcycle, he hit a truck that cut across his path. His leg was broken in two places. Before Rabin could recover, the British retaliated for the Palmah's spectacular destruction of 10 bridges linking Palestine to the rest of the Middle East by arresting almost the entire mainstream Jewish leadership, on 29 June 1946. Rabin – and his father – were among them. Yitzhak was held, and thus doubly immobilised, for five months. Nehemiah, who seems to have been picked up simply because he was there, was detained for two weeks. Then a 60-year-old widower, Nehemiah had only one complaint, Yitzhak recalled in his memoirs: the British paratroops hadn't given him time to put in his dentures before taking him away.

From November 1947, when the United Nations voted to partition Palestine between Jews and Arabs, to July the following year, Rabin was preoccupied with the battle for Jerusalem – first the main road, its lifeline to Tel Aviv and the coast, then the holy city itself, with its 90,000 beleaguered Jewish inhabitants. On 15 April, exactly one month before the British pulled out, he was appointed commander of the Palmah's new Harel Brigade, which was deployed on the Jerusalem front.

It was a fluctuating, frustrating war, pitting Rabin not only against the Arab enemy, but often against his own political masters and against the regular Haganah command in the hill city. Jerusalem was too important to be left to the generals, but Rabin chafed against what he considered misguided, ill-conceived orders. The three key locations along the Jerusalem road – Latrun in the plain; Bab al-Wad (Sha'ar Hagai), the wooded defile at the beginning of the first ascent; and the Kastel, the ruined Roman fort commanding the highest point on the road – were taken, lost and taken again, seldom at the same times. Sometimes the supply convoys got through, sometimes they didn't.

At one stage, Rabin was so short of men that he had to send a platoon of Gadna cadets, 15- and 16-year-old school-children, into battle for Latrun. "We were now paying the bloody price of years of neglect," he wrote 30 years later, his anger still blazing. "Now I knew for certain that my assessment prior to the War of Independence had been correct: the leadership of the Yishuv (the Jewish community in Palestine) had not prepared enough weapons of the quality required, and combat forces had not been sufficiently trained. No other people has charged so few, so poorly armed, with gaining and safeguarding its independence." Speaking after Rabin's death, Niva Lanir called his experience on the Jerusalem road "the most decisive experience of his life," adding "and even he said this". More than 200 soldiers from Harel lost their lives and over 600 others were wounded. "He's 26, and he has responsibility for the road to Jerusalem and for creating a state."

Rabin was equally dismayed by the local Haganah commander,

David Shaltiel, who was in overall control of the Jerusalem front. Rabin and Shaltiel presented rival plans for the conquest of the Old City. Eventually the Palmah commander yielded. Again, three decades later, it hurt and rankled. "Shaltiel," Rabin wrote, "rejected my proposal and was adamant about implementing his own. I was furious with him and told him outright that his plan was idiotic and bound to fail. But Jerusalem was much too dear to me to refuse even an attempt."

The upshot was that the Israelis failed to take the Old City. A Palmah unit captured Mount Zion, outside the walls, but lacked the men and *matériel* to seize and hold the Jewish Quarter inside Zion Gate before the starved, petrified residents surrendered to the Jordanian Arab Legion. Rabin was more successful in the new city, where his troops conquered the Katamon neighbourhood and secured unbroken Jewish control of West Jerusalem. But casualties were high and Rabin was threatened at one stage with a collapse of morale and confidence among his men. By the end of the war, the main road was secure. But it was with a sense of poetic justice, 19 years and two wars later, that Rabin strode into the Old City as Chief of Staff after East Jerusalem was conquered.

Like his parents before him, Yitzhak Rabin had little time for a private life, but he took advantage of the second of two truces in the summer of 1948 to marry Leah Schlossberg, the dark-haired daughter of cultured German immigrants he had been quietly wooing since she was a 15-year-old high school girl in 1944. "It began with a chance encounter in a Tel Aviv street," Rabin wrote in his memoirs, "a glance, a word, a stirring within, and then a further meeting..."

A romantic novelist couldn't have told it better. But Shabtai Teveth, who knew Rabin from school and Leah from the left-wing Hashomer Hatzair youth movement, remembers it differently. "Leah," he says, "was considered one of the beauties of Hashomer Hatzair. I remember when Yitzhak courted her. He followed her everywhere without saying a word. He stalked her, making himself noticeable. He didn't live far from where she lived, but there was no way they could have known each other. She came from a well-to-do, German-speaking family, leading a bourgeois Tel Aviv life. Everything was different. He just followed her, step by step, until he gathered enough courage to make himself known to her. By then she had found out who he was. It was a unique courtship, and very typical of Yitzhak. On the one hand, he was very tenacious, persistent. On the other hand, he was very shy. I think Leah was the first girl he ever dated."

Rabin was a handsome young man with his craggy face and gingery-brown hair. With the heroic aura of the Palmah thrown in, Leah did not need much persuading, but he was in uniform and leave was rare. "We grew closer in 1945," he wrote, "when Leah joined the Palmah and served in the battalion of which I was deputy commander – one of the rare occasions in our life together when *she* was under *my* command."

Rabin would have preferred a quiet wedding, but it was not to be. They were married in Tel Aviv on 23 August 1948, in the presence of the top brass of the Palmah and the beau monde of Tel Aviv. The rabbi arrived half an hour late. Rabin fretted at the ceremony. This was not his scene. Suddenly the guests heard an unscripted, but familiar, bass voice promising his bride: "This is the last time I'm getting married!"

Earlier that summer, Rabin was embroiled in one of the most painful, contentious episodes of the War of Independence: the sinking of the *Altalena*, which was carrying arms from France for the dissident Irgun Zvai Leumi, led by Menachem Begin. At the beginning of June, Begin had agreed to merge his fighters into the new national army. The state, proclaimed on the night of 14 May, was still in its infancy. Begin was agitating against Ben-Gurion's acquiescence in the partition of Palestine. Rightly or wrongly, the Prime Minister feared a *putsch* from the nationalist right. And his fears were reinforced when Begin refused on 20 June to hand the *Altalena*'s precious cargo over to the army. The ship anchored first off Kfar Vitkin, north of Netanyah, but after an exchange of fire with the newly-established Israel Defence Forces it sailed down the coast to Tel Aviv, where Begin hoped the IDF would not dare to attack it.

The Palmah was operating under the IDF command and Ben-Gurion ordered Yigal Allon to seize the *Altalena*, by force if necessary. Rabin had come to Palmah headquarters in the seafront Ritz Hotel for a meeting, arriving early to see Leah, who was working there. He knew nothing of the background, but was immediately drafted to take command on the beach. The *Altalena* was raked with machine-gun and artillery fire and eventually holed by a shell. After a show of defiance, the Irgun surrendered and ceased to be an independent fighting force, but not before 14 of Begin's fighters and one of Rabin's paid with their lives.

Rabin confided off-camera to Ilana Tsur, the director of a 1994 television documentary on the *Altalena* affair, that it was one of the most difficult moments of his life. But he stood by the Prime Minister's decision. "Woe unto the State of Israel," he said, "if Ben-Gurion had not done what he did. There is only one army, and that is the Israel Defence Forces."

Another episode that troubled Rabin ever afterwards was the expulsion of 50,000 Arab civilians from the twin towns of Lydda (today's Lod) and Ramlah, south-east of Tel Aviv. In Israeli mythology, the residents went quietly of their own accord. Thirty years on, while writing his memoirs, Rabin broke the taboo and admitted that they were driven out at gunpoint. A cabinet committee which checks ministerial memoirs for security breaches ordered that the passage be deleted. According to Rabin's ghost-writer, Dov Goldstein, Rabin appeared before the head of the committee and was told: "Yes, the story is open and true, but it can't come from the mouth of one of our heroes, from someone who was involved in it personally, who was Prime Minister of Israel, because it will ruin our claim that we acted humanely." Rabin was incensed, but agreed to delete the section, and instructed his English translator, who was already in possession of the manuscript, to do the same. But just prior to publication, the translator – an Israeli far-left activist – passed the story to *The New York Times*.

The expulsion, Rabin revealed, was ordered by Ben-Gurion and executed by Allon and Rabin. "We could not leave Lod's hostile and armed populace in our rear, where it could endanger the supply route to Yiftah [another brigade] that was advancing eastward," Rabin argued. Ben-Gurion indicated that the Palmah should drive them out toward the Arab Legion's lines near Latrun.

"'Driving out' is a term with a harsh ring," Rabin wrote. "Psychologically, this was one of the most difficult actions we undertook. The population of Lod did not leave willingly. There was no way of avoiding the use of fire and warning shots in order to make the inhabitants march the 10 to 15 miles to the point where they met up with the Legion. The inhabitants of Ramlah watched, and learned the lesson. Their leaders agreed to be evacuated voluntarily."

According to Larry Collins and Dominique Lapierre's book *O Jerusalem!*, many elderly people and small children died for lack of water during the forced march. Rabin did not mention this in his account, but recorded that the expulsion was a great trauma for

26

many of the soldiers ordered to carry it out. As a journalist, Shabtai Teveth interviewed Rabin about it. "He told me," says Teveth, "that this was something terrible. 'It was a very hot day. They had to walk, carrying their children and belongings,' he said. Rabin knew suffering when he saw it. But he was a soldier. He understood why the expulsion was necessary. But he noticed the suffering, and it stayed with him."

In the last phase of the War of Independence, after the summer truces, Rabin served as Chief of Operations on the southern front, driving the invading Egyptian forces out of the Negev and securing the route to what became the Red Sea port and resort city of Eilat. At the end of December, one force pushed across the international border into northern Sinai, capturing the strategic crossroads at Abu Ageila, then driving without authorisation on towards the regional capital, El Arish. "If El Arish had fallen into our hands," Rabin wrote, "the Egyptian army in the Gaza Strip would have been cut off; the major part of the Sinai would have been ours; and the subsequent military history of Israel would have taken a different course." But it was not to be. Ben-Gurion, under intense pressure from Britain and the United States, overruled the entreaties of Allon and Rabin and ordered the troops back.

One Egyptian unit, although surrounded, stubbornly held out at the Faluja crossroads, south-east of Ashdod. Allon, accompanied by Rabin and other senior officers, negotiated their surrender. A young Egyptian officer, Gamal Abd al-Nasser, asked Rabin how the Israelis had forced the British, who still cast an imperial shadow over Egypt, to get out of Palestine. Rabin patiently explained. "You know," the future revolutionary president mused, "we are fighting the wrong enemy at the wrong place at the wrong time."

The War of Independence confirmed Yitzhak Rabin's stature as a soldier with a mind of his own, a commander who could take and implement difficult decisions. But in the gregarious world of the Palmah, a kind of kibbutz-in-arms with its comradeship, its own songs and folk dances, its in-house poets, he remained a loner. Yigal Allon was the prototype, back-slapping Palmah hero. Rabin never was, or wanted to be.

"Yigal Allon," says retired general Uzi Narkiss, who served under both of them and was head of the Central Command in 1967, "was a leader, a friend on whom you could count until the end. He was admired by all of us. He allowed himself to express all his sentiments. First thing, he hugged you. Yitzhak Rabin never hugged you. If he wanted to punch you on the nose, he did it without hugging you first, or saying 'excuse me.' Allon's men loved him, Rabin's respected him. Rabin was not at his best around the campfire. He didn't know how to sing. Allon used to say: 'My only asset in life is my friends.' I don't think that Rabin could have said the same.

"Allon knew how to manoeuvre, to talk round things. He said he learned it from the Arabs in Galilee. Rabin never dealt with things like that. In politics, you need to know how to manipulate people. Rabin never mastered that. Even in the Palmah days, he was very tough, one-track minded. When he decided on something, he carried it out with stubbornness and perseverance. He was direct, very blunt with people. People appreciated him because of his mind. That was his main asset. He was analytical. He loved to go into details. He had a fantastic memory. He emphasised training. He wanted every corporal to think like an officer, see the whole picture. But Rabin relied on improvisation less than other Israeli commanders, like Moshe Dayan, who saw it as our main weapon. Rabin said: 'Yes, but only after thorough planning. We will rely on improvisation only if the plan does not go well.' "

Perhaps the main lesson Rabin drew from 1948, Narkiss believes, was that the big decisions have to be made at the political level. "It was Rabin who persuaded us, in a long, frosty night of discussion, to obey orders and pull back from Abu Ageila. 'The government must decide,' he told us. As Prime Minister, negotiating peace with the Palestinians, Rabin said the same thing: 'The political level decides, the army executes.' "

The primacy of the politician was easier for Rabin to swallow when he was in office than when he was in uniform. In January 1949, Allon sent Rabin to represent the southern front in armistice talks with Egypt on the Greek island of Rhodes. He was a fish out of water, differing so bitterly with his civilian colleagues that he left early without signing the agreement they negotiated. "I have had enough of diplomacy and politics," he complained to Allon.

The Rhodes conference marked the first time Rabin had to wear a tie. A more worldly Palmah comrade knotted one for him before he left Israel. Rabin kept it loosely knotted so that he could slip it over his head, but a valet at the Hotel des Roses thoughtfully undid it and pressed it for him. Yigael Yadin, the head of the Israeli delegation, found Rabin fretting in his room and refastened it. Bill Clinton trumped the story at Rabin's funeral in November 1995. "The last time we were together," the American President told the assembled mourners on Mount Herzl, "he showed up for a black-tie event on time, but without the black tie. And so he borrowed a tie. And I was privileged to straighten it for him." Once a Palmahnik, always a Palmahnik.

3

The Path to Victory

HE IS KNOWN, rightly, as the Chief of Staff who planned and oversaw Israel's most outstanding military victory – the decimation of the Arab air forces and the brilliant armoured thrusts of the Six Day War. But Yitzhak Rabin's route from Palmah brigade commander in 1949, when the War of Independence ended, to Chief of Staff of the Israel Defence Forces in 1964, was not without its setbacks, and on at least two occasions, frustrated that he was not receiving the promotions he thought were his due, Rabin seriously contemplated hanging up his uniform.

Only in retrospect, what's more, has the extent of Rabin's decisive role in the 1967 victory been fully recognised. Much of the public acclamation at the time was bestowed on Moshe Dayan, who had only been brought in as Defence Minister days before the war. It was Rabin, however, who had shaped the military doctrine, developed the training techniques and battle strategies, introduced the new weaponry, reorganised the country's limited forces to best advantage, and prepared those forces for war.

Back in 1949, Rabin's first steps in the embryonic IDF were singularly inauspicious – even though David Ben-Gurion, impressed by Rabin's leadership during the War of Independence, had earmarked him for a key army role. Rabin incurred the Prime Minister's wrath by attending a rally of Palmah veterans on 14 October 1949, called as a farewell and to protest Ben-Gurion's decree to disband the force. Officers like Rabin serving in the new IDF had been forbidden to attend the rally and Ben-Gurion, aware of Rabin's dilemma and intent on keeping him away, invited him to his home on the afternoon of 14 October to report on a number of shooting incidents in the south.

Rabin broached the subject of the rally, asking Ben-Gurion to explain the ban. Ben-Gurion replied briefly that the new army had to be united, and that there was no room for separate command structures. Ben-Gurion was also seeking to sideline Palmah chief Yigal Allon and other Palmah commanders associated with the Mapam political party, which was too leftist for the Prime Minister's tastes. Nevertheless, Rabin decided that army discipline was secondary on this occasion to loyalty to his comrades. Politely excusing himself, he rushed home to change out of his IDF uniform and into his Palmah white shirt, then headed for the rally.

Rabin and others like him who defied the ban were all court martialled. While some were relieved of their posts, Rabin got away with a dressing-down from the Chief of Staff and a reprimand in his personal file. But in the long run, his defiance of Ben-Gurion may well have slowed his military career. If it did, ironically, the delay meant he finally reached the top post in the period leading up to the Six Day War, and allowed him to orchestrate the victory that would later serve as his calling card in political life.

Still, in the autumn of 1949, when the Palmah Negev brigade under his command was disbanded, Rabin found himself effectively unemployed. Many of his Palmah comrades, including his mentor Allon, had left the military or been forced out by Ben-Gurion, who gave preference to veterans of the British army over the Palmah's locally trained officers. Rabin himself flirted with the idea of returning to civilian life and studying hydraulic engineering.

But the precarious position of the state – the Arabs had imposed an economic blockade and begun fostering terrorism immediately after the war – convinced him that his place was in the army, helping to build a fighting force that would secure the country's borders.

Rabin opted to join a battalion commanders' course being set up by British-trained Haganah veteran Haim Laskov. The course provided the ideal opportunity to mould the experience various officers had gained in the Palmah, Haganah and British army into a new, unified doctrine. Laskov was initially wary of Rabin's Palmah roots and made it clear he didn't want him dabbling in politics. But Rabin evidently demonstrated his worth, so impressing Laskov that the Haganah veteran told him to bring in as many of his Palmah comrades as he wanted. Indeed, despite his personal closeness to Allon and his Palmah membership, Rabin never clearly identified himself with Allon's or any other political party. Mordechai Bar-On, who was Chief Education Officer during Rabin's term as Chief of

Staff, says, "He was interested in tactics and strategy, not politics. He wanted to be a military commander."

Soon after the birth of his first child, Dalia, in March 1950, Rabin, by now a colonel, was appointed to take over the running of the course from Laskov, and used the post as a forum for forging strategy and tactics and shaping planning techniques and staff procedures. Within months, though, he was forced to leave: Chief of Staff Yigael Yadin appointed him to head the IDF's operations department – his first post in the General Staff.

In charge of operational planning and the reserves, Rabin now spent up to 20 hours a day working to improve the quality of the combat units and to organise the reserves more effectively. In the early '50s, though, the army was burdened with more than military tasks. Tens of thousands of immigrants were pouring into the country from North Africa and were being housed in crowded tent cities often lacking even basic sanitary facilities. The army was the only national body big enough to grapple with the mass immigration; Rabin was handed the responsibility.

The army worked to improve camp conditions. The IDF Medical Corps provided health services, and soldiers worked as teachers and social workers. It was a period that Rabin – if few of the immigrants – remembered with great pride. "No other agency or body in the country would have been capable of responding to this challenge," he wrote later. The "battle of the transit camps", as he called it, would "be recorded as one of [the army's] most splendid victories".

Rabin had tremendous battle experience for such a young man, but, like most of his colleagues, he knew little of the wider world. His first chance to travel abroad – apart from the Rhodes armistice talks in 1949 – came towards the end of 1952, when he was sent to England to study at the British army Royal Staff College at Camberley, travelling with Leah and two-and-a-half-year-old Dalia. Initially he found the course dull. "The first stage of my studies included a great deal of technical staff work," he wrote. "For example, I was charged with working out a transportation timetable for an entire division. It was boring, and bizarre into the bargain. Since when did the IDF contain any formation as large as a division?"

Rabin's poor English and his background in the Palmah, which disdained British fighting methods, might well have coloured his experience. "We lived in a different reality," explains Yeshayahu

(Shaike) Gavish, one of Rabin's Palmah comrades who was to head the Southern Command during the Six Day War. "We had fewer soldiers and less weaponry than our enemies, and our territory was tiny. That meant our strategy had to be different. We couldn't engage in frontal assaults. We had to use surprise attacks, outflank the enemy, operate at night."

It was not all that surprising then, that when Rabin graduated from the course, the recommendation from his British instructors was that he should serve in the Quartermasters Corps. Rabin's fellow officers in the IDF, fortunately, had a higher opinion of him. "He had a high forehead," says Uzi Narkiss, "and when you looked at him you had the feeling that the wheels were constantly turning inside."

One fellow student in England was Faez Maher, who was eventually to serve as Jordan's Chief of Staff. When Rabin first visited King Hussein in Jordan, during his second term as Prime Minister, he mentioned his old Camberley colleague, and asked the King what had become of him. Within half an hour, Maher was at the palace, and the reunion was warm and friendly. When Rabin toured Petra on Israel's Independence Day in 1995, Maher was his guide. Later in the year, Maher suffered a stroke, and Rabin personally approved his hospitalisation at Jerusalem's Hadassah Hospital.

After Rabin returned from Camberley, the new Chief of Staff, Moshe Dayan, appointed him to head the army's Training Branch. Rabin, promoted to major general, made a first trip to the United States as a guest of the US military – and came back with much food for thought. One immediate change he introduced was to order every combat officer to undergo a parachute or commando course after completing Officers Training School. The first to jump were the members of the General Staff, and Rabin, who did not want to worry Leah – then pregnant with their second child – kept it a secret from his wife. After the birth of their son, Yuval, Rabin left the Training Branch and returned to the field, becoming head of the Northern Command in April 1956.

There was friction at the time with the Syrians over the demarcation of demilitarised zones, but most of the tension was outside the area of Rabin's jurisdiction – on the Jordanian and especially Egyptian fronts, where there were constant terrorist raids. Overseeing the relatively calm north, Rabin found himself largely left out of the 1956 Sinai Campaign.

Though Israel had been consistently retaliating against a painful series of Egyptian-supported terrorist raids into southern Israel, casualties were mounting, and the government was keen to snuff out the incursions altogether. Secretly co-ordinating its attack with the British and French, Israel began its sweep through the Gaza Strip and Sinai on 29 October with the limited aims of curbing terror and reopening to Israeli shipping the Strait of Tiran at the entrance to the Gulf of Aqaba, closed by Egypt in the early 1950s. Within a few days Israeli forces had advanced through the Sinai and reached the Suez Canal and the Strait. When Russia threatened to intervene unless Israel withdrew, the United States forced Israel into gradual compliance. By March 1957, Israel was out and a United Nations peacekeeping force was stationed in the Sinai. Still, Israel had achieved its aims: the Strait was open and the southern border was quiet.

Far away on the northern front, Rabin's main role in the war had been merely to dispatch some of his troops to the south and to retain a defensive posture in case of a Syrian attack. Irritated at having missed the action, he did, however, have his own low-scale conflict to deal with once the major hostilities were over. The Syrians, perched on the Golan Heights, were intermittently shelling Israeli settlements below and Israeli fishing vessels on the Sea of Galilee. In retaliation, IDF naval units were sent to carry out raids on the eastern shore, destroying Syrian boats fishing in Israeli waters.

Toward the end of 1957, Moshe Dayan's tenure as Chief of Staff was coming to an end and a round of General Staff appointments awaited. Dayan summoned a few senior officers, including Rabin, for a discussion. He informed them that he had suggested to Ben-Gurion that the head of the General Staff branch, Meir Amit, take over his post and that Tzvi Tzur, head of the Central Command, become his deputy. Rabin, he suggested, should go on study leave. Needless to say, Rabin was not pleased. Again, he began to wonder whether he should remain in the army. But Ben-Gurion rejected Dayan's recommendations: Laskov, not Amit, was named as Dayan's successor; Rabin stayed on in the north.

Rabin's relations with Dayan had never been over-friendly. Dayan was flamboyant, innovative and impulsive. Rabin was cautious, pedantic and analytical. According to Shimon Peres, then Director General of the defence ministry, Dayan only named Rabin head of the Northern Command to get him out of the way. Even in 1949 there had been evidence of a coolness between the two when, as acting head of the Southern Command, Rabin had to hand over to Dayan, who was appointed to fill the post. In his memoirs, Rabin describes the atmosphere: "Everyone was silent and expressionless when he arrived, and Dayan may have felt ill at ease in the company of all those Palmah men. I transferred the command without any ceremony, and the feeling that Dayan would prefer to be rid of me as well was strengthened by our first talk. He was cold, reserved, and laconic. Moreover, he was frank. 'Thank you,' he said, 'I don't need you any longer.'"

By 1959, after another two years on the northern front, Rabin was starting to think his military career had reached a dead end. With Laskov's approval, he applied for a two-year course at the Harvard Business School. But a bizarre turn of events kept him in uniform. In April, the IDF held a major mobilisation exercise, but failed to make clear that it was only a dry run. As the mobilisation code names were broadcast over the radio, calling men to their units, Israelis, along with the rest of the world, wondered if war were imminent.

Rabin was one of the main beneficiaries of a state inquiry into the incident, which recommended that two generals – Meir Zorea, head of the General Staff branch, and Yehoshafat Harkabi, chief of military intelligence – be dismissed. Having long harboured fears that Ben-Gurion was torpedoing his advancement because of his in-discipline over the Palmah farewell rally, Rabin was delighted to be named as Zorea's replacement.

Within months, though, Rabin had learned that Ben-Gurion had not entirely forgotten the Palmah breach of discipline. Although Rabin was a strong candidate for the Chief of Staff's post, to replace Laskov, Tzur, the deputy Chief of Staff, was preferred by Ben-Gurion. "'I want to tell you why I decided on Tzur,'" Rabin recalled Ben-Gurion explaining. "'True, on one occasion you did disobey orders. And you are cautious.' (I think he meant 'over-cautious.') 'But these considerations did not affect my decision. Tzur is simply ahead of you in the military hierarchy.'" By way of compensation, Ben-Gurion did promise Rabin that he would succeed Tzur. And on 24 January 1961, Rabin was appointed Tzur's deputy.

Rabin was a hands-on commander, who wanted to know every detail of every operation. "He always stunned us," wrote former president Chaim Herzog, who served with Rabin in the General Staff. "I remember how he used to quote the number of hours the tanks in each battalion had put in. But with that, he never lost the ability to see the whole picture." A joke in the General Staff suggested that the army didn't have to worry if its computer went on the blink, because it had Yitzhak Rabin.

What Rabin lacked was spontaneity. At annual parties for the General Staff branch, Rabin could be seen standing to the side, watching. "His language was rather poor," recalls Mordechai Bar-On. "Also in terms of metaphors and allusions. Listening to him you could feel he had spent a lot of time reading military reports and summaries."

As head of the General Staff branch, Rabin actively promoted the view that Israel should begin lessening its dependency on French armaments – a result of Peres's policies as deputy Defence Minister – and move over to what he considered were higher-quality American-produced weapons. On this matter, as on many others, Rabin clashed bitterly with Peres. It was the beginning of a personal enmity that was to accompany the two until the unexpected reconciliation during Rabin's final years in office. During Rabin's tenure as deputy Chief of Staff, he even charged that Peres tried to have him replaced. "I was a thorn in his side," wrote Rabin, "and he wanted me out of the key post... Peres regarded my view as a menace to his position, and the struggle proved to be a bitter one. It never occurred to me to mix considerations of personal prestige in with such fateful matters. But Peres, I felt, fomented personal conflicts to place his adversaries under pressure."

Rabin claims in his memoirs that Peres visibly "paled" when he told him, in March 1963, that Ben-Gurion had promised him the Chief of Staff's post. Peres rejects this, asserting that Ben-Gurion had told him earlier. According to Peres, "The news came as neither a surprise nor a shock to me. His description of my ostensible reaction to it, written 16 years later, is the product of unfounded assumptions."

On 1 January 1964, at the age of 41, Yitzhak Rabin became Chief of Staff. Ben-Gurion had resigned seven months earlier, but the new Prime Minister, Levi Eshkol, honoured his predecessor's commitment to Rabin. In any case, Rabin was the natural choice. He'd served in almost all the top posts, and was the army's most respected military planner.

When Rabin took over, there was no threat of war. Syria continued to shell Israeli settlements, but Damascus wasn't about to embark on a lone military adventure. And Egypt, Israel's major foe, was embroiled in a conflict in Yemen. What did concern Rabin was that Egypt had been acquiring sophisticated Soviet weaponry, doubling its tank force to almost 1,200 and building up its fleet of jet warplanes to 350 by the early '60s.

Rabin realised that a future war would be against Soviet-trained armies with vast quantities of Soviet artillery, tanks and planes. The IDF had to begin training to combat Soviet doctrine. Under Rabin's guidance, full-scale replicas of Soviet fortified positions were built – with trenches, fences, lines of defence, dummy mines – and soldiers practised attacking them.

But Rabin had little time to ease into the job. In his first month as Chief of Staff, Israel began building its national water carrier, planned to pump 300 million cubic metres of water a year from the Sea of Galilee in the north, through pipes and canals, to the arid South. Fearing the project would boost Israel's economic power, Arab leaders held a series of summit meetings in Egypt and agreed that every step, barring all-out war, had to be taken to sabotage it. First came an upsurge in Palestinian terror attacks – some aimed directly at the water carrier. Then, towards the end of 1964, the Syrians on the Golan Heights began trying to divert the waters of the Hatzbani River – a tributary of the Jordan, which flows into the Sea of Galilee – in an effort to foil the whole project. Syria was also planning to divert the waters of the Banias River, another Jordan tributary. The aim was to force Israel into a choice between accepting the water diversions or going to war. While they didn't believe they could successfully attack Israel, the Arab states did believe they could defend themselves if attacked.

But Rabin sought a third option – to scuttle the diversion plans without causing a major conflagration. After consulting Prime Minister and Defence Minister Eshkol, Rabin called Israel (Talik) Tal, head of the IDF's armoured corps, for practical assistance. Tal informed him that tanks positioned on the Israeli side of the border could destroy the Syrian earth-moving equipment with their guns. "No one believed it would work," Tal recalls. Except Rabin, who was won over when Tal gave him a battlefield demonstration.

Sitting in his office with Eshkol, Rabin telephoned Tal to make his pitch. "I'm arguing that you can wipe out the diversion plan without war," Rabin told Tal, "but Eshkol wants to know what guarantees you can give."

"Tell him I'll do the shooting myself," came Tal's cheeky reply. And he did. The very next day, Tal took two tanks to Tel Dan, just north of Kibbutz Dan, and manning a gun himself, destroyed eight pieces of Syrian equipment two kilometres away. The operation, and similar ones that followed, were hugely successful. Each time Israeli tanks destroyed Syrian equipment, the earthworks would be moved further from the border. When the Syrians were outside tank range, the IDF simply switched to artillery fire. And when Syria had been forced to divert the works to a distance of 20 kilometres from the border, Israel sent in planes to knock them out. Syria hit back, shelling civilian settlements and forcing residents into bomb shelters. But it also eventually dropped the diversion plan. "Rabin defied the sceptics," says Tal, "because he understood that you can't dance to the tune of the enemy. He looked for a solution that was not dictated by the enemy's strategy." Still, it was a short-term victory; the ongoing confrontation over water was a major factor in the escalation towards the Six Day War.

Even now, the north was far from silent. There were dozens of incidents of gunfire to and fro across the Syrian border, and a wave of Syrian-backed infiltrations by Palestinian terrorist groups from Lebanon. Somewhat undiplomatically, Rabin told an army journal in September 1966 that Israel could counter Syrian aggression not only by acting against terrorists, but also by moving against the regime supporting these attacks. It was one of the shoot-from-the-hip remarks for which he was to become notorious.

Generally, though, Rabin was not one for bellicose pronouncements. "You never heard him say we were going to screw the enemy," recalls Gavish. "He saw it as overconfidence." In fact, the Chief of Staff was usually sparing with his words, and many found him closed and withdrawn. But there were signs of emotion behind the impregnable exterior. Once Tal brought his 12-year-old son to a major armoured exercise, but the manoeuvre dragged on into the night. "Yitzhak," Tal recalls, "understood that I didn't know what to do with my boy. He took him, spread out a sleeping bag, and they fell asleep side by side."

Tal tells another anecdote to illustrate Rabin's bashful streak. Walking together at army HQ in Tel Aviv one day, the two spotted an attractive female soldier. "I looked at her and marvelled," chuckles Tal. "But Rabin looked at her out of the corner of his eye. I shouted, 'Yitzhak, look, enjoy, it's not taboo.'"

Skirmishes on the northern borders intensified in early 1967. And in April, Israeli planes shot six Syrian Migs out of the sky. Yet even in early May, the assessment of military intelligence – shared by Rabin

– was that with Egypt still stuck in Yemen, war was unlikely. In fact, Israel's most decisive military conflict was only a month away.

Sometime in the period between 11 and 13 May, the Soviets fed false reports to the Arabs that Israel was massing forces on the northern border and was planning a full-scale attack. Syria, which had a defence pact with Egypt, called on President Gamal Abd al-Nasser to take up the challenge. Rabin ordered the Northern Command to avoid making unnecessary troop movements, lest they be perceived as a provocation.

Rabin was still feeling relatively untroubled on 14 May, when he arrived at an Independence Day reception in the Jerusalem home of Miles Sherover, a wealthy Venezuelan Jewish businessman and philanthropist. During the evening, however, he received a note. "His face became longer, sterner," recalls the Central Command chief, Uzi Narkiss. The message was from the head of military intelligence Aharon Yariv: the Egyptian army had been put on alert. The next day, presiding over an Independence Day military parade in Jerusalem, Rabin was informed that the Egyptian army was marching through the streets of Cairo on the way to the Suez Canal. He passed on the reports to Eshkol, standing nearby; reinforcements were sent to the southern border, and some reserve armoured units readied for mobilisation.

On 18 May, the Egyptian President ordered all United Nations troops out of the Sinai; UN Secretary General U Thant complied with alacrity. Over the next few days, Israel watched as Nasser extracted his forces from Yemen and dispatched them to the Sinai. By 21 May, seven Egyptian divisions were massed on the southern border. Israel faced 80,000 Egyptian soldiers. On 23 May Nasser closed the Strait of Tiran to Israeli shipping.

The Israeli political leadership vacillated, hoping the United States would step in after President Lyndon Johnson had raised the possibility of sending a US-led flotilla to reopen the Strait. Eshkol, lacking any military expertise, was totally reliant on the Chief of Staff's judgment. Rabin found himself caught between the politicians, who preferred to seek a diplomatic solution, and his generals, who urged that Israel act immediately or risk losing the element of surprise and allowing the Egyptians to dig in. "We told the government," recalls Gavish, "that we're allowing the Egyptians to organise, to bring in artillery, put in mines. And all this only 50 kilometres from Beersheba."

Initially, Rabin personally favoured a limited military operation –

a strike on El Arish, about a quarter of the way along the coastal road from Rafah to Port Said on the Suez Canal, to be followed by an effort to negotiate a mutual withdrawal. Gavish backed a far more offensive approach, seeking to destroy the Egyptian army and press on all the way to the Suez Canal – a stance Rabin subsequently came to endorse. "Israel was facing one of the most serious situations she had ever experienced," Rabin wrote in his memoirs, "and I sensed that in its perplexity the cabinet expected me not only to present and analyse the military options (which is the task of the Chief of Staff) but also to dispel any doubts by telling it which option to adopt... That made me feel very lonely..."

As the prospect of all-out conflict loomed ever larger, the public sense was of impending annihilation. References to the Holocaust were common. In some parts of the country, ground was conse-crated for cemeteries and fresh graves were dug in anticipation of massive casualties. Feeling increasingly isolated, Rabin turned to Ben-Gurion for support. On 22 May, he paid a call on the former Prime Minister. But Ben-Gurion made matters worse, railing angrily first against the political leadership and then blaming Rabin person-ally for Israel's predicament. "You've led the country into a grave situation," Ben-Gurion told him. "We must not go to war. We are isolated. You bear the responsibility."

Rabin came away shattered. The very next night, he suffered what many have called a breakdown, and disappeared for a day. Rabin himself believes it was a combination of factors, including his heavy nicotine intake, that pushed him over the edge. "Late that evening... I returned home in a state of mental and physical exhaustion," he wrote in his memoirs. "Ever since then I have repeatedly asked myself, what happened to me that evening? There can be no doubt that I was suffering from a combination of tension, exhaustion, and the enormous amounts of cigarette smoke I had inhaled in recent days. The past few days had seemed endless. Meals were taken on the run and only when the occasion arose. I had hardly slept, and I was smoking like a steam engine. But it was more than nicotine that brought me down. The heavy sense of guilt that had been dogging me of late became unbearably strong on 23 May. I could not forget Ben-Gurion's words – '*You* bear the responsi-bility.'"

Ruhama Hermon, who ran his office at the time, puts it simply. "He broke," she says. "To me it seems very human. He was alone. There was terrible procrastination among the politicians. But among the generals there was a sense of confidence and determination. Rabin had to walk between the two. When he came back from seeing Ben-Gurion it was as though an extra boulder had been placed on his back. Every day his shoulders seemed to sag lower. He was sending young men off to war and he didn't know how many would come back." After all, she says, "the man was flesh and blood. The fact that he came out of it so quickly shows what he was made of."

In his personal crisis, Rabin called Ezer Weizman, the former air force commander who was now deputy Chief of Staff, to his home. There are two versions of what transpired. Rabin wrote that he asked Weizman: "Am I to blame? Should I relinquish my post?" Weizman claims that Rabin actually asked him to take over as Chief of Staff, and that he turned it down. "I made him no such offer," Rabin insisted, "nor was I empowered to 'bequeath' the job to him or anyone else."

Both agree, though, that Weizman talked Rabin out of resigning. An army doctor was called and Rabin given a sedative. He slept for much of 24 May, and Weizman filled the breach, chairing a meeting of the General Staff and later meeting Eshkol to brief him on the latest developments. Weizman did not inform the public of the Chief of Staff's condition. But shortly after Rabin's assassination, Dov Goldstein revealed that at Rabin's official send-off to his ambassadorial post in Washington in 1968, Weizman issued him a private warning: "If you're harbouring plans in your heart for a political career when you return from Washington, don't forget that I'm here to tell the story." When Rabin battled with Peres for the Labour leadership prior to the 1974 elections, Weizman, by then a Likud politician, made good that dark promise.

On 25 May, Rabin returned to his post and resumed command, ordering the full mobilisation of all reserves – 80 per cent of Israel's armed forces. Israel, he knew, could not afford the economic cost of keeping the reserves mobilised for an extended period. Since Israel did not want to launch an attack if Johnson was about to intervene, Rabin urged that a cable be sent to the Foreign Minister Abba Eban, then in the United States, asking him to establish the American position. Rabin felt that if Washington was not going to step in to remove the blockade, Eshkol's cabinet would vote for war.

At the same time, with war increasingly likely and the public losing confidence in its political leaders, pressure was mounting on Eshkol to bring Moshe Dayan, the hero of the 1956 Sinai Campaign, into his government. On 1 June, Dayan was drafted into the cabinet as Minister of Defence. Opposition leader Menachem Begin also joined what became a National Unity Government, as a minister without portfolio. War was still a few days off. But once the American response arrived and it was clear Johnson was not going to send an international flotilla to break the blockade of the Strait, it became a matter of setting the date for a pre-emptive strike. Immediately after Dayan's appointment, Rabin and Gavish held a decisive meeting with him. Before going in, Gavish says he asked Rabin which plan he should present: the one for a limited attack or the one for all-out assault. Recalls Gavish: "Rabin told me, 'Your plan.' He'd become convinced there was no alternative to all-out war."

On 4 June, the cabinet voted for war. Israel faced a formidable constellation of forces. The Egyptian troops in the Sinai were backed up by 800 tanks and 242 fighters and bombers, half of them state-of-the-art Mig-21s. None of these planes, though, would ever leave the ground. A battle plan, drawn up by Weizman and air force chief Mordechai Hod, and blessed by Rabin, went into effect. At 7.45 a.m. on 5 June – while the Egyptian air force was eating breakfast – Israeli planes took off. Sweeping over Egyptian airfields, they destroyed runways and radar stations and wiped out combat and transport planes on the ground. Within three hours the Egyptian air force had been destroyed. It was a daring attack. Almost all of Israel's 200 warplanes – including training aircraft adapted for fighting roles – had been thrown into the strike; a mere 12 had been kept behind to protect the country's skies. But the gamble paid off, and by the end of the first day the war was essentially won. When Syria and Jordan joined in the hostilities later that morning, they received similar treatment; the Jordanian and Syrian air forces were smashed by Israeli pilots. Within 16 hours, 400 enemy planes had been destroyed; Israel had lost just 19.

With air superiority, the IDF's ground offensive swept through Sinai. Tal's armoured forces reached El Arish by the evening of the first day. By day two, Sharm al-Sheikh, the southernmost point in Sinai, had fallen without a single shot being fired. Mordechai Gur's paratroop brigade, meanwhile, was dispatched to Jerusalem, to capture the northern Arab suburbs, while the Jerusalem Brigade fought to the south of the city. Dayan initially opposed taking the Old City, home of the Temple Mount and its mosques and the Western Wall – the holiest site in Judaism – but reversed his decision.

On the morning of 7 June, Gur's paratroopers broke through Lions' Gate into the Old City. Having faced tough resistance in the Muslim Quarter, by late morning the paratroopers reached the Western Wall, revered as the last remnant of the Second Temple. The Old City was in Israeli hands. Jerusalem had been reunited under Jewish control for the first time in 2,000 years.

As soon as word came through that Israeli soldiers were at the Wall, Dayan and Rabin set off for the capital. Possessed of a keen sense of history, Dayan arrived with a battery of photographers to record his entry through Lions' Gate. At first, recalls Uzi Narkiss, the Central Command chief, "Dayan advanced alone. Then he turns round and says, 'Yitzhak, you too. Uzi, you too.'" The three entered together.

Walking into the Old City, Rabin later recalled, was overwhelming: "In 1948 we had been forced to leave East Jerusalem in the enemy's hands, and ever since the outbreak of the present war we had been dogged by the feeling we must not miss the historic opportunity again," he wrote. "As we made our way through the streets I remembered from childhood, pungent memories played on my emotions... For years I secretly harboured the dream that I might play a part not only in gaining Israel's independence but in restoring the Western Wall to the Jewish people... I knew that never again in all my life would I experience quite the same peak of elation."

Simultaneously, Israeli troops swept through the West Bank, conquering the major cities, bringing hundreds of thousands of Palestinians under what was to prove almost three decades of Israeli occupation. After the war, Rabin declared that Israel had to emphasise its military supremacy, but also had to be ready to trade the newly conquered territory for peace. It was for trying to close that circle, to pull the IDF back out of the West Bank under the peace accords with the Palestinians, that Rabin was to be gunned down by an Israeli extremist 28 years later.

Residents on the northern border were now pushing for an assault on the Golan, and both Rabin and General David (Dado) Elazar, commander of the northern front, were ready to comply. But Dayan, who feared Soviet intervention if Israel attacked, refused to give the go-ahead. Only under pressure from Rabin and Elazar did Dayan finally agree to a limited attack – the IDF was to take the ridge overlooking the Galilee, but not to advance beyond three kilometres from the border. Rabin objected, believing that the heavy casualties that he expected in a battle for the Golan could not be justified if the army was not going to take the entire Heights.

On 8 June, for the first time since the start of the war, Rabin slept at home. When he returned to the command bunker the next morning, he was greeted with the news that Dayan had changed his mind and given Elazar the go-ahead for an all-out assault on the heights. Rabin hopped into a helicopter and flew north. The fighting was fierce and casualties were high. Israeli soldiers inched their way up the rocky slopes, often engaging in hand-to-hand combat. Returning to the command bunker in Tel Aviv, Rabin now ordered Elazar to send significant forces to Quneitra, the main town on the heights, only 60 kilometres from Damascus. Dayan, however, informed Rabin that all military operations had to end by the next morning – to meet a United Nations Security Council cease-fire deadline. When Rabin re-established contact with Elazar, the general said the troops were already on their way to Quneitra. "There was something in Dado's tone that made me suspicious," Rabin recalled in his memoirs, "but I didn't expend much effort in an attempt to remove my doubts. Only after the war did I learn that at the time I was talking with Dado, the brigade was still awaiting orders miles from the Syrian border." The IDF occupied Quneitra on 10 June. That evening a cease-fire went into effect. Two days later, on 12 June, Israeli soldiers took control of the strategic outpost of Mount Hermon which had been deserted by the Syrians.

"We could have extended the areas under our control," Rabin later wrote. "There was no Egyptian force capable of halting the IDF had we intended to occupy Cairo. The same held for Amman. And on 11 June, it would not have required much effort to take Damascus. But we had not gone to war to acquire territories, and those we already occupied presented enough of a burden."

With the war over, Israel found itself in an unprecedented strategic position – with the Golan, the West Bank and East Jerusalem, the Gaza Strip and the Sinai Peninsula in its hands, the territory Israel controlled was over three times as large as it had been just a week earlier. And Israel now also controlled a hostile million-strong population. Instead of the massive losses the army grave-diggers had braced for, 777 Israeli soldiers were killed, compared to the 6,000 casualties in the War of Independence.

On 29 July, Rabin received an honorary doctorate from the Hebrew University of Jerusalem. As much as being a tribute to the

IDF, it was seen as an attempt to redress the injustice that many felt had been perpetrated when Dayan, especially in the international media, received much of the credit for the victory. While the dashing, eye-patched Dayan clearly boosted morale at a time when Israelis were fearing destruction, it was Rabin who had readied the IDF for victory. "The whole credit," says Mordechai Bar-On, "goes to Rabin. He prepared the army. The army was ready like a spring. Even during the war Dayan made only minor changes."

It was Bar-On who drafted the speech Rabin gave at the university's Mount Scopus campus, accepting the doctorate. He spoke not only of victory, but of the price of victory, of the camaraderie between soldiers, and even of the enemy's anguish. "The university," Rabin said, "has conferred this honorary title on us in recognition of our army's superiority of spirit and morals, as revealed in the heat of war. For we are standing in this place by virtue of a battle which, though forced upon us, was forged into a victory astounding the world. War is intrinsically harsh and cruel, bloody and tear-stained, but this particular war, which we have just undergone, brought forth rare and magnificent instances of heroism and courage, together with humane expressions of brotherhood, comradeship and spiritual greatness... We find more and more a strange phenomenon among our fighters. Their joy is incomplete, and more than a small portion of sorrow and shock prevails in their festivities. And there are those who abstain from celebration. The warriors in the front lines saw with their own eyes not only the glory of victory but the price of victory: their comrades who fell beside them bleeding. And I know that even the terrible price which our enemies paid touched the hearts of many of our men. It may be that the Jewish people has never learned or accustomed itself to feel the triumph of conquest and victory, and therefore we receive it with mixed feelings."

Far from delivering a euphoric victory speech, Rabin had addressed his audience on a deep moral and spiritual plane. His tone that day gave a clear indication that the outgoing Chief of Staff was destined for a second career, again crucial to his country's history, out of uniform.

4

An Unlikely Ambassador

"HOLD ME OR I'll fall out of my chair." That's how the Prime Minister, Levi Eshkol, responded when Yitzhak Rabin suggested himself as Israel's next ambassador to the United States of America. It was March 1967, three months before the Six Day War that made Rabin an international hero, but he'd been eyeing the job since at least 1963 when, during a trip to the US capital with Leah, he'd told her of his desire to succeed the urbane Abe Harman as Israeli envoy there.

The subject was pushed to the back burner as the war loomed in May. But even after the war, when Rabin renewed his lobbying for the position, he seemed a far-from-natural candidate to represent Israel in the world's most important capital. After all, the career soldier was known for speaking his mind, and he was unskilled and uninterested in chit-chat; furthermore, as Yehuda Avner, the British-born diplomat who had a senior position at the embassy under Rabin, put it, he "was not capable of telling a lie" – all characteristics hardly befitting a diplomat.

But when Eshkol questioned Rabin's qualifications, the general dismissed as immaterial his lack of diplomatic graces and lectured the premier about Israel's need to strengthen its links with the United States. The post-war French ban on arms sales to Israel was still in the future, but Rabin, as the country's top soldier, was already anticipating that the country's principal source of arms would soon dry up. It was in Washington, he was convinced, that Israel would find a fitting source of military and political support.

Rabin was scheduled to leave the army on 31 December. He said that Eshkol, despite his initial reservations, came around to support the idea fairly quickly, though he insisted that the Foreign Minister give his approval as well. In his memoirs, Rabin says that it was Abba

Eban's opposition that held up his appointment for some weeks. Yet Eban, in *Personal Witness*, published in 1990, suggests that it was *he* who encouraged the Prime Minister to send Rabin to Washington. Whatever the truth, when Rabin did finally take up the job, he and Eban not only differed on important questions of policy, but also constantly jockeyed for the political upper hand *vis-à-vis* the Prime Minister.

Arriving with Leah and 12-year-old Yuval (Dalia remained in Israel to finish high school and then enter the army), Rabin took up his post in February 1968. "He was viewed as a rough diamond," recalls Joseph Sisco, a former Undersecretary of State, who worked closely with Rabin when he was ambassador and also during his first term as Prime Minister, and remained a good friend until Rabin's death. "He knew English when he came, but not terribly well. But he had a special feeling for the US, for two reasons. For one, because his father had lived in Chicago 12 years or so, Yitzhak talked about the city all the time. Second, his whole concept – and on this we totally agreed – was that the security and survival of Israel was inextricably linked to the United States."

Nachman Shai accompanied Rabin on a number of trips to the United States when he served the then Defence Minister as media adviser in the mid-1980s. He recalls the strong feelings Rabin expressed about the country, and traces them back to his ambassadorial years: "Rabin fell in love with America when he arrived there, and he studied it. He studied it at the simplest, most superficial level at first. Sports, politics, wealth." (An American who worked closely with Rabin over many years observed less delicately that "he liked rich men". And indeed, many of the friends he cultivated, and spent his Saturdays playing tennis with, were Jews of great wealth and influence.)

Shai lists more of the qualities of American life that appealed to Rabin: "Baseball, the distances, the openness. He said to me more than once: 'Europe I pass over in flight. I don't land there.' He may also have been comfortable in America because he didn't have to rely on interpreters. But he hated the British and he hated the French too."

Ruhama Hermon, who accompanied him from the army General Staff in Tel Aviv to run his office at the Washington embassy, recalls some of the inexperienced ambassador's *faux pas* as he began his mission: "Once he stood in the ambassador's residence welcoming guests when he noticed that he was wearing different shoes on each foot. And when a female guest asked for whisky on the rocks, he filled her glass with whisky and soda, only afterward remembering the ice. When the glass was already in her hand, he threw in the ice cubes apologetically, and the drink spilled on her dress.''

Rabin's own taste for whisky, which much later in his career led to unsubstantiated charges that he had a drinking problem, can probably be traced to this period. Years after he'd left the city, he told a journalist that it was in Washington that he'd discovered that a glass of Scotch could help ease his way through many an otherwise awkward social engagement.

Uncertain as he may have been on the party circuit and the dance floor (Hermon also recalled how his office had been flooded with offers from people wanting to teach him "to dance the tango", after the appointment had been announced), Rabin had clear plans even before he embarked for the US capital. In a memorandum he prepared for the foreign ministry shortly before his departure, he outlined his views on what he believed should be Israel's goals vis-à-vis the US. Its principal message dealt with the country's defence requirements: Israel needed to upgrade its air force and other weapons systems, particularly in light of the Soviet weapons flooding into the Arab countries in the wake of their June 1967 disaster. Some of the other points he made were that Israel must co-ordinate with the Americans on its policies on any eventual peace negotiations; Israel should be ready to modify its position to take US interests into account, specifically the American concern over the uninterrupted flow of Arab oil; and the need to secure American financial aid – at the time still a far-fetched idea. Rabin's brilliance was that he eventually came to realise that he could use the inevitable clashes in interests between the two countries to extract concessions from the Americans. As long-time aide Amos Eiran, the embassy official who was responsible for working Capitol Hill during the years Rabin was ambassador, notes, "Rabin wasn't automatically opposed to arms sales to Arab countries. We knew that we couldn't always prevent the sales; so, instead, we'd try to get compensation."

The month before Rabin's arrival, the Prime Minister, Levi Eshkol, had visited the United States and secured President Johnson's promise to sell Israel 50 F-4 Phantom jets, then the most sophisticated jet fighter in the world. From the time of that oral promise until the actual delivery of the planes, however, nearly two years passed. There were those in the US administration who wanted to make the deal conditional on Israeli concessions: agreement to withdraw from territories occupied during the Six Day War in the context of a peace settlement, or agreement to sign the nuclear nonproliferation treaty.

One of Rabin's first wrangles with the administration was over the second demand. But before the issue escalated into a major policy disagreement, Johnson had second thoughts and ordered his administration to stop trying to link the Phantom deal to a particular Israeli concession. In October, shortly before the presidential election, Johnson publicly announced his support for the sale, though it was still another year before the first 16 planes were delivered.

Even if Johnson's decision helped Democratic presidential candidate Hubert Humphrey earn the Jewish vote, it wasn't enough: in January 1969 Richard Nixon became President. Fortunately Rabin had already established a relationship with him. Three years earlier, Nixon, then a lawyer in private practice in New York but setting the groundwork for his return to national politics, made a tour of key trouble spots around the world. In Tel Aviv, the American Embassy held a dinner in his honour, but most Israeli VIPs apparently considered Nixon a nobody, and the only official of any gravity who attended the party was the then Chief of Staff Yitzhak Rabin. (Explaining why he went, Rabin wrote that Nixon "had come to Israel after a visit to Vietnam, and I was naturally interested in hearing his assessments of the situation there".) Not only that, Rabin offered to "show him around", says Eiran. "And this wasn't to kindergartens. He met Nixon at the door of his hotel, and took him on a helicopter tour of military installations. Nixon appreciated this a lot."

Sisco explains that Rabin had a keen understanding of Richard Nixon's view of the Middle East. "Nixon looked at the region in two dimensions. First, in terms of East and West (that is, the Cold War); and second, psychologically, Nixon always had a feeling of identification with the underdog, and he equated that with Israel's position. I heard Nixon say, 'By God, those Israelis are tough, they can take care of the Arabs.'"

There was another figure in the Nixon administration whose relationship with Rabin took on critical importance – Henry Kissinger. Many have speculated about Kissinger's true feelings toward Israel and the Jewish people, suggesting that this refugee from Nazi Germany bent over backwards to play down his Jewishness and deny any partiality to Israel, so as to deflect charges of dual loyalty at home. But there is little evidence to support the charge that Kissinger was a "self-hating Jew". Max Fisher, the Detroit millionaire who for nearly half a century has played a crucial role in both Republican and world Jewish affairs, says people put "too much emphasis on Kissinger's being worried about being Jewish. I dealt with him a lot, and I never felt any anti-Israel tendency." He does add, though, that Kissinger is a "very complicated guy". Fisher explains that when Golda Meir became Prime Minister – after the sudden death of Levi Eshkol in February 1969 – she insisted on relating to Kissinger "as a nice Jewish boy who should do whatever she wanted". Of course, there's no suggestion that the American complied.

With Rabin, relations ran deeper. Kissinger, first as national security adviser, and then, after Nixon's re-election in 1972, as Secretary of State, saw the world mainly through the prism of the Cold War. Rabin, intending to compliment Kissinger in his memoirs, called him "a great manipulator of events and people". But it was largely through Rabin's influence, it seems, that Kissinger eventually came to appreciate Israel's importance in its own right, not simply as a crucial player in the global struggle between the superpowers. According to Yehuda Avner, Rabin perceived Kissinger as the only US Secretary of State "who understood the Arab-Israeli conflict. The two had a very intense dialogue." Fisher tells how during the tense negotiations that accompanied the question of Israeli assistance to Jordan during "Black September" in 1970, Kissinger called him to complain that Rabin and Meir "are being too tough on me".

Kissinger and Rabin first met in Tel Aviv in 1966, when Rabin invited the then Harvard professor to lecture at Israel's National Defence College. They met again in Israel two years later, before Rabin's departure for the United States, and discussed at length their views on regional and global politics. They continued their formal and informal contacts throughout Rabin's stay in Washington, and up to Rabin's death.

Nachman Shai calls Nixon and Kissinger Rabin's "two gurus". He says it was clear during Rabin's defence ministry years in the mid-'80s that "when we set up his schedule of meetings in the US, he would always visit them. In my opinion, with Nixon, it was that he wanted to show him that 'he had made it again.' " This was after 1977, when Rabin had resigned in disgrace from the Prime Minister-ship for financial improprieties, in a manner that superficially resembled Nixon's resignation in 1974.

But Shai attributes the deep relationship with the two to the ambassadorial years. Nixon and Kissinger, he says, "were hawks, but flexible ones. They were stubborn to a certain point, but after that, there was no choice, they recognised you had to talk. And Rabin did exactly the same thing," he observes, a reference to Rabin's eventual reconciliation to the idea of talking to the Palestine Liberation Organisation.

Two themes that coloured Rabin's entire tenure in Washington were the embryonic "peace process" with the Arabs and US arms sales to Israel. He was far-sighted enough to link the two, to the benefit of Israel.

Immediately after the Six Day War, as punishment for Israel's pre-emptive strike, President Johnson froze the shipment of arms to Israel for five months – even those whose sale had already been agreed upon. Rabin believed that this encouraged the Arabs to retain their belief that Israel could be vanquished militarily, and encouraged the Russians to supply them with the armaments to keep trying. Aided by such events as the virtual civil war in Jordan in 1970, during which King Hussein actually asked the Israelis to come to his aid militarily, Rabin was enormously successful in convincing the Americans that it was in their interest to help Israel defend itself. If in fiscal years 1968, 1969 and 1970, the United States awarded Israel military credits worth $25 million, $85 million and $30 million respectively, the figures jumped in '71, '72 and '73 to $545 million, $300 million and $307.5 million.

But the dynamic was a tense one, largely owing to two major plans to "bring peace" to the Middle East, and the determination of the United States not to let the Soviet Union get the upper hand in the region. Ironically, it was the Israeli cabinet, only a few days after the end of the Six Day War, on 19 June 1967, that adopted a reso-lution calling for a pullback to the international border with Egypt and Syria in return for peace and full diplomatic relations. The West Bank and Gaza, and the situation of the Palestinian refugees, were to be left to later discussions. The Foreign Minister, Abba Eban, communicated the plan within days to the US government. Two months later, however, the Israeli government modified that posi-tion. But the United States was not informed of the change, nor was the ambassador, Rabin, when he took up his position, told of either the original resolution or of the change in policy.

By November 1967, the United Nations Security Council had passed Resolution 242, which, among other things, called for Israeli withdrawal from the territories, the end of belligerency between all the states in the region, and recognition of secure boundaries. As Middle East analyst William Quandt put it, in *Decade of Decisions*, published in 1977: "The resolution fell just short of calling on Israel to withdraw from all territories and on the Arabs to make 'full peace' with Israel."

From then on, Israel had to contend with the separate peace efforts of UN negotiator Gunnar Jarring, beginning in 1968, and of US Secretary of State William Rogers, whose plan of October 1969 called for Israeli withdrawal from all the territories in return for Arab recognition and secure borders. Jarring's attempt was based on the terms of Resolution 242, which the Arab states had all rejected, but he seemed to think it was reasonable to expect Israel to withdraw from the occupied territories before negotiations with the Arabs.

As ambassador, though, Rabin's chief concern was the quiet attempt by the United States to enlist support for the Rogers Plan. He responded with a "pink sheet", in which he charged Nixon's Secretary of State with trying to impose a settlement on Israel, and pre-empting negotiations between it and its neighbours. Rogers was furious that a foreign diplomat had the temerity to criticise the US government, and his relationship with Israel was permanently soured.

The "pink sheets" were a channel Rabin used for informally disseminating his views on critical issues to the press and officials. Their origin is explained by Yehuda Avner: "One day Rabin had a contentious discussion with Kissinger about the supply of planes. We thought Kissinger was trying to link their supply to concessions, something he later denied – and I suggested we leak the story to the press. But when we came back to the embassy, it was already evening and everything was locked up. My secretary could find only pink paper, so we typed it up on that. I called Hedrick Smith [of *The New York Times*], I think it was, and said, 'I've got this interesting story.' And that was the birth of the pink sheets." The institution infuriated Abba Eban – as did a direct channel of communication that Rabin established with the Prime Minister – and he appealed to Golda Meir to order Rabin to discontinue his initiative. She did, but the pink sheets continued to go out.

Both the Jarring and Rogers plans were non-starters. The Arab states were not yet close to being ready to make peace with Israel, and Israel would not begin to consider pulling back from the cease-fire lines until its enemies at least expressed willingness to enter direct negotiations. One of Rabin's major challenges as ambassador was bringing the US to accept this position, which most American diplomats said they thought was unrealistic.

Two major events took place involving Israel and its neighbours in 1970, and both were to have a significant influence on the country's relations with the United States and on Rabin's standing in Washington. The first was the escalation, followed by a cease-fire, in the War of Attrition, the drawn-out conflict with Egypt (with a front along the border with Jordan as well) that began in 1968 and ended two years later, with a total of nearly 600 Israeli military deaths. With its vast population and constant supply of arms from the Soviets, the Egyptians could afford to keep up the military pressure on Israel, principally with steady artillery attacks across the Suez Canal. Largely due to the prodding of Rabin, who argued with the cabinet in a visit to Israel in December 1969 that the United States would not oppose such attacks (and in fact did not), the Israelis began to step up the level of their responses with deep bombing raids against military and industrial targets in the Egyptian heartland. The most significant consequence of Israel's more aggressive posture was greatly increased Soviet involvement, including the deployment of SAM-3 missiles around major Egyptian population centres and the arrival of Soviet pilots to fly Soviet planes against the Israelis.

When the Soviets went so far as to move missile launchers into the Suez Canal region, the United States issued a stern warning to Moscow (Nixon's note advised the Soviets that the two superpowers needed to "be very careful in their action to prevent a confrontation which neither wants"), and efforts to bring about an end to the fighting went into full swing. A cease-fire took effect in August 1970, and was accompanied by American guarantees that it would supply Israel with enough weaponry and equipment to maintain the balance of forces in the region.

The other major political–military event that served to bind the United States and Israel even closer occurred in Jordan that September. Palestinian terrorists, who increasingly had been acting with impunity in the Kingdom, hijacked four Western airliners to the Jordanian desert and blew them up. King Hussein went on the offensive, killing thousands of Palestinians in their refugee camps. Then Syria sent 250–300 tanks into Jordan to help the Palestinians.

Golda Meir was on a state visit to the United States. In New York with her, Rabin received an urgent call from Nixon. Former embassy official Amos Eiran recalls: "Nixon wanted to see Rabin.

He even sent a plane to bring him from New York to Washington. Using maps, Rabin gave the Americans an analysis of the situation. He had, after all, been head of the IDF Northern Command before he was Chief of Staff."

The Americans also passed along a request from King Hussein that Israel bomb the Syrian forces in northern Jordan. Furious consultations ensued, which resulted in Israel's agreeing to attack the Syrian tanks if the United States in turn would guarantee it a protective umbrella from the Sixth Fleet, stationed in the Mediterranean, should there be any reactive move by Egypt. The US agreed. Before Israel was required to act, though, Hussein himself struck the Syrian tanks from the air. The Syrians and their Soviet sponsors knew of the American–Israeli co-operation, and the combination of pressures led to a Syrian pullback across the border. Israel never fired a shot. But, as Rabin noted in his memoirs, "Israel's willingness to co-operate closely with the United States in protecting American interests in the region altered her image in the eyes of many officials in Washington. We were considered a partner."

Kissinger phoned the ambassador a few days later and asked him, according to Rabin, to communicate to Golda Meir the President's feelings that "the United States is fortunate in having an ally like Israel in the Middle East. These events will be taken into account in all future developments."

As Israel's position with the United States government became more firmly grounded, a subtle change took place in the relationship between the embassy and the leadership of the American Jewish community. In the days when Israel obtained most of its arms from France, and State Department Arabists had sway over American policy, visiting Prime Minister David Ben-Gurion was not invited to the White House, having to make do with a meeting with John F. Kennedy in a New York hotel. In that era, Israeli diplomats were happy to make use of whatever assistance wealthy or well-connected Jews could give them in Washington. Even today, AIPAC (the American Israel Public Affairs Committee, the principal US organisation lobbying on behalf of Israel) plays a critical role representing Israel's interests before Congress. But Rabin always felt that relations with the White House were another matter, and both the force of his personality and the evolution of Israel's status in Washington meant that he was able to have direct access to the President and his top aides. Rabin – both as ambassador, and during his two later periods as Israeli Prime Minister – never liked the idea of intermediaries representing his government *vis-à-vis* the executive branch. Nachman Shai explains it bluntly: "He was willing to take the $3 billion a year that was eventually obtained by this system, but he wasn't willing to accept the methods, the organisations that accompanied this."

But on the vexing issue of Soviet Jewry, Rabin found himself caught in the middle. He both resisted efforts by the administration to take a position contrary to that of American Jews, but at the same time avoided becoming too closely identified with their cause. With the full support of American Jews, Senator Henry Jackson, together with his Congressional colleague Charles Vanik, sponsored an amendment, passed in 1975, that would have linked the granting of "Most Favored Nation" status to the USSR to that country's dropping its draconian restrictions on Jewish emigration. But although, in his memoirs, the sincerity of Rabin's deep admiration for Jackson is unmistakable (Yehuda Avner says Rabin saw Jackson as "the embodiment of virtue for its own sake"), so is the ambivalence he felt about the bill that carried Jackson's name: "Israel had not written the Jackson amendment; but once it had been placed on the agenda of the American public, she certainly was not about to oppose it."

The problem for Rabin was that the American administration, then deeply involved in the process of *détente*, pressured him to lobby in Congress *against* Jackson–Vanik. He says he refused, but makes clear at the same time that he did not actively campaign on behalf of Soviet Jewry.

American Jews have traditionally always supported the Democratic presidential candidate and been strongly behind the liberal causes of the day. Many were among the leaders of the organised opposition to the Vietnam War. Though Richard Nixon had run in 1968 on a platform of bringing the Vietnam War to an end, his tactics involved widening the war. Well before he arrived in Washington, Rabin understood that he would do well to keep his views on the conduct of the war to himself. It was, of course, an issue that was dividing America, and he certainly had no interest in taking sides. But the presence of a former Chief of Staff who had led his country's army in a brilliant victory on three separate fronts was a temptation too hard for many Americans to resist.

In the course of his five years in Washington, Rabin was asked to lecture on numerous occasions at various American military academies and other venues. (Later, when he returned home and ran for Knesset, he was attacked for accepting fees – totalling up to $90,000,

according to journalist Robert Slater, the author of *Rabin of Israel* —
for speaking engagements during his time as ambassador. He even
took money for speaking at bar mitzvahs.) Though his nominal topic
was invariably the Middle East, questions from the audience focused
primarily on the way the United States was handling the war in
South-East Asia. At the same time, Rabin was granted unprecedented access to the Pentagon and a variety of military installations,
and on numerous occasions was sought out by members of the
military for his comments and advice.

In his memoirs, Rabin describes one characteristic conversation he
had with the noted Washington pundit Joseph Alsop. He recalls
how he asked Alsop if the Americans had precise military and
political objectives in Vietnam. Rabin writes: "The expression on
Alsop's face was of the 'I thought you'd never ask' variety... 'We
must eliminate the fighting power of the Vietcong and North
Vietnam!' he thundered. 'There's no other way.'"

Rabin writes that that sort of talk reminded him of what he'd
heard from French officers in 1960 during the war against the FLN
freedom fighters in Algeria. He responded to Alsop, "'If that's the
way you see the concept of winning, you'll lose the war in Vietnam.
There's no way of eliminating the fighting capacity and spirit of tens
of millions of people who are dedicated to the sanctity of their
cause.'" The same thought must have crossed Rabin's mind again
two decades later, as he came to realise that Israel could not destroy
the fighting spirit of the Palestinians by breaking their bones.

Nevertheless, Rabin had a hard time comprehending the spirit of
revolution that was sweeping America during his time there.
Leonard Fein, the founding editor of *Moment* magazine, describes a
meeting of the General Assembly of Jewish Organisations in 1970
when Rabin encountered "a group of young liberal Jews who were
inside the hall protesting American involvement in the Vietnam
War. He went over and started berating them. I remember that we
were all taken aback that the Israeli ambassador would involve
himself in the issue, even taking it upon himself to lecture American
citizens on how they should act toward their own government."

When the 1972 US election came around, it was clear to anyone
who took an interest in the matter whom Yitzhak Rabin supported
for president. One Washington insider, a Democrat, says the
ambassador "worked unashamedly for Nixon against George
McGovern... McGovern wasn't anti-Israel, he was anti-settlements"
in the occupied territories. (At the time, the type of settlements

being established by the Labour-led government were limited to the areas that Rabin's mentor Yigal Allon had deemed critical to Israel's security.) "McGovern talked about peace with the Palestinians, and because he was a peacenik, he irritated Rabin no end."

Paul Berger, a prominent Washington lawyer and today a member of the Jewish Agency executive, recalls speaking with Rabin at an embassy party that year. "I said I thought that Nixon would, in the long run, be bad for Israel. 'Israel,' Rabin responded, 'lives in the short run.'" Berger adds: "I voted for McGovern, but in retrospect, I can see how he would have been terrible for Israel. He just didn't understand the situation, and his sympathies were with the Palestinians. But I should add that Rabin never suggested to me or anyone I know that we should not support the Democrats. It was very simple: he felt he could count on the Republicans."

Berger recounts an incident that occurred around the dinner table at his Chevy Chase home shortly before Rabin's departure from Washington, in 1973: "It was a small dinner. Bill Douglas [the late, intensely liberal Supreme Court justice] was among the guests. The two of them had a violent argument about Cambodia," where the US was carrying out a bombing campaign, and supplying South Vietnamese troops with arms and equipment. "Rabin told Douglas: 'It's nice that you have such liberal views. But if the US pulls out, millions of Cambodians will die.' The two argued so fiercely that the next day each one called to apologize for his behavior." Of course, a few years later, after foreign troops did withdraw from Cambodia, the Khmer Rouge regime murdered an estimated 4 million of their countrymen.

In any case, in June 1972, on a visit to Israel, Rabin gave an interview to Israel Radio in which he said, with respect to the forthcoming presidential election in the US, "While we appreciate the support in the form of words which we are getting from one camp, we must prefer the support in the form of deeds which we are getting from the other." Nixon, of course, had not yet been nominated for a second term, nor had McGovern received the Democratic nomination, yet the Israeli ambassador could be understood as having endorsed the incumbent. Yuval Elitzur, the Jerusalem correspondent for *The Washington Post*, heard the interview, and thought it was worth reporting to his paper. It created a major fracas back in Washington. The Israeli Embassy denied that Rabin had been properly quoted and released another version of his remarks. Elitzur says that the newspaper's publisher, Katherine

Graham, "said that she wanted to see a transcript of the interview. If I was wrong, I could look for another job; if I was right, the paper would run an editorial." It ran an editorial, titled "Israel's Undiplomatic Diplomat".

There's a telling postcript to the story. A few weeks later, says Elitzur, he had occasion to be in Washington, and he dropped in at the embassy. Staff warned him to keep away from the second floor, where Rabin worked, telling him the ambassador was furious with him. "I figured," he recalls, "OK, he doesn't want to see me, I won't go upstairs. But soon after, I had to fly to New York. And who is on the same plane as me – Yitzhak Rabin. As he passed me on his way to first class, he nodded and greeted me curtly." After the trip, in front of the LaGuardia arrivals terminal, Elitzur found himself passing the ambassador's limousine. Rabin's driver stopped him and said the ambassador wanted to see him in the car. "I came to the door and Rabin said, in his flat style, 'Elitzur, you're going to Manhattan? I'll give you a ride.' That's it. I got in, and we talked the entire ride. He never mentioned the incident, and thereafter we had very good relations, as we had had before the radio interview."

Yitzhak Rabin's tour of duty in Washington came to an end in March 1973. A few months earlier, he and Soviet envoy Anatoly Dobrynin had been named "Ambassadors of the Year" by *Newsweek*. But a colleague back in Jerusalem described receiving a letter from him at the time in which he wrote that it didn't matter what *Newsweek* thought of you, when your own government was working behind your back. He went on to complain that the Foreign Minister, Abba Eban, had been conducting a two-year defamation campaign against him. Eban, for his part, has written that Rabin, "during his service in Washington [showed] incomprehension of the ambassadorial role... A study of his cables to Jerusalem showed periods of thoughtfulness and moderation interrupted by sudden outbursts of aggressiveness."

Eban's thoughts notwithstanding, Rabin's time in the United States was clearly a success, both personally and for Israel in general. Just before he left the country, Golda Meir came on another official visit. Her last meeting with Nixon at the White House turned out to be Rabin's parting visit to the President as well. Nixon told the Prime Minister that Rabin was the most capable ambassador in Washington, and asked her what position she expected to appoint him to when he returned home. "That depends on how he behaves," Rabin recalled her saying, embarrassing him terribly. Little more than a year later, circumstances conspired to make him Israel's first sabra – native-born – Prime Minister.

By the time he left the United States, the relationship between the two countries was on an entirely different footing than it had been on his arrival, and at least part of the credit for this must go to him. The days when Israel needed some influential American Jew with good contacts in Washington to speak on its behalf were – at least until the acrimonious years when Yitzhak Shamir was pitted against George Bush – a thing of the past. The doors to the White House and the State Department were open to the Israeli ambassador, and the little nation could now state its case for itself. The days when Israel had to beg the Americans for arms and equipment, too, were history. Israel was now perceived by the American superpower as a strategic asset in the Middle East.

5

Instant Prime Minister

WHEN HE TOOK the oath of office as Prime Minister on 3 June 1974, Yitzhak Rabin was a political novice. He'd been in the Knesset for less than six months; he'd been a junior minister for only three months in a government, haunted by the disaster of the Yom Kippur War, that did little but try to postpone its own demise. He had suddenly become the leader of a party in deep crisis, whose previous leader had won the election but was pressured to resign soon afterwards because of the Yom Kippur failures. And he'd faced severe difficulty in stitching together a coalition government, which commanded a perilous 61 votes in the 120-member Knesset.

Rabin had returned from the United States in the spring of 1973 a bright prospect, who might eventually be groomed as a successor to the incumbent Labour Party Prime Minister, Golda Meir. In September, he was chosen as 20th on his party's list of 120 candidates for the Knesset, due to be elected on 31 October, and introduced to campaign meetings as a future cabinet minister. But the Yom Kippur War changed everything. Israel managed to turn back the joint offensive launched by Syria and Egypt on the holiest day of the Jewish year, but only after it had suffered over 2,200 dead and 5,500 wounded. The war's cost could also be calculated in money – more than $9 billion – and in the public's loss of confidence in the political and military leadership, which had not been ready for the surprise attack.

In the aftermath of the war, the elections were delayed until 31 December. Labour won, but its percentage of the popular vote slipped from 47 per cent to under 40. It took several months for Meir to form a government; when it finally took shape in early March, Rabin, who had been mooted as a candidate for Defence Minister, was named Minister of Labour. "All my life," he told a reporter, "I have been collecting ex's. I am now ex-Chief of Staff, ex-ambassador to the United States, and now an ex-potential Defence Minister."

A month later, the government commission of inquiry investigating the Yom Kippur War failures submitted a preliminary report exonerating Meir and the Defence Minister Moshe Dayan, and placing the blame on army Chief of Staff David Elazar. The report was greeted with a new wave of public fury, and Meir resigned. There was no clear successor in line. Rabin, whose role in the war had been confined to unofficial defence adviser, was virtually the only top Labour figure untouched by the public reaction to the failures; with the support of Pinhas Sapir, Golda Meir's Finance Minister and power-broker, he defeated Shimon Peres 298–254 in a Labour central committee vote. He thus became Labour's candidate for Prime Minster, a shoo-in for the top post.

"Rabin was thrown into the job of Prime Minister before he was ripe for it," says Dan Pattir, a former newsman who served as Rabin's media adviser during that first premiership. "He had virtually no political experience; if he'd been, say, Defence Minister for a term before he became Prime Minister, things would have been very different."

The Rabin cabinet represented a new broom for the Labour party, but that also meant it lacked the top party people, the experienced leaders of previous governments. There was no Golda Meir, no Sapir at the finance ministry, no Abba Eban at the foreign ministry, where Rabin installed his old Palmah mentor, Yigal Allon. And there was no Moshe Dayan at the defence ministry. In his stead was Shimon Peres.

Rabin was not happy about the last appointment. "I did not consider Peres suitable," he wrote later, "since he had never fought in the IDF, and his expertise in arms purchasing did not make up for that lack of experience." But Peres was the Labour No. 2, and had to be given a commensurate position. In the years to come, Rabin came to regret the appointment bitterly – and often in public. "The Prime Minister's great strength was military," says Pattir, "but he wasn't Defence Minister. In fact, the Defence Minister was his political rival. And, to put it delicately, the two ministers did not operate in complete harmony."

Replacing Sapir at the finance ministry was Yehoshua Rabinowitz, a colourless party man who'd been mayor of Tel Aviv. Rabinowitz proved competent in dealing with the overwhelming financial problems the country faced – the Yom Kippur War had cost it a full year's gross national product – but lacked Sapir's legendary political acumen. Not only did Rabinowitz fail to inspire confidence; he had little confidence himself. In private conversations, the new Finance Minister gave Rabin's government little chance of surviving for more than a month. In the event, Rabinowitz proved to be a fairly successsful Finance Minister, but he wasn't a popular one. A political joke playing on the word ra, "bad", asked how to say "bad, worse, worst" in Hebrew and answered: "Ra, Rabin, Rabinowitz."

Despite the predictions of doom, the Rabin government survived three years. But these were years of great pressure on Rabin, who spent much of his time maintaining a razor-thin parliamentary majority – slightly boosted by the inclusion later in 1974 of the National Religious Party, in exchange for concessions on religious legislation – and protecting his own flanks from thrusts by the opposition and senior members of his own cabinet. Rabin himself considered this first term in office, marked by dissension in his own cabinet, unrest in his party and public disillusionment with his administration, to be a period of personal failure. He blamed himself for not stamping his authority firmly enough on his government. And when he returned to power in 1992, he was determined not to repeat that mistake, and therefore ran his cabinet more like a president than as a first among equals.

In retrospect, the impact of his first term can be seen in much of Rabin's behaviour and many of his attitudes during his second administration. Two experiences stand out as particularly formative: the arduous hammering out of the 1975 interim agreement with Egypt, under which Israel pulled back from part of the Sinai Peninsula; and his first eye-to-eye encounters with the zealots of the Israeli religious right, who pushed him into allowing Jewish settlement throughout the West Bank.

Rabin had been Prime Minister for only two weeks when he received a visitor in Jerusalem: Richard Nixon, the first American President ever to come to Israel. Nixon was trying to salvage his foundering presidency by emphasising his international accomplishments, paying separate visits to China and the Middle East. It was in vain; as Rabin observed sadly, "The fate of one of the most pro-Israeli Presidents had already been sealed."

Nixon resigned at the end of the summer. So Rabin's first visit to Washington as Prime Minister, in September 1974, was to meet

Gerald Ford. In talks at the White House, the two leaders discussed the Israeli position in future negotiations with the Arabs, and Israeli requests for arms and aid to fill immediate military needs, and replace stocks expended during the Yom Kippur War.

Rabin the soldier was in his element during the strategic discussions – but not at the state dinner that followed. After the meal, speeches and a concert, came the dancing. Ford invited Leah Rabin for the first dance, and swept her on to the floor. "I was in a spot," wrote Rabin later. "If only I could dance – even poorly! If only someone would get in ahead of me and invite Mrs Ford on to the dance floor. But miracles of that nature do not occur at the White House. Deciding to adopt the tactics I follow in every sphere, I strode over to Mrs Ford, who rose at my approach, obviously convinced that I was about to ask her to dance. But swallowing hard, I explained. 'I'm sorry, Mrs Ford, but I simply don't know how to dance. And I wouldn't dream of mauling your toes.'

"Now that the worst was over (or so I deluded myself) I was pleased to see the First Lady rewarding me with a warm smile. But that smile carried a double meaning. 'When I was a young woman, I used to teach dance, and I protected my toes from men less skilful than you. Come along.'" It was Henry Kissinger, the Secretary of State, who diplomatically extricated the Prime Minister from the dance floor – a rescue, Rabin said, for which he would be eternally grateful.

In the months to come, Rabin would have much more to do with Kissinger. The following March, the Secretary started his famous Middle East shuttles to work out an interim agreement between Israel and Egypt. Kissinger's technique was to fly back and forth between Rabin in Jerusalem and Egypt's Anwar Sadat in Cairo, Aswan or Alexandria, exchanging proposals and trying to narrow the gaps between the two sides. Sometimes he would do a little more, exercising his own judgment on what to pass on to the interlocutors. During one session in March, Pattir recalls that Rabin told Kissinger he would offer Sadat a non-belligerency agreement in exchange for the bulk of Sinai, apparently a line extending from El Arish on the northern coast to Ras Muhammad at the southern tip of the desert peninsula. There was no answer from Sadat.

Then Rabin offered Sadat all of Sinai, in exchange for a separate and full peace agreement – much the same deal as Sadat accepted in 1979. Still no answer. Finally, Kissinger told Rabin that it was pointless to talk about Israeli concessions of this order, because Sadat couldn't conclude a separate peace with Israel. Says Pattir: "I'm not sure that Kissinger ever presented these options to Sadat, perhaps because he felt that it was too early to bring about that kind of decision." It may even be, Pattir believes, that Kissinger didn't *want* Israel and Egypt to reach a deal so fast, since that would have eliminated his own mediation role.

The forthright no-nonsense Rabin and the subtly manipulative Kissinger were an improbable match, but the relationship they had started during Rabin's years in Washigton continued when Rabin returned to Jerusalem. Kissinger admired Rabin's analytical power, and would sometimes sound him out on non-Middle East matters – like the strategic arms limitation talks with the Soviets, or the winding down of the Vietnam War.

Kissinger would go to great lengths to gain the upper hand in the shuttle talks. Meetings often stretched deep into the night and the Israelis, who had worked a full day before sitting down at the negotiating table, felt that the Secretary had rested in the afternoon and was trying to tire them out. So, on one occasion, they planned a countermove. Before a scheduled session with Kissinger, the entire Israeli team – Rabin, other ministers and key aides – left work at noon and went home to sleep. The talks that night dragged on, but the Israelis showed no signs of fatigue. Kissinger was visibly upset.

At times, the talks produced angry exchanges and raised voices. One of the worst came in late March 1975, when Kissinger was winding down an unsuccessful shuttle, frustrated by Israeli stubbornness. In the middle of a meeting of the Israeli cabinet, Rabin received a harsh letter from Ford, in which the President expressed "profound disappointment over Israel's attitude in the course of the negotiations" and announced a "reassessment" of US policy toward Israel. Rabin, peeved, told his colleagues he was convinced Kissinger had written the letter for Ford.

At the end of that failed mission, Rabin escorted the Secretary of State to the airport, trying to explain his caution by saying that he saw the danger of resumed hostilities with Egypt as more than merely a political problem. "I regard every IDF soldier as my responsibility – almost as if he were my son. You know my own son is in command of a tank platoon on the front line in Sinai. My daughter's husband commands a tank battalion there. I know what their fate might be. But Israel is unable to accept the agreement on the present terms, and there is nothing I can do but carry that heavy burden of responsibility – the national as well as the personal."

Kissinger took the point to heart. Later on, he told Rabin that on "that day at the airport, I just couldn't control myself. All of a sudden I found myself crying."

Rabin was very interested in Kissinger's characterisations of the Egyptian leaders. The Secretary, he wrote, "was astonishingly well acquainted with the principal figures on both sides, and he would regale us with descriptions of the Egyptian, Jordanian and Syrian leaders he had met." Needless to say, Rabin added, "I am also certain that he gave the Arabs reciprocal – and equally gifted – descriptions of us."

An interim agreement between Israel and Egypt was ratified by the Israeli cabinet on 1 September 1975; it included greater flexibility on Israel's final line of withdrawal, in exchange for an ending of Ford's "reassessment" and the promise of a generous US aid package. The pullback of Israeli troops allowed Egypt to reopen the Suez Canal, closed since 1967, and operate its oil fields in the Gulf of Suez. An accompanying memorandum of understanding between the United States and Israel opened the way for a resumption of the supply of arms, including F-16 warplanes, and Washington's written consent on several key political issues, including the promise not to recognise or negotiate with the Palestine Liberation Organisation unless it renounced terror. That promise was steadfastly honoured for almost two decades, until the Bush administration opened contacts with the PLO in the early 1990s.

Involved in the drafting of every detail of the interim agreement with Egypt, Rabin insisted that the document include a clause saying that it would be superseded by a full peace agreement. "It was," says Amos Eiran, director general of the Prime Minister's Office at the time, "the first written acknowledgment, in an agreement between Israel and an Arab state, of the possibility of making peace." Rabin was greatly pleased when Kissinger brought back word from Alexandria that Sadat had accepted the clause.

In his memoirs, Rabin accentuates the point. "The 1975 agreement with Egypt was never meant to be an end in itself. As its title implies, it was designed to advance the 'momentum' toward peace, and in that sense it achieved its objective – no minor accomplishment in Middle Eastern politics. I can only hope that the next achievement along that road will prove to be as durable and successful."

A noble hope. But during the period following the signing of the interim agreement, Rabin was doing more than just hoping. In secret, he launched a series of meetings with Arab leaders, designed to open up channels for making peace. One such channel was to King Hussein of Jordan, Israel's neighbour to the east, with whom Rabin's predecessors had also met in secret. Most of the sporadic meetings were held in the Aravah desert, running from the southern end of the Dead Sea to the Gulf of Aqaba. The Israel–Jordan border – long the quietest of Israeli–Arab frontiers – ran down the middle of the valley, with nothing but wasteland separating the Israeli highway to Eilat and the parallel Jordanian road to Aqaba. The talks were held at different spots, in a special mobile-home-like structure with a dining room and a conference room, or at sites closer to Tel Aviv. Usually, Eiran says, Israel brought a second trailer, occupied by a team of experts analysing the conversation, often using closed-circuit television, and sometimes proposing responses in "real time" before the end of a session.

All but one of the meetings took place on the Israeli side of the line. Eiran says that the King would pilot a Jordanian army helicopter just across the border, sometimes on his own and sometimes accompanied by a senior Jordanian Air Force pilot, a man who was to die in the 1977 helicopter crash that took the life of Hussein's Palestinian-born third wife, Queen Alia. "I would come to the border to pick up the King," Eiran recalls. "Then we would take one of our helicopters, or go by car, to the meeting place." Over dinner – the food would be brought in from the kitchens of a nearby hotel – there would be political small talk but no negotiations; afterwards, the participants would settle down to serious discussions until late in the night. Rabin's premiership ended before anything concrete could result, but the basis had been laid for a real friendship that developed rapidly in the last 18 months of Rabin's life, when the two could finally meet in public.

There were also contacts with King Hassan II of Morocco. In early 1977, Rabin himself visited Morocco in secret, for several days, travelling via France, disguised in a shaggy, dark wig. The purpose of the meetings was to examine the possibility that Hassan would act as a conduit for contacts with Egypt. That was precisely what happened, when Menachem Begin's subsequent government used the Moroccan connection to help take the leap towards peace with Egypt.

Rabin felt the Moroccan monarch wanted to establish an alternative channel to the one conducted by the Americans, whose interests were not always identical with those of the Arabs and the

Israelis. Rabin didn't accept the King's approach, and said he didn't want to give Hassan the impression that he was abandoning the Americans. "On the other hand, I wanted to establish a direct channel, as the King had suggested," he would later tell Pattir.

Hassan also offered to try approaching Syria with Israeli peace feelers, offering to pass on a letter from Rabin to President Hafiz al-Asad, explaining why Israel was ready for an agreement; Rabin did jot down a handwritten note, but there was no reply from Asad.

There was no immediate response from the Egyptians either. But during the changeover after Labour lost the May 1977 election, Eiran showed accounts of the secret meetings with Hassan to Begin and to Eliahu Ben-Elissar, who succeeded Eiran as director general of the Prime Minister's Office. Eiran presumes that Moshe Dayan, as Begin's Foreign Minister, used the Moroccan conduit to set up his talks with Sadat aide and confidant Mohammed Hassan Tohami – secret contacts that paved the way for Sadat's historic visit to Jerusalem in November 1977.

Rabin consistently spoke in favour of the principle of "territorial compromise" in an eventual peace settlement with the Arabs, and insisted that there should be no dialogue with the PLO, hewing to the policy of Labour Party governments before him. But in keeping with his practical image, he rarely went into detail on what he saw as the shape of a future peace agreement since at the time it was no more than a vague dream.

Still, he was quite specific in one conversation reported by Shlomo Avineri, who served as director general of the foreign ministry under Yigal Allon. In an article published a month after Rabin's death, Avineri recalled that in January 1976, he had asked Rabin how he thought peace might be achieved. Rabin responded with an hour-long lecture that explained the caution of his first term – but also the strategy he would follow, after years in the political wilderness, when he returned to the premiership in 1992. "Rabin made it clear," Avineri recalled, "that an Arab-Israeli peace arrangement would involve withdrawal from most of the territory the IDF conquered during the Six Day War, except for Jerusalem, the Jordan Valley and specific points of strategic importance. Areas with heavy Arab populations could not remain under our rule forever, and in order to assure maximum negotiating flexibility, we should refrain from establishing Jewish settlements on them."

Rabin emphasised that the time was not ripe to move ahead on major territorial concessions; they couldn't take place in the shadow of Arab successes in the Yom Kippur War. Israel's mission then was to improve its strategic, diplomatic and psychological position following the trauma of October 1973, "and only afterward – he indicated a period of five years – from a position of Israeli strength, to move toward peace arrangements along those lines".

Rabin explained to Avineri that he did not see his government's task as reaching peace arrangements, and this was one reason why he had refused to consider an interim arrangement that would transfer Jericho to Jordanian control. He saw his role as improving the morale and the armaments of the military, enhancing American support of Israel politically and militarily, and most of all, "to get the idea out of the Arabs' heads that a weak Israel could make concessions. Only a strong Israel can make concessions."

This position was simultaneously both "hawkish" and "dovish", in Avineri's interpretation: generous in concessions that might be made to the Arabs in the framework of a peace arrangement, but stubborn and determined on the manner in which such an arrangement might be reached. Avineri argues that this is exactly how Rabin remained through the election of 1992: he inspired the confidence of the right and the mistrust of parts of the left with his hawkish and unyielding public image; both were misreading him. He was, argues Avineri, unable to reveal his true strategy without endangering his chances of carrying it out.

Very few people understood his real stance, not even ministers in his cabinet; but Avineri suggests that it was known in the military. Only after the Oslo accords in September 1993, was Rabin's real thinking to emerge in public.

During Kissinger's second shuttle mission in August 1975, the government arranged a gala reception for the Secretary of State at the Knesset. Angry crowds of supporters of Gush Emunim (the Believers' Bloc), a year-old organisation of Orthodox rightists who passionately opposed yielding a single inch of Israeli-held territory, did their best to disrupt the reception, laying siege to the Knesset building and rampaging through Jerusalem's streets. It was a scene that would be repeated two decades later.

The protesters were particularly incensed that a Jewish Secretary of State would ask Israel to make concessions. They jeered him as a "Jew boy", using a classic anti-Semitic phrase to express their contempt at what they saw as his obsequious behaviour; the spiritual father of Gush Emunim, Rabbi Tzvi Yehudah Kook, reviled Kissinger as "the husband of a gentile woman".

Rabin was "shocked and ashamed", and said there were no words to express his embarrassment before the Secretary. "I doubt that I shall ever witness more deplorable or misguided behaviour on the part of my countrymen," he wrote later. "If Gush Emunim had an axe to grind, it was with me and my cabinet, not with a guest who had given so much of himself in pursuit of stability and peace in the region. In fact, there can be no excuse for Jews anywhere to stoop to such obscene behaviour. I might not be able to teach Gush Emunim the rudiments of good manners, but I did have a say where rioting in the streets was concerned. The next day I called in the inspector general of the police and ordered him to put a stop to it – by force, if necessary."

But Rabin went to great lengths to avoid violence in dealing with Gush Emunim's efforts to expand settlement into the area of Biblical Samaria, the West Bank hills north of Jerusalem. In the years after the Six Day War, Labour governments had allowed limited Jewish settlement in the West Bank, restricting it mainly to the Jordan Valley and to the Etzion Bloc, an area of pre-state Jewish farming communities between Bethlehem and Hebron, which had been conquered by the Jordanian Arab Legion in 1948. Under a plan devised by Yigal Allon for the future of the territories taken in 1967, both areas were to remain under Israeli control for strategic reasons, while those parts of the West Bank with large Arab populations – like the Samarian hills – would be returned to Jordan under a future peace agreement. Though the Allon Plan had never been officially adopted, it was unofficially the policy of the Rabin government. And yet Labour had allowed settlement in Kiryat Arba, an all-Jewish suburb of the Arab city of Hebron.

Kiryat Arba was established after a group of Orthodox Jews spent Passover at an Arab-owned hotel in Hebron in the spring of 1968, and then refused to leave until the government gave them permission, more than 18 months later, to settle on land abutting Hebron. This provided the impetus for a new thrust of attempted settlement in Samaria, starting in the summer of 1974. Repeatedly, would-be settlers and their supporters arrived at a prearranged site and demanded to stay. One of these early sit-ins was attended by Ariel Sharon, then a Likud Knesset member, and several other members of parliament. Rabbi Kook, then in his eighties, was also there.

"The soldiers came to evacuate us, there were about 50 or 70 demonstrators," recalls Yehuda Ben-Meir, a former member of the top echelon of the National Religious Party who, together with Zevulun Hammer (later to become leader of the NRP), provided much of the early political backing for Gush Emunim. "They moved us out gently, respectfully, and they didn't even touch Rabbi Kook." The general heading the Central Command, Yonah Efrat, who was in charge of the operation, deployed a large group of soldiers around Kook, to make sure no one touched him.

"Those protests were real passive resistance," says Ben-Meir, who a decade later left the increasingly hawkish NRP and joined Meimad, a dovish movement of Orthodox Jews. "We didn't curse the soldiers, or try to sneak back after we'd been moved on. We just went limp, like a sack of potatoes." Ben-Meir is drawing the unmistakable distinction between those settlers of two decades ago, and the often-violent settler demonstrations during Rabin's second term of office.

The settlement attempts culminated when thousands of Gush Emunim activists gathered at the abandoned railroad station in Sebastia, west of Nablus in December 1975, determined to stay put until they were granted the right to establish a settlement in the Nablus area. Pattir says Rabin wanted to solve the problem by talking the would-be settlers into leaving, but it didn't work. "He recruited Ariel Sharon to talk to the squatters, and Haim Guri, the 'poet of the Palmah'. They went to Sebastia separately, and came back with one conclusion. They told Rabin: 'Peres [the Defence Minister] offered the settlers much more than you can ever do.' Rabin had been encircled from the right." Yehuda Ben-Meir confirms that Peres, who at the time was more hawkish than Rabin on the settlement question, was the main government contact for Gush Emunim and its political sponsors.

Rabin was adamant that the settlers had to leave, but wasn't willing to risk using force. He asked Mordechai Gur, then Chief of Staff, how many soldiers it would take to move the squatters out; Gur said a brigade. According to Pattir, Rabin recoiled. "He said, 'If it takes 3,000 soldiers, and only one fires a bullet by mistake – which is reasonable to assume, with so many guns around – it would be terrible.'" Gur agreed. The general had been counselling against the use of force throughout the confrontation, and at one point reportedly threatened to resign if Rabin ordered him to evict the settlers. "Gur said that it would be proper to use force if the settlers undermined the government's ability to govern, or if they tried to paralyse the country," Ben-Meir says. "Then he'd have no qualms about obeying the order."

Rabin could not stand the pressure, and permitted 30 families of settlers, living in mobile homes, to move into the IDF base near the village of Kaddum a few kilometres east of Nablus. The agreement was billed as a temporary measure, to end the confrontation with the settlers, but Rabin never tried to move them out – perhaps because he lacked the political will to do so, or perhaps because, at that stage, he did not want to risk a confrontation with the 10 NRP Knesset members who solidified his coalition. But it was not an arrangement that pleased Rabin. "He always said that his basic mistake was that he gave in to pressure, that he compromised," says Ben-Meir. Rabin felt that the Kaddum arrangement was forced on him by a Minister of Defence – Peres – who was not working with him, both because he was more hawkish at the time and because they were political rivals.

The experience of Kaddum – which became the settlement of Elon Moreh and where, on 18 May 1977, the day after winning the election, the Likud's Menachem Begin set the tone for his government's settlement policy by declaring that there would be "many more Elon Morehs" – made its mark on Rabin. It is seen by many as the reason why he insisted on holding the defence ministry for himself after winning the 1992 election, and where he first developed the concept of "political" and "security" settlements, a key distinction for him during his second term as Prime Minister. "It is certainly possible," says Amos Eiran, "to see that period as setting the pattern for Rabin's future relations with the settlers."

Along with ideological confrontation and political intrigue, the first Rabin administration was also marked by high drama – the brilliant rescue, on 4 July 1976, of 104 Israeli and foreign Jewish hostages from the hands of a gang of hijackers at Uganda's Entebbe airport.

News that Air France Flight 139 from Tel Aviv to Paris had been hijacked after a stopover in Athens came during the regular Sunday morning meeting of the cabinet, on 27 June 1976. Rabin quickly suggested that the hijack was connected with Wadia Haddad, operations chief of George Habash's Popular Front for the Liberation of Palestine. Not long before, Haddad had sent a similar gang to attack a plane belonging to El Al, Israel's national air carrier, in Nairobi, Kenya. Agents of the Mossad espionage agency had thwarted that attempt at the last moment, and secretly brought the terrorists to Israel.

The Nairobi gang, which included Arabs and Germans, was taken into custody on the airport perimeter. "They were ready to shoot rockets at the plane, which had many passengers, many Israelis, on it," says Amos Eiran. "We'd tracked them for a year, in a continuing operation. Our people moved at the last moment; they almost had blood on their hands, they were that close." According to Eiran, there was a heated debate about what to do with the terrorists, and someone suggested that "to avoid international complications, they should be disposed of on the way, thrown into the sea. Rabin objected forcefully, and said they had to be brought to Israel for interrogation and trial. 'That might be difficult,' he said, 'but we are a country of law and order, and I won't, under any circumstances, have any part in something like that.' "

This time, Rabin correctly guessed who was behind the Air France hijacking because the terrorists were again a mix of Arabs and Germans. The cabinet soon learned that 83 of the 230 passengers on the plane were Israelis. It reminded France that all of them were under sovereign French protection, and waited for Paris to act. In the meantime, after a stop in Benghazi, Libya, the hijacked plane flew south to Uganda, to the Entebbe airport not far from the capital city, Kampala. On landing, the Jews were separated, and most of the others allowed to leave. Rabin assembled a team including the Foreign Minister Allon, the Defence Minister Peres and the Chief of Staff Gur to manage the crisis.

Two days after the hijack, the terrorists presented their demand: over 50 "freedom fighters" must be released, most of them from Israel, and flown to Entebbe. In his memoirs, Rabin writes that Peres expressed surprise when the Prime Minister asked Gur about the possibility of a military operation. The "deplorable truth" was that 53 hours after the hijack, the Defence Minister had not consulted the Chief of Staff about rescuing the hostages. That's one side of the story. In his own memoirs, Peres claims the initiative for the military operation was his, and that Rabin was hesitant in approving it. The top officers involved in the operation have also squabbled for years over credit; success has many fathers.

From the beginning, Rabin followed two paths. On the one hand, he looked for a way to satisfy the terrorists' demands to free prisoners, putting together a list consisting of people "who did not have blood on their hands". On the other, he explored the military options. "But his assessment was always that they would not accept our list and would insist on their own," says Eiran, "and that there was no choice but to get ready for a military operation."

Over the next few days, cabinet debate centred not on whether there should be a rescue bid, but on what shape it should take. One of the first suggestions was to drop 1,000 paratroopers over nearby Lake Victoria. Rabin turned that down, saying that it "reminded him too much of the Bay of Pigs", according to Eiran. Another idea was to land a small Israeli force on the Entebbe airstrip. Again, this was rejected by Rabin. "What came into play was his personal perfectionism, as well as his knowledge and experience," says Eiran. "He was very worried about the time on the ground, worried that if the operation took too long, the Ugandan forces on the field would have time to organise. It would have been enough to sink the entire operation if one rocket had hit the first Israeli plane when it landed on the airstrip."

In the meantime, Israel was busy gathering intelligence. A number of Israelis who had been in Uganda were called in and interviewed, including those who had at one stage trained Ugandan armed forces, and employees of the Solel Boneh construction company that had built the Entebbe airport. Rechavam Zeevy – who became a Knesset member and leader of the far right-wing Moledet party, but was at the time Rabin's anti-terror adviser – went to Paris to interview the plane's freed non-Jewish passengers. On Friday night, 2 July, a rehearsal for an Israeli assault raid, called the Hercules Plan because it involved landing Hercules transport planes at Entebbe, was held at Sharm al-Sheikh, at the southern end of the Sinai Peninsula. The next day, Nahum Admoni, head of the Mossad, brought in black-and-white photographs taken from a light plane that had flown over Entebbe 24 hours earlier.

When Gur informed him that the dry run had been successful, Rabin ordered the planes carrying the assault force to take off on the seven-hour flight from Sinai to Entebbe even before the cabinet had convened; they could turn back later if the cabinet did not authorise the plan. This was necessary because the hijackers had set a deadline, and time was running out.

Before the special cabinet meeting on Saturday 3 July, scheduled for 2 p.m., Rabin asked Eiran to come to his home. "I saw him pacing around, in his small office, weighing the decision. He said to me that the operation could be a failure even if we got the hostages out," Eiran recalls, "and that if there were more than 25 casualties, he'd take the responsibility." Later, after the cabinet had given the green light, Rabin took two or three of his closest aides into a small room next to his office. Reports Pattir: "He said, 'Gentlemen, if this operation fails, there'll be a new Prime Minister tomorrow.'"

But the operation didn't fail. Most of the passengers were rescued, the terrorists were killed, the planes returned safely. Four more people were killed – three passengers and Yonatan Netanyahu, the commander of the small force that killed the terrorists and freed the hostages (and the older brother of the Likud's leader, Benjamin Netanyahu). But complete disaster had been only narrowly avoided. At the Israeli airbase where the planes first triumphantly landed, the pilot of the lead aircraft, a reservist, came up to Rabin and told him that "God worked overtime last night." Proceeding to debrief the assault team, like a military commander, Rabin learned how right the pilot was. The lead plane had landed a few metres from a ditch. A little farther and it might have been unable to take off. A Ugandan jeep with a recoilless gun was on the airstrip when the Israeli planes landed; for some reason, the crew did not fire. Two soldiers whose job it was to refuel the planes on the ground at Entebbe couldn't find the fuel faucets on the airstrip, which had been pointed out by the Solel Boneh team that built the field. So some planes in the rescue force had to make an unscheduled refuelling stop in Kenya on their way home.

The rescue planes flew on to Ben-Gurion Airport, to a tumultuous public reception. Opposition leader Begin was on the shoulders of a dancing crowd, though he had only been informed of the operation after it was approved by the cabinet. "Begin got a lot of the public adulation, as though he was the main mover," says Eiran. "All the while Rabin, who had been at the heart of things, was still taking care of the nitty-gritty, examining the details of what happened. The public hardly saw him."

Entebbe took place in the summer of 1976. Elections were due the next year, in the autumn. With Rabin's popularity sky-high, no one dreamed that by the following July, Labour would no longer be Israel's governing party, and Begin would be Prime Minister. It was a year marked by political intrigue, police investigations and criminal trials, scandal that reached the highest levels of government, and growing public anger with Labour, which had learned nothing from the Yom Kippur failings. In the end, there was also an acceptance of personal responsibility that is rare in Israeli politics.

In the autumn of 1976, Rabin nominated Asher Yadlin, a long-time party man and head of the Labour-dominated Histadrut trade union federation's vast health maintenance organisation, to be Governor of the Bank of Israel. But it quickly turned out that the government's nominee for the country's top professional economic task was under police investigation on suspicion of corruption. The nomination was withdrawn, but the affair had a deep impact on public confidence, reminding everyone that Labour was still the same old party machine that ran the Histadrut, provided health care, specialised in patronage, and hadn't changed much after the 1973 débâcle.

Yadlin was sentenced to five years in jail in February 1977. But even before his trial, scandal had reached Rabin's cabinet itself. Housing Minister Avraham Ofer was being investigated on suspicion of embezzling funds for Labour Party use when he was an official of the Histadrut's Shikun Ovdim housing company; the probe dragged on for months, without charges being filed. On 3 January 1977, Ofer killed himself. "To my mind," Rabin wrote in his memoirs, "the trigger of his gun had been pulled by an intemperate public and a press that permitted itself to condemn a man before he was even accused of a crime. It was a tragic and sobering experience."

At the same time, the running battle with Peres continued, often on the front pages of the daily press. There were clashes over the defence budget, over settlement policy (Rabin's cabinet policy still rejected settlement in heavily populated Arab areas of the territories; Peres backed "settlement everywhere" and was in close contact with Gush Emunim), over leaks from cabinet meetings. Rabin suggested that Peres had been running for Prime Minister since he had lost the contest for the party leadership in February 1974, and was preparing for the next confrontation. "There can be no greater threat to the public's confidence than having cabinet squabbles splashed across the front pages of the daily papers," he observed. "On a number of occasions, however, the Defence Minister behaved as if he was out to challenge the cabinet's authority by taking his differences to the public."

The pre-election contest between Rabin and Peres for the Labour Party leadership should have taken place in the spring of 1977. But events – of a kind that could only happen in Israel – pushed it forward. The National Religious Party, a minor coalition partner, failed to support the government in a Knesset no-confidence vote on the grounds that an official ceremony marking the arrival of Israel's first F-15 warplanes had caused violation of the Jewish

Sabbath. Possibly orchestrating the crisis to facilitate early elections –
a terrible misjudgment – Rabin dismissed three NRP ministers and,
rather than try to govern without a majority in the Knesset,
submitted his resignation and called new elections. He stayed on as
caretaker Prime Minister and voting, which should have taken place
in the autumn, was set for 17 May.

On 22 February, Rabin was chosen as Labour's candidate – over
Peres, naturally – by the slim margin of 41 votes, out of over 2,800
cast in the Labour Party convention. And he began gearing up for
the anticipated strong challenge of the Likud.

But in March, before the campaign got into full swing, Rabin
went to Washington to meet the new President, Jimmy Carter. His
wife, Leah, took advantage of a break in their busy schedule to go to
the Dupont Circle branch of the National Bank where she wanted
to close two accounts the Rabins had held there since their days at
the embassy. There was a total of $2,000 in the two accounts and
Mrs Rabin asked to withdraw it all. Under the strict currency
regulations in effect at the time, an Israeli citizen was not allowed to
hold a foreign account unless living abroad, or to take more than
$450 in cash on an overseas trip. The existence of the account was a
violation of Israeli law, punishable by a fine or a jail sentence.

A few days after the Rabins returned to Israel, media adviser Pattir
got a phone call from Dan Margalit, then the Washington correspondent of Ha'aretz, Israel's most prestigious daily newspaper.
Margalit – who had verified the existence of the account, by
depositing $50 in it before Leah Rabin closed it – asked him if he
knew that the Rabins had an illegal account in the United States.
Pattir said he would look into the matter. He checked, and Rabin
told him not to react, only to say that he did not deal in private
matters. Ha'aretz published the story, and the finance ministry began
an investigation.

The inquiry disclosed that over the years Leah Rabin had made
periodic withdrawals from the account, a clear violation of the law.
Attorney General Aharon Barak (today Chief Justice of the Supreme
Court), saw no alternative but to refer the case to the courts. (Leah
Rabin never forgave Barak for insisting on a court proceeding; even
in 1995, at her husband's funeral, she did not shake the Chief
Justice's hand.) It was also suggested that a distinction be made
between the Prime Minister and his wife, who Rabin said was the
family's "finance minister". He would have to pay a fine; she would
have to stand trial. "To this day," Rabin wrote in 1979, "I cannot

understand the legal justification for drawing that distinction, and at the time I sensed a growing resolve to reject the offer with a resounding no. I would do everything possible to share full responsibility with my wife."

He continued: "Friends tried to dissuade me from taking any fateful steps, but a man is always truly alone at such times. And alone, my conscience and I came to three interconnected decisions: I would withdraw my nomination as the candidate for Prime Minister; I would share full responsibility with Leah; and I would try to resign my post as Prime Minister," enabling the Labour Party's new candidate to fill that post in the interim.

Rabin announced his decision on the night of 7 April. The resignation was unprecedented in Israeli public life, but Pattir says it was typical of Rabin. "He would not take any advice, and say that it was human error or something." Pattir adds that standing at Leah's side, sharing the blame with her, was "what a military commander does, not leaving wounded soldiers on the field of battle".

The law did not actually allow Rabin, as caretaker Prime Minister, to resign. Instead, he took a leave of absence, and Shimon Peres became "chairman" of the cabinet. A month later, 1.8 million Israelis went to the polls, and, demanding clean government, swung dramatically away from a Labour Party wounded by the scandals, challenged by a short-lived new centrist party Dash [the Democratic Movement for Change], and lacking a clear message on the future of the territories. The Likud won 43 of the 120 Knesset seats to Labour's 32, and President Ephraim Katzir asked Begin to form a new cabinet. The Labour movement, which had formed every government in the 29 year history of the State of Israel, was out of power, and Yitzhak Rabin was that marginal figure, an opposition member of parliament.

6

The Long Road Back

EVEN IF HE didn't know it at the time, Yitzhak Rabin's resignation in 1977 was a decisive act that marked the beginning of a long road back to the pinnacle of power. The way in which he resigned – taking the initiative, standing by his wife, insisting that the Prime Minister must be above all suspicion – created a significant pool of sympathy among the public, most of whom regarded the Rabins' crime as more of a technical oversight than a significant moral transgression.

On the Saturday after his resignation announcement, Rabin showed up at a soccer game at Tel Aviv's Bloomfield Stadium. Far from reviling the disgraced leader, the crowd gave him a standing ovation. Niva Lanir says that the moment was pivotal for her. "It was then I realised that, despite what had happened, he was the only one who could lead Labour back to power." The sentiments expressed at the Tel Aviv arena were apparently widespread. Some 2,000 letters of support poured into the Rabin household, and Leah Rabin responded personally to each one.

Micha Goldman, a longtime Rabin ally, concurs with Lanir. "After 1977, whenever he travelled around the country," he recalls, "Rabin received public feedback of support. It was a response that didn't have its parallel within the party. That's why he worked for years to change the electoral system – so the choice wouldn't be made by dealmakers, but by the public at large. He wanted the American system in Israel, open primaries, because he knew the competition within the party a priori gave him limited chances, being dependent on machinery that didn't like his method of operation."

Still, the hasty departure from office was painful and embarrassing for the Rabins. Shortly after his announcement, but before he took the leave of absence that made Peres the acting premier, Rabin attended a conference of the kibbutz movement at Kibbutz Ein Gev, on the Sea of Galilee. Only after Rabin's death did his friend Dov Goldstein describe to the daily *Ma'ariv* what happened on the way back from that meeting. At Leah's request, Goldstein and his wife had accompanied the Rabins to Ein Gev; Yitzhak had been reluctant to face the public, even a very select one that was naturally in his camp, and Goldstein came along to offer moral support. In fact, the reception Rabin received was lukewarm, and, as Goldstein recalled it, he left feeling "that his wish of being enveloped in warmth, or being embraced, hadn't been fulfilled". After their small air force plane took off for the return journey to Tel Aviv, the pilot turned on the radio news. The top story involved the decision of the Attorney General Aharon Barak that an administrative fine would not suffice for Leah Rabin; she would have to stand trial. According to Goldstein, Leah Rabin "gets up and it's as if she's going to the opening of the plane, which is in the air. We don't know where she's going or what she intends to do. But we hear her say: 'I'm killing myself. I can't survive this, because of Yitzhak.' And then I see Yitzhak get up, grab her by both shoulders, embrace her, pull her tightly toward him and say: 'Absolutely not, we'll fight this together, and we'll win. There's no "you and I", there's just the two of us.'" Goldstein stresses that though Leah's distress was genuine, it was clear to those on the plane that she wasn't actually intending to jump.

Though Rabin had considered relinquishing his Knesset seat along with the Prime Ministership, aides convinced him not to do so, and when the party went to the polls on 17 May, he was, by his own request, in the No. 20 position on its Knesset list, a virtual guarantee of a seat even if electoral disaster struck. And strike it did. Labour was out, the Likud was in. And the new Prime Minister was the man, who since the beginning of the state three decades earlier, had been the perennial opposition leader, Menachem Begin.

Despite Begin's deserved reputation as a hard-liner when it came to territorial compromise in the West Bank, he will go down in history as the first Israeli Prime Minister to sign a peace treaty with an Arab country, the man who returned the whole of Sinai to President Anwar Sadat after his dramatic visit to Jerusalem in November 1977. In his memoirs, published shortly after the March 1979 signing of the Israel–Egypt treaty, Rabin's ambivalence about those events is clear. He blames Begin for discontinuing a longstanding Israeli policy of co-ordinating positions with the United States (when it became clear to Begin that his position on the West Bank and Gaza could not be reconciled with that of President Carter he "proclaimed, with what was undoubtedly meant to be a reassuring smile, that Israel and the United States had 'agreed to disagree'"). And he blames Carter for acting as though the Soviet Union had significant influence over the hard-line states in the Arab world, and could help it foster a comprehensive peace between Israel and all the Arab states. Both these developments, suggests Rabin, convinced Sadat that if he didn't act quickly, he would be pushed into an international peace conference, where he would be forced to toe a Soviet–Syrian–PLO line. Jimmy Carter, concludes Rabin, by announcing his intent to work together with the USSR to sponsor a peace conference, had defaulted on historic US policy. Therefore, concludes Rabin ironically, the Carter administration could "actually claim credit for President Sadat's historic decision to come to Jerusalem".

Rabin, now a rank-and-file opposition Labour Knesset member, was on the Ben-Gurion Airport tarmac to greet Sadat in 1977, and Begin was magnanimous enough to invite him to the March 1979 treaty signing at the White House. But on the whole, the period from 1977 to 1984 can be accurately described as "wilderness" years. This is particularly true of the period until 1980, when Yigal Allon, Peres's main competitor for Labour's leadership, died, and his widow asked Rabin to take up his torch. (Allon had been unofficial head of the camp within Labour that represented the kibbutzim, whereas Peres's camp controlled the party machinery.) Micha Goldman says that he pitched in to help Rabin whenever he could, because the former Prime Minister had no other assistants. "He had a small office in the Kiryah [the government's complex of offices in Tel Aviv], and a secretary. Rabin got involved in a lot of public work. He didn't look to become the chairman of a business or economic concern," as many ex-politicians and generals do when they want to make some fast money, "he spent the majority of his time on trips on behalf of the UJA [United Jewish Appeal] and the Israel Bonds," which presumably didn't pay as well. "And other voluntary organisations – Tel Aviv University, hospitals, the Weizmann Institute – asked him to help raise money."

Although, in the long run, the affair of the dollar account probably helped Rabin more than it hurt him by establishing an image of the scrupulous politician, it continued to have negative reverberations for some years. Yitzhak, as co-holder of the account, had to pay a fine of $1,600, which was imposed administratively. Leah, on the other hand, had to face court proceedings, and could actually have been sentenced to jail for three years. In fact, the Tel Aviv District Court gave her the choice of paying a fine of 250,000 Israeli pounds (about $27,000) within 45 days, or going to jail for a year. Needless to say, she chose the former option, but the Rabins did not have that sort of money lying around. They borrowed it from relatives in Israel and from friends abroad.

Shortly before the elections for party leadership in the Labour central committee in December 1980, rumours that had been circulating quietly for years began to resurface. They involved the charge that Rabin's fine had been paid by an alleged leader of Israeli organised crime, Betzalel Mizrahi. When she'd first heard the story, Niva Lanir talked to Rabin about it. He told her that he knew about the rumour. "'There's no equivocating on this one,'" she recalls him telling her. "'If anyone asks you about it: lay into him hard.'" He then detailed for her the arduous loan arrangements he had made to pay the fine. In order to bring in the money he borrowed from abroad, he'd had to get permission from the authorities since, as he had already painfully learned, Israeli citizens were not permitted to hold foreign currency.

Now, nearly four years after the fine had been paid, Rabin had announced his intention to challenge Peres for the party leadership, and suddenly, every journalist in Israel seemed to be on to the Betzalel Mizrahi story. At the time, Rabin was in South America raising funds for Israel. "Dan Margalit calls, the same guy who broke the story on the dollar account," Lanir recalls. "I said: 'Listen, Margalit, Rabin's abroad, but I'm not even going to ask him for a reaction. I will tell you already that if Ha'aretz publishes that story, with or without a reaction from Rabin, it will be taking upon itself the biggest libel suit in history. I won't even deny it, because it's absurd, an invention from start to finish.'"

Ha'aretz held the story, as did every other paper in Israel. Shortly afterwards, Rabin returned from his foreign tour, and a few days after that he and Lanir travelled to the southern working-class town of Dimonah to campaign. In the car, during the long drive from Tel Aviv, Rabin told her he didn't think they'd heard the last of the story. "'Too many people have been working on this story too many years,'" he predicted ominously. "'They won't give it up. Three days before the elections to the convention, they'll publish it abroad,'" Lanir recalls him saying. "I remember the scene. It was in the car, and dark. I said, 'Wow, what they say about you really is true. You really are paranoid.' 'Would that you were right,' he answered. That was a Tuesday. On Saturday, *L'Express* comes out with a cover story: 'The Israeli Mafia Pays Rabin's Fine'."

Rabin sued the French weekly and won, but the experience was a humiliating one for him. Once the story had been broken in France, it was immediately picked up and reported on Israeli radio, and he held a press conference in Tel Aviv the same night to deny it. Lanir moderated the proceedings. "I understood for the first time in my life how these things work," she recalled, 15 years later. "Though it was a Saturday night, the entire domestic and foreign press corps was there, as if war was breaking out. It was clear they had had advance knowledge that the story was about to be published." A few days later Rabin appeared before a committee of Israeli newspaper editors. In hand he had all the documentation proving how the fine was financed. "It was the first time I actually saw tears fall from his eyes," says Lanir, "and his voice trembled. It was such a deep insult. Some things he always took personally. He may have become less innocent with time, but he never became cynical."

Rabin's introduction to the more sordid aspects of Israeli politics had come rather late in the game. His military career lasted nearly three decades. When it ended, not even three months had passed before he was off to Washington to be ambassador. Only months after his return he was serving as a government minister, and events then conspired to elevate him into the Prime Minister's Office. When he fell, he fell far and he fell quickly. Suddenly he was part of the camp that no longer controlled the Labour Party. The forces that were in charge didn't go out of their way to make his progress in the party any easier. For example, when Rabin competed for the party chairmanship in 1981, he wasn't even allowed to see the lists of registered party members.

And then there was the time, just after Rabin's memoirs were published in Israel, that nearly identical letters showed up at the offices of most of the nation's newspapers, some of which were printed. The letters included a quote from the diaries of former Prime Minister Moshe Sharett that spoke disparagingly of Rabin.

Lanir, who was then working for the Labour-sponsored paper *Davar*, followed the letters back to their source and discovered that they had all come from a particular advertising agency – which was in the employ of the Labour Party. The names on the letters belonged to various low-level employees at the agency, and the quote from Sharett was a forgery. The defamatory phrase did appear in the Sharett diaries, but it described Ariel Sharon, not Rabin.

Lanir explained that to Rabin, "it was clear that it was always Peres" behind the dirty tricks. But, she continued, "he never mentioned Peres by name. He understood that Peres had henchmen. The night that the article came out in *L'Express*, Peres called to express his shock and disbelief, and said, 'I never would have believed that such a thing could happen.' When Rabin hung up the phone he said, 'I doubt it.' But he didn't say: Liar, scumbag. It wasn't hatred he felt, it was animosity."

Whatever the exact quality of the animus Rabin bore against Peres, he had the opportunity to give vent to it when he started work on his memoirs shortly after leaving office. As ghostwriter he chose Dov Goldstein, a veteran *Ma'ariv* writer and editor, with whom he'd been meeting on a weekly basis for years to discuss politics off the record. During the two years they worked on the book, they met three times a week, for seven or eight hours a sitting. The result was a transcript of about 1.25 million words, some 1,500 pages. Goldstein edited that down to a two-volume Hebrew book of 550 pages, which was published in 1979. Later that same year the book appeared in the abridged English version entitled *The Rabin Memoirs*.

It was Goldstein who came up with the book's most famous phrase (which doesn't actually appear in the English version), in which Rabin described Peres as "an inveterate schemer". Goldstein recalled later that when Rabin saw the expression, "he was beside himself with joy. He hugged me and said: 'That's exactly what I meant. I didn't know how to express it.'"

Though writing his memoirs may have served as a catharsis for Rabin, the book was undoubtedly received more warmly in the ruling Likud than in Rabin's party. No one could have accused him of pulling punches. Even if Rabin lets the reader in on some of his sense of humour in the book (a quality he was often accused, wrongly, of lacking), he also reveals an arrogance and a surprising degree of pettiness. Not only Peres had to take it on the chin. Rabin also accused David Ben-Gurion of bad judgment during the War of Independence and of general manipulativeness. And he criticised Abba Eban, Foreign Minister during the Six Day War and when Rabin was ambassador to Washington. (Rabin describes his proposal, when named Prime Minister, to transfer Eban, a man generally perceived outside Israel as one of the country's most brilliant diplomats, from the foreign ministry to the minor job of Information Minister: "During his many years as Foreign Minister, he had essentially explained policies formulated by others, rather than generate his own political thinking." Eban refused the offer, and didn't serve in Rabin's cabinet.)

Rabin never expressed regret about the book, and never took back any of the things he said in it. In fact, at the time of the 1981 general election, he even resisted party pressure that he endorse Peres, who had trounced him in the election held by the central committee to choose the party chairman.

Labour, with Peres as its standard-bearer, lost to the Likud again in 1981. In 1984, though it had a slight lead over the Likud in Knesset seats earned (44 against 41), it was unable to form a coalition of its own. After months of deadlock, the two blocs entered into a "national unity government". According to the terms of the coalition agreement, Peres and Likud leader Yitzhak Shamir would rotate the Prime Ministership, each serving for two years (first Peres, then Shamir), and Rabin would remain Defence Minister for the entire period.

That Labour wasn't able to muster the necessary number of Knesset members to form a government under its exclusive leadership was evidence of the problem Peres had always had at the polls. Three times he had been at the top of the Labour list (1977, 1981, 1984), and three times he had failed to form a Labour-led government.

Israel in 1984 was a country in distress. Two years earlier, under Begin's leadership, the IDF had entered Lebanon in what was announced as an operation to knock out the PLO presence in the south of the country and secure a quiet border for the settlements in the north of Israel. Instead, the Israeli army rolled on as far north as Beirut, and the war's architect, Defence Minister Ariel Sharon, stood accused of having misled even the Prime Minister about his true intentions. The population was divided in its support of the war, and that division, to a large extent, reflected the ethnic split between Ashkenazi and Sephardi Jews, with the latter constituting a major component of the Polish-born Prime Minister's support. An angry, frustrated atmosphere prevailed.

In September 1982, while Israeli troops maintained their grip on the Lebanese capital, Christian militiamen aligned with Israel entered two Palestinian refugee camps there, Sabra and Shatilla, and murdered, by Israeli estimates, up to 800 people. (Other estimates run into the thousands.)

Though it was not Israelis who pulled the triggers, the massacre had happened on their watch, and there was outrage and shock both at home and internationally. Under massive public pressure, an extremely reluctant Begin agreed to the appointment of a judicial commission to investigate the massacre, and the publication of its results in February 1983 forced Sharon's resignation from the defence ministry, though he stayed on in the cabinet. Little more than half a year later, Begin himself resigned, entering a sort of permanent hibernation, from which he never emerged to the day of his death, in March 1992.

A futile attempt to force peace on to the Lebanese had not succeeded, and when the unity government finally took office in September 1984, it found its army facing an increasingly hostile Lebanese population, bogged down in the country with no clear exit in sight. Economically, too, Israel was in dreadful shape, with inflation running close to 500 per cent a year. A joke at the time was that it was more economical to take a cab than a bus: you paid for a cab at the end of the ride, when your money was worth less than at the start.

Though the Labour members of the cabinet, principally Peres and Rabin, felt they had a mandate to extricate Israel from Lebanon, Rabin still had to live down behaviour during the early stages of the war that bore a pretty strong resemblance to support of the campaign. When, in the late summer of 1982, Israel had besieged Beirut, Rabin made a number of visits to the city in the company of Sharon, and even advised the then-Defence Minister on how best to tighten the siege in order to drive out Yasser Arafat and the PLO. (To the end of his life, Rabin confounded expectations on the left by maintaining good relations with Sharon, meeting with him regularly to discuss politics. Niva Lanir explains it partially as the lifetime bond of two soldiers who had served together on the General Staff, and partly as political calculation on Rabin's part: "Being seen with Sharon made him seem more a centrist figure in the Labour Party. But it wasn't a friendship. I have no memory of Sharon being at the Rabins' home.") By January of the following year, however, Rabin was already calling the war a mistake.

Nachman Shai, Rabin's media adviser at the beginning of his term in the defence ministry, says that Rabin "thought the war was a catastrophe". Haim Yisraeli, a senior aide to every Defence Minister since Ben-Gurion, has explained that a public perception over the years of Rabin as a "hawk" was incorrect: "He was a security man." He could advise the Begin government on tactics that would best vanquish the despised PLO in Beirut (and minimise Israeli casualties), but when he came to see that there were far-reaching strategic goals for the war that essentially called for Israel imposing its vision of a political settlement on Lebanon, he realised it was a losing battle, and that Israel had to get out.

The IDF brass, on balance, came to share his feelings once Chief of Staff Rafael Eitan, Sharon's partner in the conception and pursuit of the war, had departed. Moshe Levi, who took over the senior army job in April 1983, explains that even before the 1984 election, when the government was a Likud-led coalition, the army had come up with plans for a partial withdrawal (which the cabinet turned down). Even when Likud was joined by Labour in the unity government, it was clear to the Labour cabinet ministers that they would have to convince at least one Likud minister to come over to their side and vote for withdrawal.

Niva Lanir worked with Rabin during his first year in the defence ministry. She describes how Rabin gradually built up government support for withdrawal: "It was no accident that Rabin would regularly invite senior army officers to be present at cabinet meetings. I'm not saying that the army was involving itself in politics. But I think that David Levy [the Likud housing minister] was convinced to vote for withdrawal because he heard what senior officers had to say. There were officers who spoke in favour [of pulling out] and those who testifed against, and each would explain why. I think that every week there was a discussion in the cabinet on Lebanon."

Moshe Levi confirms Rabin's *modus operandi*. There was a variety of opinions within the army, he says, and it was only after extensive and open discussion that the General Staff decided to present the proposal Levi himself supported to the government: "We said to them, there are different opinions, and we brought the holders of those different opinions to explain them. In addition, there were also personal conversations with key people, in particular David Levy, who had the personal and political courage to go with his own understanding, even though it stood in contradiction to the declared position of the Likud, of which he was a senior minister." The plan finally approved called for a staged withdrawal from Lebanon (which began in January 1985, and went on until June) with a small remaining presence in a security zone just north of Israel's border, meant to keep that border quiet. Control of the security zone was to be in the hands of the South Lebanon Army, an Israeli-controlled Christian militia.

Rabin presided over another process in the defence ministry that may have been far less obviously dramatic than the pullout from Lebanon, but was perhaps just as risky and far-reaching in its implications. As part of the comprehensive economic plan devised by the government to cut public spending and bring inflation down to double-digit figures, Rabin pledged the defence ministry to cutting some 20 per cent from its budget. Moshe Levi describes Rabin's readiness in this area as an example of his statesmanlike quality, not only in his willingness to put the national interest before the internal needs of his ministry, but also in the way he and the Prime Minister Shimon Peres worked together on the issue. "People say that the tension between Rabin and Peres dissipated only in recent years [during the peace process], but I would have to say that their co-operation, in both the economic realm and the security sphere, was complete." Niva Lanir almost echoes Moshe Levi's words: "Apparently the responsibility of being in charge of a ministry took precedence over all the games of the party. Rabin and Peres talked all the time, they worked together. It was fine. I realised that when they could get beyond the party rivalry, they could achieve great things."

Typically, after a war, the army requests – and receives – increased budgets. The lessons of the war are analysed, and the required changes and improvements invariably demand significant invest- ment. Here, though, the army was bringing a war to an end, and carrying out the costly act of withdrawal from Lebanon, and at the same time voluntarily cutting expenditures in a big way. "We let some 7,000 career soldiers go," Levi recalls, "and thousands of civilian army employees. The process was very painful. And for Rabin, as a security man, it was particularly so. The most painful part came when he had to fire people."

The cutting was risky too. As Levi notes, "This wasn't a marginal budget reduction. And the starting point for the cuts was not security. The economy was about to fall apart." Even senior people in the security establishment understood that. "We arrived at a formula that struck the right balance. But I'm sure that if Yitzhak Rabin had not gone along, and the entire General Staff and I hadn't joined him, it would have been impossible to make the cuts. I don't think the government could have imposed cuts of such magnitude on the Defence Minister. If you ask whether we endangered Israel, I think the answer is no, but we were walking a fine line, balancing the interests of the country in general and its net security needs."

Even after his death, the question of Rabin's personal sensitivity is still a subject of spirited discussion. Undoubtedly, he was capable of making tough decisions, decisions that could affect people's lives in the most fundamental way. He had, in fact, been sending young men into battle since he was in his twenties. Yet whatever toughness, even gruffness, he became famous for in public as a lifetime military man, his colleagues say that he never lost his sensitivity to the feelings of the families of fallen soldiers, and remained constantly accessible to those whose sons were missing or in captivity. Lanir recalls an appearance by Rabin before the Knesset Foreign Affairs and Defence Committee soon after he became Defence Minister. "He was handed a slip of paper informing him about a helicopter accident. I think maybe three were killed. He looked at the slip and then continued to talk. Then it happened again, he got another slip of paper saying that three soldiers had been killed in Lebanon. He folded up the slip and said to the committee: 'Okay, that's too much for me. I have to bring the meeting to an end.'"

Nachman Shai says: "I think that as the years went on, Rabin became more vulnerable to the casualties. How much can you stand? The first time, in the first war, it's your friends. The second time, it's the sons of your friends, as in Yom Kippur. The third time, it's the grandchildren – it's Rabin's grandson who's in the army, in the paratroops, and his grandson might be at Beit Lid junction when the bomb goes off. It's already three generations of blood he sees spilled before his eyes."

On 20 May 1985, Israel released 1,150 Palestinians who were being held in Israeli prisons for terrorist activity within Israel – the so-called Jibril exchange, because it was engineered on the Arab side by Ahmad Jibril, head of the Popular Front for the Liberation of Palestine–General Command. Though the army Chief of Staff had recommended not to make the deal, which led to the release of three Israeli soldiers captured in Lebanon and being held by Jibril's group, all but one member of a circumscribed 10-man "inner cabinet" that dealt with crucial policy matters, including Rabin, voted to go ahead with it. The Defence Minister justified the exchange by saying that "when there is no military option... and after all the possibilities have been thoroughly examined, there is no alternative but to enter into negotiations and pay a price".

In retrospect, most observers see the exchange as disastrous. Earlier exchanges had let even larger numbers of "terrorists" go free, including the release in Lebanon of more than 4,000. But, as Moshe Levi recalls, "They weren't terrorists who'd committed attacks in Israel and were being released from here. They acted principally in Lebanon, and remained in Lebanon. But I think that those big numbers confused the decision-makers a bit," when it came time to vote on the Jibril exchange.

What's more, the terrorists released in May 1985 went back to their homes in the West Bank and Gaza, and many immediately took up arms against Israel. There were numerous attacks on Israeli targets – both civilian and military – before the uprising known as the Intifada broke out a year and a half later at Gaza's Jabalya refugee camp.

7

Fighting the Intifada

"BREAK THEIR BONES." Whether Defence Minister Yitzhak Rabin did or didn't utter those three infamous words while directing soldiers in the field during the early weeks of the Palestinian uprising seems destined to remain a mystery forever. The phrase, widely attributed to him at the beginning of 1988 – but which he later denied having used – gained Rabin notoriety in the farthest flung corners of the world. The full story has probably gone with him to the grave.

Dan Shomron, Chief of Staff at the time, says he personally never heard Rabin say the words. "Maybe he did, but it would only have been as a manner of speaking; what he meant was to use force. 'Breaking bones' was just an expression – Dado [Chief of Staff David Elazar] used it during the Yom Kippur War."

Amram Mitzna, at that time head of the Central Command, which included the West Bank, also never heard Rabin issue the apocryphal order. "But I did hear him say riots should be dispersed with physical force," he adds, "and some of the soldiers took it the wrong way."

Others maintain that even if Rabin didn't explicitly tell soldiers to go out and break bones, that's exactly what he intended them to do. Whatever the case, the words themselves soon became immaterial. In the first year of the Intifada, there were 12 recorded deaths by beating in the Gaza Strip, and many more broken arms and legs there and in the West Bank. There were also over 260 deaths by shooting, but somehow, the sight of Israeli soldiers physically beating Palestinian civilians stirred more revulsion and outrage, both at home among liberal-minded Israelis and abroad, than all the rounds of live fire and rubber bullets put together.

And the sight was there for all to see. In one of the most

memorable scenes of the Intifada, a CBS cameraman caught four IDF soldiers on film on a bleak hillside near Nablus while they were pounding away with their rifle-butts and rocks at the heads, arms and legs of two Palestinian stone-throwers captured during a riot. The footage appeared on TV screens all over the world at prime time in February 1988 and led to a major uproar, though it later emerged that none of the Arabs sustained broken bones. Later, when soldiers and officers under investigation for breaking Palestinians' bones testified that they had been following the Defence Minister's instructions, Rabin declared in front of the Knesset that to the best of his recollection, he'd never issued illegal orders or told anyone to go and break bones. Still, if one image of the Defence Minister of the Intifada stuck, it was that of Rabin the Bone-breaker.

The first hours, weeks and months of the Intifada can hardly be counted among Rabin's finest. It was a period of confusion, of miscalculation, and to an extent, of trial and error. The break-their-bones controversy was only one of several grim episodes. Another was the live burial of four more troublemakers in the northern West Bank. Soldiers had ordered the four to lie down in a clearing while a bulldozer covered them with heaps of earth. They were rescued alive shortly afterwards, but the horrific image lingered on. The Israelis seemed to have lost their senses.

And yet, for Rabin, even this experience was not completely devoid of value. It was as if everything that happened had to happen for the Israeli–Palestinian struggle ever to begin to reach some sort of conclusion. "The Intifada was Rabin's school," remarks Ze'ev Schiff, a leading Israeli defence analyst and co-author, with Ehud Ya'ari, of the definitive book *Intifada*, published in 1989. At first, Schiff says, "Rabin believed that the Jordanians would bring the Palestinians to the negotiating table. The Intifada taught him that the opposite was true." In other words, it was the education that led Rabin away from a vague and passive notion of Jordan as the key to resolving the Palestinian issue to an active search for Palestinian partners with whom Israel could deal – a search that ultimately ended up at the PLO's front door.

Until December 1987, the status quo in the West Bank and Gaza Strip was about the last thing on the Israeli defence establishment's mind. The months before had been far from quiet, but the sharp increase in the incidence of stone-throwing, firebombing, strikes, demonstrations and rioting had failed to set off any alarm bells. The military, Dan Shomron recalls, was preoccupied with other, "more actual" things: trouble along the northern border with Lebanon, a surge of terrorist infiltrations from Jordan in the east, the growing threat from Iraq, and the regular building of the army – training and preparation for war. After all, only two years later Saddam Hussein was vowing to annihilate half of Israel with chemical weapons and Jordan's King Hussein was his best friend.

To Rabin himself, the territories he had conquered in 1967 remained somewhat alien. He never had much patience for the Jewish settlers, was positively infuriated by the vigilante elements among them, and had few sentiments for the area's Biblical past. As for the almost 2 million local Palestinians, he displayed no particular knowledge of them and spent as little time as possible with them. The only material he used to read about the Palestinians were intelligence reports that usually painted them in their worst light. Although he was convinced of the worth of territory from a military point of view, he never expected to hold on to these particular territories for ever, according to Schiff. He never forgot that they weren't empty, and he was always mindful of keeping the occupation as benign as possible. Thus, in 1985, he appointed Ephraim Sneh, a brigadier known for his liberal views, to head the Israeli Civil Administration in the West Bank.

Still, until the Intifada, Rabin subscribed to the Labour Party staple, the "Jordanian option", as the key to dealing with the future of the territories, regarding the Allon Plan, with its provision for continued Israeli settlement along the Jordan Valley, as the best guarantee of Israeli security. Foreign Minister Shimon Peres had taken it upon himself to reach a secret London Agreement with Jordan's Hussein in April 1987, with the aim of holding an international conference on the Middle East conflict. Rabin, however, was never interested enough to go into the details of what a political settlement brokered by the Jordanians might actually entail.

So on the evening of Tuesday, 8 December 1987, when the Palestinian throngs in the Jabalya refugee camp in Gaza confronted an unwitting bunch of Israeli reservists, in unprecedented numbers and buoyed by a sense of daring and defiance that was extraordinary even by their own standards, it was little wonder that Rabin, usually such a stickler for details, misread the situation – or rather, didn't bother reading it at all. The day had started out normally enough. There was certainly no reason to suspect that a mass civilian uprising was in the air – and indeed, the Shin Bet internal security agency charged with assessing the day-to-day situation in the territories had suspected no such thing. The only mildly unusual event had been a traffic accident in the afternoon, in which an Israeli truck driver ploughed into a car carrying Palestinian labourers returning to the Gaza Strip after a day's work, killing four.

With hindsight, it is obvious that the Intifada was just waiting to happen, and the car accident was all it took. From the crash site, a wild rumour fanned through Gaza that the "accident" had in fact been a wilful revenge attack, perpetrated by the cousin of an Israeli who had been stabbed to death in Gaza a couple of days before. Israelis had become so demonised in the eyes of the occupied Palestinians that they were perceived as being capable of almost anything. By the time the residents of Jabalya returned home from the crash victims' funerals that night, the revenge theory was accepted as indisputable fact. First, crowds converged on the Israeli outpost, a hated symbol of the occupation at the heart of the camp, hurling curses and stones into the compound. Soon, the whole of Jabalya was in uproar. Stones and firebombs rained down on the army patrols that ventured into the streets. The rioting went on for hours, and resumed early the next morning.

The uprising spread rapidly to the Rafah refugee camp, down by the Egyptian border, and from there to other parts of the Gaza Strip. Some of the small army units unlucky enough to be on duty felt that they had lost control. And still, the military and defence establishment – as well as the Palestinian leadership, which was similarly taken off-guard by the spontaneous popular explosion – were unaware that anything fundamentally new was afoot. Requests from the field for troop reinforcements with which to douse the flames and prevent them from spreading were turned down.

So sanguine was Rabin that on 10 December he left the country: after some initial hesitation, he went ahead with a long-planned trip to the United States. In his absence, the Intifada jumped over to the West Bank. "Had appropriate action been taken on that day, it might still have been possible to block the spread of violence from the Gaza Strip to the West Bank," wrote Schiff and Ya'ari. "But the sad fact is that Rabin and his aides had their sights set so firmly on Washington that they failed to see what was happening at their feet." Mitzna recalls two or three long-distance phone conversations with the Defence Minister, who wanted to be kept fully abreast of events on the ground. Nevertheless, when Rabin did finally return to Israel on 21 December, his first public comments only served to underline his ignorance of what was going on. He categorically blamed Syria and Iran for fomenting the unrest – accusations that were "based on nothing", says Schiff.

The truth is that in the immediate aftermath of 8 December, neither the Israelis nor the Palestinians were in a position to understand fully the import of the events as they occurred. The pattern of Palestinian protest had taken a quantum leap, but the realisation only dawned on Israel's top security and political echelons, and the PLO alike, at a crawl. Shomron argues that the uprising had actually been building up for the whole of the year before, and that 8 December was an arbitrary date for its "official" start. Mitzna reckons it took himself, Rabin, and everyone else involved, several weeks to understand once and for all that this was not just another flare-up of protests that would quickly and spontaneously burn out.

Perhaps Rabin and the rest of the defence establishment simply underestimated the Palestinians. "We didn't expect it to go on for long because we didn't think they could hold out," Shomron recounts. "They didn't have stockpiles of provisions or anything. But it seems that in a popular uprising, people are prepared to suffer." In the past, violence had flared up and died down within days. This time, it stayed there. There was another crucial difference as well. What distinguished the Intifada from the previous kind of unrest was the nature of the enemy. The Israeli army was no longer confronting armed terrorists, political agitators or student activists. It was now having to do battle with whole families. Elderly men, women and children swelled the ranks of the stone-throwers. Israel was facing a genuine, unarmed civilian rebellion.

Once it had been established that Israel had a new problem on its hands, Shomron and Mitzna immediately set about arguing that military means alone were insufficient to bring the uprising to an end, rooted as the Intifada was in Palestinian poverty, rage and hatred of the occupation. A political strategy, they maintained, was essential. Rabin didn't disagree. But he had priorities, and his first was to try to restore some semblance of order. "The message was to use more force," Mitzna recalls. At that time, the military sorely lacked the basic equipment needed for quelling riots. Rubber bullets were in very limited supply, and the army's small reserve of tear gas had been gathering dust for years. Soldiers facing angry mobs used what they had – guns, although army guidelines allowed them to open fire only in life-threatening situations. It was, necessarily, left to the discretion of the soldier to determine at what point a rock, a concrete block or a Molotov cocktail became life-threatening. The front line was everywhere, the scenes were chaotic and the casualties, particularly on the Palestinian side, rose. "Not only didn't we have the physical means to deal with the Intifada," Mitzna relates, "we didn't have any clear procedural guidelines either. For example, who was the enemy and who wasn't? Were all the Palestinians enemies? Could they only be punished through the judicial system? It was a constant dilemma."

Despite his initial dismissiveness of the Palestinians' ability to wage a popular war, Rabin did rise to the challenge. Soon after his return from the United States, the Defence Minister took on the Intifada as his personal campaign; the Palestinians had found themselves a flesh-and-blood adversary. Each Thursday, Rabin would convene a special forum of the Chief of Staff, the area commanders, Prime Minister Yitzhak Shamir's military secretary and delegates from all the other bodies that dealt with the territories. Every week, Mitzna reports, was the same. Rabin would first go around the table gathering information from everyone present. He wanted to hear details about every demonstration: where exactly it was, how many people took part, and how it ended. From all of these details he would build up a picture. Then he would decide what to do.

He didn't even rely on his Chief of Staff to report to him on the state of the army. Rather, he would go out into the field practically every week to hold sessions with soldiers on Intifada duty. He would first survey the surroundings, then quiz them about their feelings, about their daily routines, about how they handled the situations they faced. He also listened to their bitter complaints – how they were being humiliated by kids with stones, how infuriating it was to be spending their days playing cat and mouse in the alleyways, and how they didn't even have any means with which to fight back.

It was both in response to the rapidly rising number of Palestinians killed (22 had died by the end of December), and to the alarming dip in army morale, that batons were first distributed. Rabin told the Knesset on 20 January 1988 that the Intifada would be fought with "might, power and beatings". Mitzna says the idea was to have soldiers barge into a riot or demonstration and actively break it up. It was not to use the clubs for punishment once an offender had been captured. To the subsequent horror of the defence establishment, however, a surprising number of soldiers displayed a predilection for dealing potentially lethal blows long after the heat of the riot had subsided. That sent Rabin and his commanders rushing back into the field to try to explain the difference.

Yitzhak Rabin was steering a course fraught with obstacles at every turn. There were the Palestinian women and children; the frustrated soldiers; the Israelis killed by Palestinians in the territories (two soldiers and five civilians in the first year of the Intifada); and an Israeli public that was squeamish about army excesses, but which demanded drastic action whenever Jews were killed. And then there were the Likud ministers in the national unity government, the hard-liners like Ariel Sharon, then Minister of Trade and Industry, who constantly criticised the IDF, and later Rabin himself, for being too soft. They saw Rabin's iron fist as a kid glove. They wanted to see the uprising smashed into the ground, whatever it took. Rabin was hardly a liberal when it came to security matters. But neither did it enter his head to send in the tanks against unarmed civilians, or to strafe Palestinian refugee camps from the air – as some opposition figures were suggesting.

Soon after the outbreak of the Intifada, Rabin and Shomron were invited to attend an academic forum at Tel Aviv University to delve into the historical precedents for dealing with civilian uprisings. Shomron remembers a particularly powerful analysis by Professor Shimon Shamir, a Middle East specialist who served as Israel's ambassador to both Egypt and Jordan. The academics concurred: history taught that wherever an occupying authority acted with a strong hand, it had always regretted it later. Not because the action wasn't effective, but because it had made a sworn enemy of the brothers, cousins and parents of every victim. The status quo ante, as the French experience in Algeria had shown, could never be restored. In short, excessive might was rarely right.

Rabin listened more than he spoke, but he agreed with the academics' conclusion. "We consulted, and decided to tread delicately, not to take irreversible steps and actions that we would later regret," Shomron recalls. "While using a strong fist on the one hand, we would allow life to go on in the territories on the other. We would let the schools and institutions stay open wherever possible, and we would allow Palestinians to continue working in Israel. We did so all the way through the Intifada."

Rabin was also concerned by international opinion, although some of his public relations blunders might have given the impression that he didn't care at all. Perhaps most of all, though, he was bothered by his inner conscience. His aim was always to fight the uprising as effectively as possible, while minimising the casualty figures as much as possible. By the spring of 1988, he realised that the

Intifada could not be quashed militarily, and started fighting for its containment. Some of the measures Rabin used in his war stretched the Israeli justice system to its limits – or beyond, his critics would say. He utilised the Emergency Regulations of 1945, that had remained on the statute books since the British Mandatory period, with gusto. These included non-judicial punishments such as the demolition of suspects' homes, the deportation of Intifada ringleaders and mass detentions without trial.

Although Rabin sought legal counsel and always stayed within the bounds of the system, he was reined in on more than one occasion by the judiciary. In July 1989, for example, the High Court of Justice ruled in favour of a petition by the Association of Civil Rights in Israel, and against the defence establishment position, that house owners must be able to appeal against demolition orders issued by area commanders before they were carried out. The number of demolitions dropped sharply – not because a significant number of orders were overturned by the courts, but because the army, feeling that demolition had lost its effectiveness as a swift deterrent, resorted to it less often. Mitzna, for one, had little stomach for meting out collective punishments. In general, he was a commander with more qualms than most. The potential for conflict with Rabin, who mostly just wanted to get the job done, must have been awesome.

Two nights before the Israeli elections in November 1988, a bus was making its way from Tiberias to Jerusalem. On the outskirts of Jericho, the pitch darkness was pierced by a flash. It was a Molotov cocktail being thrown at the bus, which burst into flames. A mother and her two children were killed; a soldier who had tried to rescue them died later. Rabin soon joined Mitzna at the scene, and he was furious. "We had an argument then," Mitzna recalls. "Rabin wanted action. He needed something to be done." Mitzna was reluctant to rush in, put the whole of Jericho under curfew and round up the menfolk. In the end, it wasn't necessary. "It was our luck that we caught the three perpetrators within 24 hours. They turned out to be three Africans, members of a small African Muslim community living in Jericho. Nobody had sent them. They simply got up on their own initiative and decided to lay in ambush with a Molotov cocktail. Then, Rabin understood. You can't punish everyone – if good and bad get the same treatment, then there'd be no point in being good."

Even throughout the wildest days of the Intifada, Yitzhak Rabin had one very notable success. He managed to keep the army, one of

Israel's most vital organs, within the public consensus. "There were days when I most feared that people would refuse to serve," says Dan Shomron. But although dozens of reservists and a few conscripts did balk at serving in the territories, Shomron says that "there was even an increase in numbers of those volunteering for élite combat units. Rabin took a line the army could live with. The extremes didn't catch on."

And he didn't stop at that. Rabin had always been of the opinion that the Palestinian issue would eventually require a political solution, but he publicly declared at every turn that he would only pursue a framework for negotiations once calm had been restored on the ground. From the start of the Intifada onwards, however, he quietly went about learning the subject. At the beginning, his contacts with the local Palestinian leadership, whom he seemed to be noticing for the first time, were mainly for the purpose of gathering information. Slowly, they took on a more political hue.

Sari Nusseibeh, a Palestinian academic from Abu Dis, near Jerusalem, was a prominent member of the "local leadership". He was a known political activist and thinker, and a scion of an aristocratic family with a long history of political involvement. The Israelis assumed he was helping direct the Intifada, setting the tone and serving as a link between the "inside" − the so-called Palestinian "Unified Command" orchestrating protests in the territories − and PLO headquarters in Tunis. Nusseibeh is always wary of saying anything about that period that could be even vaguely incriminating. Sitting in the offices of his Palestinian research consultancy on East Jerusalem's Saladin Street − the same rooms that the Israelis closed for two years in 1989 because of the secret activities allegedly going on there − he speaks in a code of ambiguity about how the Intifada was run.

Academic discussion groups, which just happened to include representatives of the various Palestinian factions, produced papers whose concepts found their way into leaflets printed and distributed by local cadres of the Unified Command in the Palestinian towns, villages and camps. The leaflets, declaring strikes, calling demonstrations and defining the means of fighting the occupation in any given week, were the manna that fed the uprising. Although the leaflet writers were usually rounded up by their third or fourth publication, the loose chain of command, based on a system of dissociation and deniability, ensured there were always more.

Nusseibeh was the kind of person who people around Rabin

assumed he was meeting. Though Israeli sources say that the Defence Minister met with a handful of local leaders over the years, Nusseibeh reports that, to the best of his knowledge, Rabin didn't personally meet with anybody. He did, however, send military representatives into the prisons, in his name, to hold a series of talks with the grass-roots activists – the leaflet writers. A lawyer who was in contact with the prisoners kept Nusseibeh, who remained outside prison walls, informed.

To Rabin, the PLO was an open book in the late 1980s. Its thinking was relayed almost simultaneously to Jerusalem by a large network of informers planted within the organisation. The PLO bosses in Tunis were also considered anathema as far as being suitable negotiating partners was concerned. Even after King Hussein cut his administrative and legal ties with the West Bank in July 1988, renouncing any claims of sovereignty and leaving the way open for the PLO, Rabin's opinion didn't change. The PLO was despised by most of the Israeli public; it also represented the Palestinian diaspora, a whole can of worms involving refugee rights of return that Rabin had no intention of opening up.

But he was a realist. He knew that the local Palestinians didn't have the strength or credibility to move without an endorsement, at least, from Tunis. The military figures holding talks in the prisons therefore encouraged the activists to use their connections to present their ideas to the PLO bosses abroad. And a Labour Knesset member, Rafi Edri, now acknowledges that he was holding secret meetings at around this time with PLO officials, in Morocco – apparently with Rabin's approval.

Following the November 1988 Knesset elections, another national unity government was formed and Rabin retained the defence portfolio. In January 1989, the first reports emerged in the media of the Rabin peace plan. The concept was for a deal with the local Palestinians based on elections and an expanded autonomy for an interim period, in return for cessation of the Intifada. It was adopted by the Prime Minister Yitzhak Shamir and by mid-year it had become, to all intents and purposes, the Shamir Plan.

"I was surprised when the Shamir Plan came out," Nusseibeh relates. Several elements of it – concepts like elections, the staged implementation of a settlement that would include self-rule and the withdrawal from Palestinian population centres – bore more than a passing similarity to ideas that came out of the prison talks. But there were fundamental differences as well, and the plan was doomed from the outset. Shamir was obviously not eager to see it through, and he was helped by the fact that the PLO rejected it out of hand. In March 1990, the unity government fell after Shamir failed to meet a Labour deadline for deciding once and for all to proceed to the first stage of the peace plan – a seemingly innocuous three-way Israeli–Egyptian–American meeting.

The Intifada, by then, had passed its peak. Its nature had changed. The mass outpouring of rage of the first two years had given way to an activists' war – small groups attacking Israelis with guns and bombs. The local leadership was diffused. Some members, like Jerusalem leader Faisal Husseini, had spent the first two years more or less permanently in jail; dozens more had been deported; and others, like Nusseibeh, had been slipped enough veiled threats by the Shin Bet to be intimidated into playing an ever more ambivalent role. The PLO had fully reasserted itself, and the local momentum that had sparked the uprising was lost. Activists saw collaborators with the Israeli authorities everywhere and had already begun hunting them with a vengeance, and the people's struggle degenerated into an internecine trial of factional fighting, mutual suspicion and blood-letting. For Rabin, though, the Intifada had already served its purpose. It had turned the Palestinian people into a proper enemy. And as such, they had earned the right in Rabin's eyes to a proper peace.

8

Second Chance at the Top

EARLY IN 1990, Labour Party leader and Finance Minister Shimon Peres decided to break up the national unity coalition between Labour and the Likud. Peres was convinced that as long as Yitzhak Shamir was Prime Minister, there would be no progress toward peace. In 1987, Shamir had torpedoed Peres's London Agreement with King Hussein for an international peace conference. Now he was blocking progress with the Palestinians. The Prime Minister and Finance Minister of Israel were hardly on speaking terms. Peres believed he could make a midterm deal with the ultra-Orthodox Shas party that would leave him as Prime Minister and put Shamir in the opposition.

Rabin found himself facing an acute dilemma. True, Shamir was not moving the peace process forward. But the idea of his perennial party rival emerging as Prime Minister again was anathema to him. He distanced himself from Peres's behind-the-scenes machinations and tried to keep the hopelessly riven unity government afloat.

Secular Labour leaders wearing skull-caps began making furtive nocturnal visits on behalf of Peres to the homes of influential Shas rabbis. Haim Ramon, a Peres protégé, and the young Shas party leader Aryeh Deri reached a secret understanding on a political alliance and a timetable for action. In early March, Shas's spiritual leader Rabbi Ovadiah Yosef made his move. In a dramatic television appearance he denounced "warmongers" in the Israeli cabinet, declared that peace was more important than territory and repeated his well-known ruling that saving human lives took precedence over the integrity of Greater Israel.

Rabin realised which way the wind was blowing and was not pleased. "There are some in Labour who seem to be in a great rush to bring the government down," he thundered in a party forum, "and it isn't the peace process that's uppermost in their minds." Peres, he told his close aides, was simply obsessed with the idea of becoming Prime Minister, and he wouldn't play along. But two things happened that made him change his mind: Shamir showed just how uninterested he was in peacemaking, and Peres assured Rabin that he had an alternative Labour-led peace government sewn up.

In a stormy cabinet meeting on 11 March, Shamir, dead-set against any hint of negotiations with the "terrorist PLO", angrily rejected a compromise formula for Palestinian representation in peace talks with Israel. Rabin, the architect of the 1989 Israeli peace initiative, had personally worked hard for language he thought Shamir could readily accept and was devastated by the Prime Minister's table-banging obduracy. "We did all we could to find a formula," he said after the meeting. "But Shamir didn't want to know."

To put pressure on Shamir, Peres had scheduled a Labour Party central committee meeting for the next day. Here, for the first time, Rabin strongly backed Peres's decision to bring the unity government down. On 15 March, with five Shas Knesset members staying away during the vote, the Knesset approved a Labour motion of no-confidence in the Shamir government – by a majority of five. Peres's path to power and peacemaking seemed clear.

But the Labour leader was foiled by one of the most bizarre episodes in Israel's political history. First he was betrayed by Shas. Only four days after bringing the Shamir government down, the ultra-Orthodox party did an about-face: it informed President Chaim Herzog, who was canvassing parties prior to deciding whom he should ask to form the next coalition, that it would back the Likud leader, not Peres. What had happened in the interim had to do with the primacy among the devout of Ashkenazi (Eastern European) rabbis over Sephardi (North African and Middle Eastern) ones. For its religious legitimacy, Shas depended on the sanction of a nonagenarian Ashkenazi sage, Eliezer Menachem Schach. And Schach, although he had issued dovish rabbinic rulings in the past, now vetoed Labour. In a vitriolic speech to an ultra-Orthodox audience packed 10-deep in a Tel Aviv basketball stadium, the rabbi accused the Labour movement of lacking any trace of Judaism and its kibbutzim of raising "pigs and rabbits". A humiliated Rabbi Yosef – the Sephardi authority – wasn't ready to challenge his more powerful Ashkenazi counterpart.

Peres still managed to cobble together a coalition without Shas, dependent on a Likud defector (the former minister Avraham Sharir), and another ultra-Orthodox party, Agudat Yisrael. But on the morning of 12 April, when the new government was to have been approved by the Knesset, two of the Agudah members, Eliezer Mizrahi and Avraham Verdiger, went into hiding. An ashen-faced Peres had to concede that he did not have a parliamentary majority. The eventual upshot was the formation of a narrow-based government led by the Likud. Shamir easily wooed the Likud defector back, pried away a Labour dissident and, backed by Shas, formed a new administration, leaving Peres and the Labour Party in inglorious isolation, chastened and in total disarray. The way was open for Shamir to continue stonewalling peace proposals. Eighteen months later, after eight exhausting trips to the Middle East, US Secretary of State James Baker did finally manage to set up a regional peace conference in Madrid. It opened in October 1991 amid much fanfare, but no progress whatsoever was made on any of the four peace tracks – with Syria, Lebanon, Jordan and the Palestinians. And in a frank newspaper interview after he was voted out of office in June 1992, Shamir admitted that, had it been left to him, he would have dragged out peace negotiations for another 10 years.

Peres's political miscalculation had cost Rabin his beloved defence ministry. But the news was not all bad. On the contrary, the chance he had awaited for 13 years had come, and he seized it with both hands. No one could say he hadn't given Peres a fair crack. He had even gone to the rabbis on Peres's behalf, once to Schach who, he was told, was blind, deaf, dumb and senile. Rabin had found him nothing of the sort. He was very sharp, Rabin said, and he knew what he wanted. And he didn't want Labour.

Peres, Rabin felt, had made every mistake in the book. Because of overweening personal ambition, he had humbled the party; and he had kowtowed to the Orthodox and received a resounding slap in the face. Rabin, intensely secular, hated the wheeling and dealing, especially the fawning over the rabbis. He resolved not to go on being a compliant No. 2 to a man who had made such grave mistakes and who, besides his other failings, was far less electable than he was.

Rabin dubbed Peres's failure "the stinking manoeuvre". The term stuck and added to public perceptions of Peres as too clever by half and too tricky for his own good. Peres retorted that Rabin had been party to the "stinking manoeuvre" from the very beginning, and that had it succeeded he would have been happy to stay on as Defence Minister. Only because it had failed was he opening up old political wounds.

Rabin was unfazed. Just two weeks after Peres's humiliation in the Knesset, he addressed the party's 150-member leadership bureau and formally challenged Peres for Labour's top spot. "My mistake," he said, "was in putting party harmony above other more important issues." The uneasy truce, declared at the climax of the 1984 election campaign, was over. Rabin was demanding a showdown in the central committee, the 1,200-member supreme party body which elected the leader, and Peres was ready to take him on. "I didn't ask for a fight with Rabin," he said, "but if he wants one, he'll get it."

Political pundits were quick to write Peres off. No one but the Labour leader himself thought he would be able to stave off Rabin's challenge. Many of Peres's closest political supporters advised him to step down gracefully. And when he didn't, some, like former party secretary general Uzi Baram and Ephraim Sneh, who had joined Labour after leaving the army, crossed over to the Rabin camp. Even Haim Ramon, the loyal Peres acolyte who had helped engineer the initial deal with Shas, announced that he wouldn't turn up for the central committee vote and would go to the beach instead.

The only question on party lips seemed to be whether the 70-year-old Rabin should take over, or whether both he and Peres should step aside for the younger generation. Many agreed with veteran Labourite Ora Namir that the two of them were "tearing the party apart", and somebody else should be given a chance. Avraham Burg, another young Peres disciple, put it succinctly: "50 per cent want Peres, 50 per cent want Rabin and 100 per cent don't want either." But Rabin and Peres bestrode Labour politics like two immovable colossi. "As long as they're around, nobody else has a chance," was Ramon's rueful assessment. With his back to the wall, Peres lobbied the central committee members, all seasoned politicos, as only he knew how. He had spent his career learning to manipulate the machine – to recruit the party hacks rarely seen by the public – and Rabin, never one for back-room politics, was hopelessly out-manoeuvred. When the central committee met on 22 July, Peres carried the day by 582 votes to 504.

Peres was not invincible, though. Larger forces had been set in motion and the Labour leader had merely managed to postpone the day of reckoning. In the wake of the "stinking manoeuvre" and the political horse-trading by both major parties, a grass-roots movement for electoral reform was gathering pace. Half a million Israelis petitioned President Herzog in favour of direct election of the Prime Minister – in the belief that this would clean up politics and rule out midterm, defector-engineered government collapses. The national mood galvanised earlier tentative moves for democratisation of the Labour Party. Micha Harish, the party's general secretary, had long been advocating a membership drive and party-wide primaries. Peres was not keen. He saw the proposed reforms as a thinly veiled attempt to unseat him. But the national mood was such that he, of all people, could not afford to oppose the trend. Rabin welcomed the changes. If Peres could control the central committee, he certainly could not manipulate the entire party membership. The membership drive, vigorously conducted by Binyamin Ben-Eliezer, a Rabin stalwart, was an outstanding success. By the time the next battle for the party leadership came round in February 1992, in advance of that year's scheduled elections, over 150,000 people had joined the party and were eligible to vote.

Rabin's loyalists were convinced that the bigger the turnout the better. They spoke of a new conviction in the party, a growing belief that it could fight its way back to power. Rabin, they said, gave the Labour grass roots something they had not had for some time: a sense of hope. "People are convinced that with Rabin at the helm, we would have a winning ticket," declared his campaign manager Avraham Shochat.

Rabin ran on the simple slogan that he was the only candidate who could beat the Likud in a national election. Peres campaigned on his long service to the party and his undisputed political talent. No one gave the other two aspirants, Yisrael Kessar, the Histadrut trade union boss, and Knesset member Ora Namir any chance. Their importance was only in how many votes they would take from each of the two main contenders, and whether they would force Peres and Rabin into a runoff, by denying either of them 40 per cent of the vote in the first round.

As polling day approached, tension between Rabin and Peres grew. At a Labour Knesset delegation meeting in January, Peres complained about character assassination – Rabin supporters had branded him a loser, and a man obsessed with his own political aspirations. Rabin countered sharply that "playing the abject victim is no substitute for leadership".

By this time, most party insiders had been won over by Rabin's campaign message. Rabin might not be the better man, Uzi Baram noted, but he would certainly make the better candidate. With his brilliant military record and blunt, straight talk, he was strong where Peres was weakest: in public credibility. He would be more likely to win an election against the Likud, and then, because he was more hawkish than Peres, better able to sell Labour's peacemaking strategy to a sceptical public. That was why doves like Baram and veteran Labour leftist Aryeh Eliav supported him.

On the night of the leadership vote, 19 February, Labour's Hayarkon Street headquarters in Tel Aviv were abuzz with expectation. Camera crews from all over the world had set up on the third floor, where computer screens were installed to relay the results from 700 polling stations across the country. Knesset members paced nervously, mingling informally with journalists.

Rabin closeted himself with family and a few friends at his home in Tel Aviv's Neveh Avivim neighbourhood, chain-smoking. Everyone was on edge. When his trusty aide Shimon Sheves discovered that someone had presumed to put a bottle of champagne away to chill, he threw it out of the window. "It might bring bad luck," he said.

As soon as the first results came through, it was clear Rabin was going to win. The only question was whether he would clear the 40 per cent mark. If he didn't, he knew Peres could win the runoff by taking most of the Histadrut vote that would go to Kessar on the first ballot. For hours, as the votes were counted, Rabin's share hovered between 39 and 40 per cent. At one stage it was 39.99 per cent. In the small hours of the morning, it became apparent that he had made it – barely. Of the 108,000 votes, Rabin won 40.6 per cent to Peres's 34.8 per cent. Kessar had taken just under 19 per cent and Namir about 5.5 per cent.

Fifteen years after his ouster, Rabin had regained the leadership by a hair's breadth. At 3 o'clock in the morning Peres phoned to congratulate him. The call had been initiated by radio journalists covering the story and was broadcast live. The conversation was stilted and strained. But the next day the two rivals shook hands and vowed to co-operate.

Two weeks before Rabin's Labour leadership victory, the Knesset had voted to dissolve itself after three small far-right factions broke away from the Likud-led coalition, and to set an early election date in June. By April, Rabin's election campaign was in full swing. It was run with military precision by the ever-faithful Sheves, who had been his right-hand man since the early 1980s. The campaign slogan was "Israel is waiting for Rabin", a play on a well-known Six Day War song, "Nasser is waiting for Rabin", recalling Rabin's role of military saviour.

With his cellular phone always at the ready, Sheves orchestrated the hectic push for power, arranging over half a dozen appearances a day. Rabin was obsessed with winning. He drew on seemingly limitless reserves of energy. At 70, he was running his staff, many of them less than half his age, off their feet. He criss-crossed the country several times, chain-smoking, often having only a beer for lunch, burning with desire to be elected. He wanted to wipe out the memory of the failures of his first term as Prime Minister and to prove to the country and to himself that he was the right man for the top job. His deep craving for a second chance turned the shy, introverted man into a formidable campaigner.

Rabin was no wheeler-dealer politician. But he was a sharp political analyst. Labour, he reasoned, could no longer count on any support from the religious parties. The "stinking manoeuvre" seemed to bear him out. "Given the choice," he said, "they will always go with the Likud." The only way for Labour to win power, therefore, was to capture more of the centre, the political ground between left and right, between Labour and Likud. Rabin's aim was to get a "blocking majority" of at least 61 in the 120-member Knesset, comprised solely of Labour and parties to the left. That would stop the Likud from forming a coalition and force the religious parties to work with Labour or languish in opposition. To win on this strategy, Rabin needed to gain no less than five seats from the right – 150,000 wavering Israeli right-wingers. Peres scoffed at the strategy: "I doubt whether there are 150," he said.

Rabin, though, had the tough soldier image to appeal to the security-minded centre. He also had enormous credibility and a convincing alternative programme. Very early on, he realised the Likud was letting many of its traditional supporters down. Most Israelis wanted a better life, more security and improved economic prospects. Many realised the key to it all was peace, and giving up the Likud obsession with the Greater Land of Israel. On 1 March, he told the Labour central committee that people felt the Likud was missing opportunities and would continue to do so. Moreover, it had its socio-economic priorities all wrong. Simply put, the Likud and its leader were out of sync with changing times. The 1991 Gulf War, Rabin argued, had opened up a window of opportunity for peace in the Middle East. But it would not remain open for ever.

Labour would do its best to seize the chance; the Likud would almost certainly squander it.

The Likud's other cardinal sin, according to Rabin, was its huge spending on settlements. Not only did this complicate the peace process and hurt Israel's standing in the world, but the billions wasted there could be put to much better use inside sovereign Israel. This argument made deep inroads in the traditionally Likud urban blue-collar neighbourhoods and the neglected outlying townships populated by immigrants of the 1940s and '50s.

As the campaign heated up, Rabin boldly carried his message into these Likud strongholds across the country. This would have been unthinkable in any of the elections after the 1977 political revolution that first brought the Likud to power. But now he was received with open arms. And the highly charged chants of "Ra-bin, Ra-bin" that greeted him were reminiscent of the "Be-gin, Be-gin" of a decade before − shouts of adulation the dour Shamir could never hope to elicit.

The crowds loved Rabin's straight talk, his sincerity, and his commitment to what he believed was best for Israel. "The Likud took your money, the money you paid in taxes, and threw it away in the territories," Rabin bellowed to a working-class crowd in Beersheba. "They did nothing for sovereign Israel. In 15 years they never built a single factory in Beersheba!" When Shamir came to Beersheba, by contrast, a group of disaffected ex-Likud members raised a banner reading: "Shamir hates Moroccans. We're all Moroccans here." Shamir stormed out, calling the hecklers terrorists. He couldn't have done more to alienate the Sephardi vote. At a Rabin gathering in Tel Aviv, Nahman Mizrahi, a former paratrooper and a typical grass-roots Likud supporter, now middle-aged with curly, greying hair hanging down to his shoulders, gold chain around his neck and designer dark glasses, spoke for many when he said: "We Sephardim raised the Likud to power in 1977, and we will be the ones to bring them down."

For the waverers, Rabin struck exactly the right note: he would deliver peace with security and he would reorder national priorities. Instead of pouring money into the settlements, he would put it to work on infrastructure, education, fighting unemployment, absorbing immigrants and helping discharged army conscripts get a better start in life. The Likud would sanctify the status quo, Labour would make far-reaching changes. "The electorate," Rabin declared, "must choose between stagnation and hope."

In the battle for the middle ground, Rabin made some tough-sounding campaign statements, and declared that in peace negotiations with Syria he would not give back the Golan Heights. "Anyone who comes down from the Golan," he roared, "will compromise Israel's security." It was a statement that would come back to haunt him later, as opposition to his government's peace-making efforts grew. But it was a statement that was largely misunderstood. Rabin never said he rejected *any* compromise on the Golan. His campaign message was deliberately vague. When pressed, he explained he would be ready for withdrawal "on the Golan", but not "from the Golan". The bottom line was that while he was a stickler on security, he was prepared to make far-reaching territorial concessions. "I am not ready to give up an inch of security," he declared, "but I am ready to give up many inches of territory."

Besides the disaffected Likud voters, Rabin targeted two other important potentially right-tending groups: the 400,000 Russians who'd arrived in the new wave of immigration from the disintegrating Soviet Union, and young first-time voters. In both groups, Labour surprised the pundits and outpolled the Likud. Among the immigrants, post-election analysis showed that support for Rabin had reached a dramatic, and possibly decisive, 47 per cent; the Likud, which after all had been in government when most of the immigrants won their freedom and came to Israel, scored just 18 per cent of the Russian vote.

Rabin was Labour's election strategists' trump card and they played it for all it was worth. The campaign was the most leader-oriented in Israeli history. It was as if the law for direct election of the Prime Minister was already in force. The formal name of the party's list of Knesset candidates was even changed from "Labour" to "Labour led by Rabin", ensuring that Rabin's name was on the ballots, breaking with Israeli tradition of voting for a party rather than a personality. Huge photographs of the leader's earnest countenance looked down from the sides of buildings all over the country. Rallies, resplendent with lights, music, banners and balloons, reflected the reinvigorated party's newfound energies and incongruously presented the awkward and bashful Rabin almost like a pop star.

In contrast, the Likud did its best to hide Shamir, and projected the young leaders around him instead. It was not a winning strategy and the party knew it. Smear tactics against Rabin became a last desperate throw of the political dice. Allusions were made to his

24-hour crisis as Chief of Staff in the run-up to the Six Day War, and there were crude insinuations about a drinking problem. But to portray the exalted war hero as a closet drunk with feet of clay was no easy task. "The mudslinging," said Uzi Baram, "might titillate the Likud's inner circle. But it won't wash with the general public." Likud campaign managers knew they were skating on thin ice. Rabin, they complained, was not only "Mr Security," he was "Mr Teflon" too.

Rabin used the attacks to play his trump card, his credibility. In a tell-all interview with the mass circulation *Yediot Aharonot*, he conceded that he had been "depressed" for that one day before the outbreak of the Six Day War, but that the very next day he was back in charge, planning for the decisive victory. As for his drinking, he told a reporter that, "like everybody else", he took a shot now and then, but that hardly made him a drunk.

As Rabin went from strength to strength, the Likud's fortunes ebbed. In late April, with the campaign in full swing, the state comptroller came out with a damning indictment of Likud govern-ment management, especially at Ariel Sharon's housing ministry. Nor was Shamir's limited appeal as a candidate helped by incessant infighting among his Likud would-be successors as party leader. Moreover, the party was seen to be out of touch with popular feeling when it went back on earlier promises to support electoral reform. It was also seen to be dragging its feet on peace, and as a result to have hurt Israel's relations with the United States. Shamir's insistence on continued building in the territories had led the administration to withhold $10 billion in loan guarantees for immigrant absorption. Unemployment soared to over 11 per cent, costing still more votes. Finance Minister Yitzhak Moda'i made things worse by defiantly declaring that even if unemployment reached 16 per cent, Israel would not bow and scrape for the loan guarantees. After 15 years of Likud government, growing numbers of Israelis felt the time had come for a change.

On 23 June 1992, 2,657,327 people went to the polls. The result was a sweeping victory for Labour and for Yitzhak Rabin. Not only did Labour win a record 906,126 votes, giving it 44 Knesset seats to the Likud's 32, but Rabin also got the "blocking majority" on which his strategy had been based. With 44 seats for Labour, 12 for more dovish Meretz and five for two small left-wing parties elected mainly by Arabs, he was assured that at least 61 of 120 members would block any attempt by the Likud to set up a coalition.

Rabin was at home with his family when the first exit poll findings came through. Leah Rabin burst into tears as TV anchorman Haim Yavin announced there had been another *mahapakh*, the term he himself had coined to describe the political turnabout when the Likud first ousted Labour in 1977. Now he was using it to describe Labour's return to office. Rabin, in his cautious way, warned that it was only a television straw poll. But soon the result was beyond doubt. The wheel had come full circle. Rabin was the Labour Prime Minister who handed over power to the Likud's Menachem Begin. Now, in his own mind, he had regained from the Likud the premiership lost through no fault of his own. He would show the Israeli people that, given this second chance, he could be a great leader. He would show them that he could define strategic goals and that he had the political skills to achieve them. If he had been raw the first time round, now he was politically mature, ready for the great tasks ahead.

At the Labour Party's Dan Hotel campaign centre, there was pandemonium. It was the first election Labour had won outright in almost two decades. Champagne corks popped; there was dancing, hugging and singing. The ecstatic party workers chanted "Rabin, Rabin." Someone turned on the recorded jingle. "Rabin is the right man," the sound system blared. "Israel is waiting for Rabin."

At 11.20 p.m., Peres arrived looking jubilant. "It's the best thing that could have happened to Israel," he said, twirling a small red flower. Party workers gathered round to share their rejoicing in the victory. But Rabin's aides misinterpreted the scene. When Rabin arrived at 1 a.m. after the count was clear, someone whispered to him that Peres had resuscitated his camp within the party. Rabin smiled, shook hands all around and seemed to enjoy the celebration. But he was irate about the false news on the Peres faction and determined to show who was boss. "*I* will lead the coalition negotiations," he declared in his victory speech, red-faced, with neck veins bulging. "And *I* will appoint the cabinet ministers." Peres was left standing alone and sad-faced, the flower wilting in his hand.

Rabin wanted a balanced coalition with Labour as the fulcrum between left and right, secular and religious. He did not want to be dependent on the five Arab votes for his majority. And he wanted to keep his main natural coalition partner, the left-wing, secular Meretz, in check. He resented the Meretz boast that once in a coalition with Labour, it would set the tone. He hoped the right-wing Tsomet would balance Meretz's dovishness, and the ultra-

Orthodox Shas its secularism. By setting up a broad-based government of political opposites, he would be able to play them off against
each other and enhance his freedom of action.

He didn't quite bring it off. The appointment of Meretz leader
Shulamit Aloni as Education Minister kept out Tsomet, whose
leader Rafael Eitan, the former Chief of Staff, had wanted the job for
himself, and almost scared Shas off, because of Aloni's outspoken
secularist views. But Shas's spiritual mentor Rabbi Ovadiah Yosef
saved the day. He took the unprecedented step of leaving home to
meet an underling on his turf, going to the interior ministry, where
he ordered wavering party leader Aryeh Deri, the outgoing minister,
to sign the coalition agreement. The upshot was a Prime Minister
well-pleased with his handiwork, at the head of the most peace-
oriented government in Israel's history, without right-wing ballast,
but with the secular-Orthodox balance he'd sought.

Most of all, though, Rabin had wanted a government without
Peres. He hoped rumours spread by his own people, that Peres was
being considered for the post of "minister for the Jewish world",
would persuade him to retire. But Peres refused to bow out,
knowing he had enough clout within the party to force Rabin to
take him aboard. Rabin balked at giving Peres the defence portfolio.
It was from that post that he believed Peres had "tirelessly schemed"
against him during his first administration. So they compromised on
the foreign ministry. But Rabin clipped Peres's wings from the start.
The key bilateral peace negotiations between Israel and the neigh-
bouring Arab states, and between Israel and the Palestinians, would
be handled by the Prime Minister's Office. Peres would have to
make do with the ethereal multilateral negotiations on the future of
the Middle East after the achievement of peace.

As the new government started work, relations between the two
were as strained as ever. But to everyone's surprise, they were soon
working closely on the peace process; first out of a balance of terror
and gradually out of a grudging mutual respect. Their weekly tête-à-
têtes were relaxed encounters, and aides said they often heard the
pair laughing loudly behind the closed doors. Still, in March 1993,
Rabin began to fear that Peres was plotting again. Sheves warned
him to be on guard. Rabin retorted that he knew what was going
on. "I'm not a child," he declared. Peres had resuscitated his Friday
meetings with members of his faction. They had totally out-
manoeuvred Rabin in party infighting. Although Rabin had packed
the cabinet with his supporters, Peres had managed to get his own

people into key elected party positions: Eli Dayan as Labour whip in the Knesset, Nissim Zvili as party secretary general and Ezer Weizman as the party's candidate for the largely ceremonial office of President.

But Peres insisted that future relations with Rabin would be judged by one yardstick – the peace process. As long as Rabin gave it his best shot, Peres promised he would show unswerving loyalty. But if there were foot-dragging, "I will not hesitate to raise the banner of rebellion," he warned.

The antipathy between the two was not only the result of a struggle for power. There was an abiding clash of personalities. Comments Kalman Gayer, a close policy adviser to Rabin who knew both men well: "An analyst tries to take things apart and to find a way to put them together again after he understands them. That's Rabin. An integrative person can deal with vagueness. If he sees an obstacle, he tries to avoid it, to keep away from details and move on. That's Peres. The different approaches inevitably clash. In the case of Rabin and Peres, an extraordinarily strong rivalry was created."

In fact, the great wars between them were over. Rabin was 70 and Peres 69; they were at an age where one-upmanship mattered less than real achievement. Peres had been Prime Minister before, felt he had nothing to prove, and was resigned to serving out his career as Rabin's No. 2. More importantly, both Rabin and Peres were obsessed by the same big idea – making peace. The personality clash that had torn them apart became an asset; Israel's unlikeliest duo came to complement each other as the serious work of peace negotiation began.

9

Making Peace

SOON AFTER HIS new coalition was sworn in on 13 July 1992, Rabin predicted it would take just nine months to reach an agreement with the Palestinians. He believed the Intifada had led to a shift in the balance of power among the Palestinians, away from Yasser Arafat's PLO in Tunis, known as "the outside", to the local leadership in the occupied territories, "the inside". In Israel, a broad consensus ruled out any contacts with Arafat and his organisation, and the peace plan Rabin had formulated as Defence Minister in 1989 was designed to circumvent the PLO and create a credible local leadership by holding elections in the territories. He was convinced the elections would have taken place long ago but for Yitzhak Shamir's obduracy. And he was sure that once elected, local Palestinian leaders would be able to deliver.

But he was in for a rude awakening. In mid-September 1992, Israeli negotiators met in Washington with a team of "inside" Palestinians for the sixth round of talks since the 1991 Madrid peace conference – the first since Rabin had come to power. And the conduct of those talks clearly showed the PLO pulling the strings from the "outside" – or, rather, stymieing progress because it was not officially involved. The negotiations were going nowhere.

Foreign Minister Shimon Peres was quick to draw conclusions. He urged Rabin to reconsider his stand against negotiating with the PLO. Rabin refused. But he gave Peres permission to put out feelers to the PLO through Egypt. In messages to Egyptian presidential aide Osama al-Baz, Foreign Minister Amr Moussa and President Hosni Mubarak himself, Peres floated the "Gaza-First" idea – a plan for granting the Palestinians of the Gaza Strip self-rule, on an experimental basis, with the promise of West Bank autonomy if it worked – knowing it would make its way to Tunis. At about the same time

Above left Yitzhak Rabin, aged five, with his parents Nehemiah and Rosa, and his sister, Rachel, in 1927. *Above right* in 1940, the year he graduated from Kadoorie Agricultural School, just before enlisting in the Palmah. *Below* with the football team from Kadoorie (standing, third from right).

Above Yitzhak Rabin with Leah Schlossberg. *Below left* with daughter Dalia, in 1952 and *right* 25 years later, with grandson Yonatan (watched by Labour politician, Ora Namir).

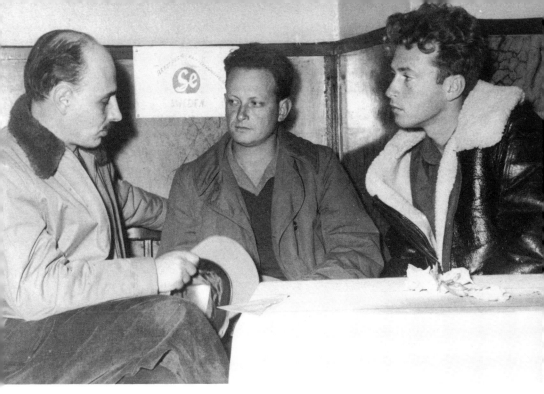

Rabin the soldier: *above* as a young brigade commander with his mentor Yigal Allon, head of the Palmah (centre), and Deputy Chief of Staff Yigael Yadin (left) in 1948; *below left* as Chief of Staff with Northern Front Commander David Elazar during the Six Day War; *right* entering the Old City of Jerusalem on 7 June 1967 with Defence Minister Moshe Dayan (centre) and head of Central Command Uzi Narkiss (left).

Rabin with colleagues: *above* as Prime Minister with his predecessor Golda Meir in 1976; *below left* on the beach with Foreign Minister Yigal Allon in 1977, the last year of his first term as Prime Minister; *below right* as Defence Minister with Prime Minister Peres in November 1984.

Posing for a sculpture in 1992.

Rabin at play.

The Jerusalem Report writing team, including David Horovitz (standing, third from left) and Hirsh Goodman (back row, right).

Rabin, the peacemaker: *above* a word in his ear from PLO chairman Yasser Arafat with Shimon Peres looking on; *below* receiving the Nobel Peace Prize with Shimon Peres and Yasser Arafat in 1994.

Enemies at home, friends abroad: *above* vitriolic opposition to the Oslo accords amongst Israelis; *below* lighting up with King Hussein of Jordan.

After the assassination, a memorial poster in Jerusalem quotes from the Kaddish, the Jewish prayer of mourning, "He who makes peace in his heights. . ."

Rabin made it clear that he was ready to make major territorial concessions for peace: "It is time to give up the religion of Greater Israel," he said in a speech in early September. Encouraged, the PLO responded by looking for ways to make direct contact with the new Israeli government. Abu Mazen, head of the PLO's Israel desk, made an approach through Egypt in October. It was too early, Moussa cabled back. Rabin was not yet ready.

But in early December – unknown to Rabin and Peres – there was a dramatic breakthrough in Israeli–PLO ties. Deputy Foreign Minister Yossi Beilin – derided by Rabin as "Peres's poodle" – had set up an as-yet unauthorised secret channel through top Norwegian officials. In September, during a visit to Israel, Norwegian deputy Foreign Minister Jan Egeland had met Beilin and offered to provide facilities for secret Israeli–Palestinian contacts. Beilin thought little of it until the PLO approached Yair Hirschfeld, a history professor and close associate of Beilin's, in London. Beilin gave Hirschfeld the go-ahead to meet the PLO's top economic expert, Ahmad Qurei, better known as Abu Ala. Terje Larsen, a Norwegian researcher who knew both Beilin and Abu Ala, helped to set up the first of two meetings in London in early December, to break the ice. Hirschfeld and Abu Ala decided to meet again under Larsen's auspices near Oslo on 21 January 1993.

By this time, after six months in power, Rabin was starting to doubt whether the "inside" Palestinians would ever be able to deliver. He had signalled his genuine desire for an accommodation with the Palestinians by calling a halt to new housing construction at West Bank settlements, but received little encouragement in return. The seventh and eighth rounds of talks in Washington had been a frustrating waste of time. Then, in retaliation for Rabin's December expulsion of 415 Hamas fundamentalists to Lebanon after the brutal killing of an abducted Israeli policeman, the Palestinians had suspended the Washington peace talks altogether.

For better or worse, secret diplomacy was now simply the only game in town. If Rabin wanted to make good on his election pledge to accelerate the peace process, he would have to play. He began sending out feelers to the PLO through Labour's Haim Ramon and Ephraim Sneh and Yossi Sarid of Meretz, as well as Shlomo Gazit, a former head of military intelligence. And in January 1993, when Peres came to him again with a specific proposal for the PLO – urging that Israel suggest to Arafat that he come to Gaza and arrange elections, to produce an elected Palestinian leadership with which

Israel could negotiate – Rabin heard the Foreign Minister out. Peres argued that as long as the PLO leader remained in Tunis, he would deliberately block progress. And, having now been briefed by Beilin on the Hirschfeld–Abu Ala talks, Peres told Rabin of the impending meeting in Norway between the pair. The Prime Minister intimated grudging approval.

At that meeting, held at Sarpsborg near Oslo, Peres's idea of launching Palestinian self-rule in Gaza immediately became the main focus. Abu Ala proposed an Israeli withdrawal from the Strip and a mini-Marshall Plan for the Palestinians. Hirschfeld was excited. "Start with Gaza," he enthused, knowing that the vast majority of Israelis held no sentimental attachment to the impoverished, over-populated, terrorist hotbed the Strip had become. An Israeli pullout from Gaza could serve as a confidence-building first step toward wider Palestinian autonomy, while enabling the most sensitive issues at the heart of the Israeli–Palestinian conflict – the status of Jerusalem, the fate of settlements, the return of Palestinian refugees, and the final delineation of borders – to be deferred long into the future. "That's something for which the government can get support."

At the next Oslo meeting in February, Abu Ala and Hirschfeld produced a seven-page paper, known as the "Sarpsborg document", which provided for the transitional handover of Gaza to the United Nations. Peres hit the roof when he saw it. "It's a terrible paper," he said to Beilin, flatly rejecting any UN role. "But something serious is going on." For the third meeting in March, Peres drafted amendments to the Sarpsborg document. Most importantly, he declared that Israel would be ready for the PLO to move its headquarters from Tunis to Gaza. The PLO and Israel were beginning to find a common language. In mid-April, Rabin met Mubarak in Ismailiyah and was shown a map Arafat had just left with him. On it Gaza and Jericho were boldly circled. The "Gaza-First" idea, planted by Peres, had come back as "Gaza-and-Jericho-First," with Arafat claiming the copyright. For the PLO leader, a foothold in the West Bank was imperative, to ensure that Israel was not cunningly seeking to fob him off with the poisoned chalice of Gaza alone. But Rabin was taken aback by the Jericho element, especially the inclusion of the Allenby Bridge across the Jordan River in the proposed autonomous area. If the Palestinians controlled a crossing-point from Jordan, there would be nothing to halt an inflow of either weaponry or refugees. Rabin told Mubarak the idea was a non-starter.

The Prime Minister was still harbouring faint hopes that a deal on limited self-rule could yet be struck with the Palestinians "inside", excluding the PLO. He felt Israeli public opinion would not tolerate open talks with the PLO, let alone a full-fledged peace deal with the terrorist organisation. He continued to regard the secret contacts as an adjunct to the public negotiations, which could feed into the main Washington talks and take them forward. Rabin pinned his faith on Faisal Husseini, scion of a famous nationalist family and the most respected Palestinian leader in the territories. Shamir had kept Husseini out of negotiations on the grounds that he lived in East Jerusalem and that his involvement might be taken to indicate Israeli readiness to negotiate on redividing the city. In April, Rabin gave the green light for Husseini to join the official Palestinian negotiating team.

It made no difference. From Tunis, Arafat continued to block all progress, holding out for an official role for the PLO. When the Washington talks reconvened on 27 April, after a four-month break because of the expulsions, they immediately came to a deadlock. For Rabin, Husseini's inability to take charge and move things forward was a major disappointment – and probably marked the point when he accepted that, if a deal were to be made, Arafat would have to be openly involved.

In Oslo, meanwhile, Abu Ala was energetically pushing what he called "the Gaza-and-Jericho project". Hirschfeld told him that Mubarak had raised it with Rabin, and that Rabin had balked at the Jericho details. Undeterred, Abu Ala insisted this was the way to proceed.

The combination of the PLO biting so strongly on Peres's "Gaza-First" bait, and Husseini's failure to do anything useful in Washington, led both Rabin and Peres to see the Oslo connection in a new and more serious light. The turning point came in mid-May. Peres told Rabin that he wanted to go to Norway to see Abu Ala himself. Rabin said it was too dangerous. They had to retain deniability, and they couldn't commit other members of the cabinet to a negotiating process they knew nothing about. Instead, the two agreed to send the new foreign ministry director general, Uri Savir, a Peres protégé, to assess just how serious the Oslo channel really was.

Rabin's gradual conversion to making the PLO his peace partner was a long time in coming. The start, strangely enough, was with the expulsion of the 415 Hamas and Islamic Jihad fundamentalists in December. There was much talk then in the cabinet of a two-

pronged policy serving the cause of peace: weakening the fundamentalist rejectionists, who were responsible for almost all the
terrorist activity against Israel, to strengthen the PLO-supporting
moderates. In a subtle conceptual breakthrough, the distinction
between fundamentalist rejectionists and PLO peacemakers was
firmly established in Rabin's mind.

The next major shift in Rabin's thinking followed his closure of
the territories in April, after a string of terrorist attacks had left 10
Israelis killed in three weeks. The closure, barring the 100,000-plus
Palestinians with jobs in Israel from reaching their places of work,
showed in a vivid and concrete manner that separation between
Israelis and Palestinians could work. Not only did it improve the
security situation, it pointed to the contours of a final political
settlement and singled out Gaza as a potential testing ground. Still,
he was not sure Arafat could be trusted.

The urbane Savir, formerly Israel's consul general in New York,
returned optimistic from his first encounter with Abu Ala at the
Thomas Heftye cottage in Oslo on 21 May. He felt he had
established an excellent rapport with Abu Ala, that Abu Ala had
Arafat's full backing and that the PLO wanted a deal. He told Rabin
and Peres the channel had serious potential. But Rabin wanted a
sterner test. Yoel Singer, a high-flying, Washington-based international lawyer, was brought in. He was someone whose judgment
both Rabin and Peres trusted. Singer had spent 20 years in the IDF's
legal department and had a hand in framing the disengagement
agreements Rabin and Peres had negotiated with Egypt and Syria in
the mid-1970s. He had also drafted laws for the occupied territories
during Rabin's first stint as Defence Minister. Now Peres wanted
him as the foreign ministry's legal adviser.

In late May, Peres and Beilin brought Singer to see Rabin at his
defence ministry office in Tel Aviv. Singer had seen a version of
the Sarpsborg document and described it as "half-baked". Blunt
and straight-talking, he alone among the Oslo players spoke
Rabin's language. Rabin said he wanted him to go to Oslo to test
the PLO's seriousness. "I want to hear from you that the PLO offer
is real," he said. At the seventh meeting in mid-June, Singer
interrogated Abu Ala, firing a long series of questions he said were
from Rabin. "From now on, what is happening here is official," he
told the Palestinians. Although he resented Singer's tone, Abu Ala
realised the future of the channel depended on his answers. Singer
returned to Rabin satisfied. "They are serious," he said. "They are

ready to postpone negotiations on the settlements and on Jerusalem."

Now Rabin actively entered the negotiating process himself. He
went over the minutes with a fine-tooth comb. Then he gave Singer
permission to write a full-fledged official Israeli proposal. On 3 July,
the Palestinians exploded when Singer arrived for the eighth Oslo
meeting with a totally new Israeli paper, a new draft of a Gaza–
Jericho deal that departed markedly from the papers Hirschfeld and
Abu Ala had been fine-tuning for months. Singer quietly suggested
they go through it word by word, with the Palestinians writing in
their objections and counter-proposals. The most intensive 36 hours
in the history of Israeli–Palestinian negotiations followed, bringing
the two sides very close to an agreement. But the good work ended
abruptly in a bitter argument over Jericho's precise status, with both
sides banging doors, shouting loudly that it was all over and driving
off to the airport.

Rabin was unfazed. He sent his team back a week later with more
demands for the security of the Jewish settlements and the safety of
Israeli settlers on the roads. The Palestinians responded with a
counter-proposal of their own and 25 new demands. The talks again
broke up in disarray. And this time it was serious. Rabin was
flabbergasted that the PLO had taken a leaf out of Israel's book and
introduced a completely fresh document at a time when the previous
paperwork was so close to being mutually acceptable. To him it
seemed to show a lack of seriousness and good faith. He told Peres
he had had enough and was going to call the whole thing off.
Fortunately, a Norwegian delegation led by Johan Jörgen Holst, the
Foreign Minister, had just seen Arafat in Tunis. Only pleading by
Peres, and a letter to Peres from Holst underlining Arafat's seriousness, persuaded Rabin to let the Oslo talks go on. At the same time
Haim Ramon, now Minister of Health in Rabin's cabinet, reported
independently to the Prime Minister on a meeting he'd had with
Arafat's Israeli–Arab adviser Ahmad Tibi in Jerusalem on 14 July.
Ramon said Tibi had convinced him that only Arafat could deliver
and that he was truly interested in a deal. But further meetings in
Oslo failed to bridge the gaps. Savir defined 16 points of contention
and proposed that each side make concessions on eight: the
Palestinians on security issues, Israel on all the rest.

Rabin was still sceptical, and extremely wary of Arafat. But in
August, Arafat publicly agreed to postpone discussions on Jerusalem,
catching the official Palestinian negotiating team for the Washington

talks completely by surprise. The "insiders" – Faisal Husseini, Sa'eb Arekat and Hanan Ashrawi – announced they were resigning in protest. Arafat was unmoved, and Rabin began to believe that he meant business.

A week later, Peres left for a preplanned visit to Scandinavia. He wanted to use the opportunity to wrap up the accord. Holst cut short a visit to Iceland and travelled to Stockholm to meet Peres on 17 August. Peres asked Holst to make contact with Arafat in Tunis by phone, so that he and his negotiating team could finalise the deal with the PLO leader. Holst obliged. Negotiations over the phone between Stockholm and Tunis started just after 10 p.m., and lasted for eight hours. Arafat, Abu Mazen (who had been quietly orchestrating much of the PLO negotiating strategy so far), Abu Ala, Oslo negotiator Hassan Asfour, PLO spokesman Yasser Abd-Rabbo and a Lebanese lawyer Muhsen Ibrahim camped in Arafat's office in Tunis. Holst, Peres and Singer spoke in turn from the Haga Palace in Stockholm. Rabin was on standby throughout the night in Tel Aviv, Savir in Jerusalem. The Israeli negotiators woke Peres three times in the small hours of the morning to ask him for fresh instructions. On one occasion, playing on the PLO's constant fear that Israel would conclude a deal with Damascus and leave the Palestinians in the cold, Peres growled sleepily: "Tell them we'll go with Syria." By morning the deal was done.

In the small hours of 20 August, at the Oslo Plaza Hotel, Abu Ala and Hassan Asfour signed for the Palestinians, Savir and Singer for Israel. The Declaration of Principles (DOP) provided for a five-year "interim period" of Palestinian self-rule in the occupied territories. As a first stage, Israel would withdraw its troops from Gaza and Jericho. Further West Bank redeployments would follow, and the Palestinians would hold elections. In short, the DOP promised to set in motion a process that, if carried through, would end Israel's 26-year-long occupation of more than 2 million Palestinians in Gaza and the West Bank.

Peres had been the driving spirit, Rabin the security-minded pragmatist who could sell the deal to an Israeli public that still believed the PLO was its most implacable foe. Amazingly, given the traditional Israeli loquacity, the eight months of negotiations in Norway had remained secret, their existence not known even to men like Elyakim Rubinstein, blithely continuing to lead the redundant public talks with the Palestinians under US auspices in Washington. The news that Israel and the PLO had been deeply involved in face-to-face negotiations, and had reached a framework agreement on transferring power in the occupied territories, was only made public in late August – prompting widespread international astonishment and disbelief.

For Rabin, the hardest part of all came now: Israel would have to recognise the PLO as the sole legitimate representative of the Palestinians. The men Rabin had spent most of his adult life fighting, and who had been responsible for some of the worst terrorist outrages against Israel and the Jewish people, were the same men who had negotiated the DOP. As the price for Israel's recognition, Rabin made tough demands: the PLO had to desist from all forms of terror and declare that it recognised Israel's right to exist. The Palestinian Covenant, the effective PLO constitution, had to be altered to eliminate clauses calling for Israel's destruction (a demand still unfulfilled by the end of 1995). And the PLO had to call on all Palestinians to turn away from violence and fight those who refused to comply. Arafat balked at the last demand. He couldn't call off the Intifada until there had been progress on the ground. And he wouldn't include a PLO commitment to fight other Palestinians in the PLO's letter of recognition addressed to the Israeli government. But Rabin was adamant. Unless the commitment against violence was absolute, there would be no deal. The compromise was a separate letter, from Arafat to Holst, promising to stop all Palestinian violence.

On 10 September 1993, Israel and the PLO exchanged their letters of mutual recognition. Holst brought Yasser Arafat's signed letter from Tunis to Jerusalem, where Rabin signed the Israeli recognition of the PLO with a cheap pen. It was one of the toughest days in Rabin's life. His letter to Arafat did not convey the slightest hint of friendship: it did not even use the customary "Dear" in the opening greeting, addressing Arafat simply as "Mr Chairman". Intellectually, Rabin realised that mutual recognition meant the end of a hundred years of conflict; emotionally it was almost impossible for him to come to terms with the fact that he was dealing with yesterday's terrorists. After a deliberately low-key signing ceremony at the Prime Minister's Office, Rabin walked slowly back to his own bureau, deep in thought, and sat down wearily, as if all the energy had drained out of him. Aides came in talking animatedly about the historic day. Rabin stared silently into space. He never questioned whether he had done the right thing. But the psychological barrier he was surmounting was immense.

The next day, Clyde Haberman of *The New York Times* came to interview Rabin at his official Jerusalem residence. While Haberman was there, the phone rang. It was ABC's Barbara Walters wanting to do a repeat of her famous 1977 Begin–Sadat joint interview in the Knesset – with Rabin and Arafat at the White House, after the ceremonial signing of the DOP scheduled for 13 September. Rabin told her he wasn't keen, and wouldn't promise anything. On the plane to Washington on the 12th, Rabin did not try to catch up on lost sleep as he usually did on long flights. He spent the time working on his White House speech. The next morning, although he hadn't slept, he gave interviews to all the networks, but not to Barbara Walters. She had a crew standing by at the White House all day. But Rabin couldn't bring himself to sit down with the PLO leader.

Rabin took several victims of terror attacks and their families with him for the Washington signing. It was his way of saying that Israel would not forget what the Palestinians had done during the years of conflict, and that it was this terrorist reality that he insisted on changing. It was also aimed, of course, at generating domestic support by showing that terror victims backed the deal. One of those invited, Smadar Haran, stayed behind. PLO terrorists, landing from the sea, had burst into her home in Nahariyah in April 1979, shot her husband and smashed her 5-year-old daughter's skull. Her baby had suffocated while hiding with her in their tiny attic. She could not face having to shake Arafat's hand. "You do it for me, Prime Minister, you are my messenger," she told Rabin.

In his speech on the White House lawn, Rabin declared: "...We who have fought against you, the Palestinians – we say to you today in a loud and clear voice: enough of blood and tears. Enough." That was the essence of his message on that historic day. A farewell to arms – on both sides. Suddenly, just as the applause after his speech was subsiding, there was the outstretched hand. Arafat, in military uniform and *keffiya* was moving toward him. Rabin cringed. His body language spoke repugnance. For a moment he hesitated. But, like the disciplined soldier he was, Rabin was ready to do what was necessary in the cause of peace. As Smadar Haran had so perceptively reminded him, it was not Yitzhak Rabin who would be shaking Arafat's hand, but the Prime Minister of Israel, the messenger of his people. He took Arafat's hand and shook it hard for a long moment. Then he turned to Peres and muttered with all the mock-humour he could muster: "Now it's your turn."

For the deal to succeed, of course, the handshake would have to be followed by the development of a solid, working relationship. Yet although he understood they were "partners in destiny" now, for better or for worse, Rabin found his first meetings with Arafat, in Cairo that autumn and winter, hard to take. He struggled to repress his true feelings, hiding behind an uncustomary mask of exaggerated courtesy. He always called Arafat "Mr Chairman", and Arafat always called him "Your Excellency". Rabin learned all he could about Arafat, and as he got to know the PLO leader better, he found their encounters less of an ordeal. Although he was fastidiously correct in the way he treated the PLO leader, he put forward his case with his usual bluntness, and invariably got his way. Quips Oded Ben-Ami, Rabin's spokesman at the time: "For Rabin, seeing Arafat was like going to the dentist. The anxiety before was much worse than the treatment."

The beginnings of the real process of change in Rabin's attitude to Arafat occurred when army intelligence told him that the PLO had ceased all terror activity. Arafat was keeping what was, for Rabin, his most important commitment and, in Rabin's book, that made him a legitimate partner. Still, he did not think the PLO leader was doing nearly enough to fight continuing radical Islamic terrorism. Until he did, Rabin's faith in him was strictly limited. At every opportunity, Rabin pressed the PLO leader to crack down on the militants. But he was aware of Arafat's limitations. "Even we don't stop all the terror in the areas we control," he used to say in Arafat's defence. For his part, Arafat developed a respect and fondness for Rabin over the years. "With Rabin, you always know where you are," he told his aides.

For King Hussein of Jordan, the breakthrough Israeli–Palestinian deal of September 1993 provided the full legitimacy he'd always wanted for Jordan to make peace with Israel as well. No longer would anyone in the Arab world be able to accuse him of selling the Palestinians short. What's more, it was clear that Jordan would have to move fast if it wanted to keep the peace process headed in the right direction. The King feared that if he stayed on the sidelines, he could face rampant Palestinian nationalism spilling over into Jordan and destabilising the kingdom. So move fast he did: on 14 September, just one day after Rabin and Arafat shook hands on the White House lawn, Jordan's negotiators in Washington initialled a peace agenda with Israel they had been holding up for almost a year.

Two weeks later, on 26 September, Hussein invited Rabin to a secret rendezvous aboard the royal yacht in the Gulf of Aqaba. The King wanted to discuss the implications of Israel's peace deal with the Palestinians. Would the White House handshake herald a change in Israel's perception of Jordan's strategic role in a final peace deal with the Palestinians? Who would control the Jordan River bridges during the self-rule phase – Israel or the Palestinians? And how would the inclusion of the Palestinians in Dead Sea development projects on the Israeli side of the border affect similar projects on the Jordanian side? Rabin's questions were simpler – he had really only come to find out if Hussein was now ready for formal peace. "Do you mean business?" Rabin asked the King. "Yes, I do," was the reply. Rabin was immeasurably relieved: the King's answer meant there were going to be very tangible political benefits for Israel from the deal with the Palestinians.

For years, Israel and the Hashemite Kingdom had enjoyed a special, surreptitious relationship, based on a common interest in channelling Palestinian national aspirations in directions that did not threaten either's survival. Rabin was only too happy to reassure the King that the deal with the PLO would not be at his expense, and that Israel saw a key role for Jordan in a final peace deal, as the senior partner in a confederation with the Palestinians.

Rabin and the King were no strangers. They had met several times in secret over the past two decades. On one occasion, though the two countries were still formally at war, Rabin had given the King an Israeli-made Galil assault rifle in an olivewood case. The two men understood each other well, and enjoyed each other's company. Shimon Peres had also had secret meetings with the King. In April 1987, he had achieved what he thought was an historic breakthrough in a secret negotiating session in London, only to see it torpedoed by the Likud Prime Minister Yitzhak Shamir.

Five weeks after Rabin's tête-à-tête with the King aboard the royal yacht, Peres met Hussein secretly at the Hashemiyah Palace on the outskirts of Amman, to review progress in the negotiations and outline economic aspects of a prospective peace deal. He returned to Israel euphoric. "Put 3 November in your calendars as an historic date," he told journalists, indicating that a peace treaty with Jordan was very near. "All that's needed is a pen to sign it," he said.

It didn't require too much intelligence for the Israeli media to conclude, and report, that Peres must have had a meeting with the King. The Jordanians were furious at Peres's indiscretion. Hussein warned Rabin that there would be no more meetings if they could not be kept secret. So Rabin decided to do the peacemaking himself from then on. For all Peres's optimisim, though, Hussein was moving hesitantly, waiting to see how the implementation of the deal with the Palestinians would turn out. And progress on this was painfully slow. One reason was Rabin's concern with detail; another was terror.

The Israel–PLO deal incensed both Rabin's and Arafat's domestic opponents. The extremists on both sides – and especially the radical fundamentalists of Hamas and Islamic Jihad – resorted to violence, sowing hatred and chaos in an effort to subvert the peacemaking. From the outset, Rabin saw continuing fundamentalist terror as the biggest danger – "a strategic threat" to the process. His solution on the tactical level was to pursue Hamas and the other Palestinian fundamentalist groups ruthlessly. On the strategic level, he wanted a peace deal that entailed strict separation – a minimum of contact, to ensure a minimum of friction – between Israelis and Palestinians.

The fundamentalists stepped up their terrorist activities after the September 1993 agreement, attacking a series of Jewish settler targets in the West Bank and Gaza. The fact that the PLO was not involved did not stop the Israeli right-wing opposition and Jewish settlers from blaming the government's peace policies. There was a division of labour on the Palestinian side, they claimed: the PLO was using diplomacy to divest Israel of its best security assets, and the fundamentalists were using force. There was total co-ordination between them, and the government was naive not to see it.

The massacre of 29 Arabs praying in a Hebron mosque, by settler extremist Baruch Goldstein on 25 February 1994, almost shattered the brittle process of reconciliation. It sparked an outcry in the Arab world, and Arafat, blaming anti-peace elements in the Israeli security forces for the crime, broke off the talks on implementation of the peace deal with Israel. Eventually, Rabin was able to convince the PLO leader that it would be wrong to give the men of violence a veto over the process. But no sooner had the talks resumed than there was another attack, this time from the fundamentalists on the Palestinian side. A suicide bomber killed eight Israeli civilians in the northern town of Afulah on 6 April – the first of a series of threatened revenge attacks for the Hebron killings. A second suicide attack followed a week later, in Haderah, with five victims. Goldstein's suicidal attack had provoked the Islamic suicide bombers. Violence had escalated to a new level. Rabin insisted on continuing the peace process, undeterred by opposition on both sides. "We will continue the process as if there is no terror," he said. "And we will fight the terror as if there is no process."

But he was not making it easy for the negotiators on either side. They had reached the Oslo deal because they had been able to rise above details and to put off thorny questions like borders, Jewish settlements, Palestinian refugees and the future of Jerusalem. But now Rabin was demanding a new level of detail and precision, especially on security matters. Even before the signing of the Declaration of Principles in 1993, he criticised it as having "more holes than Swiss cheese". Now he was insisting that all the holes be filled before going ahead with the implementation. Peres bore the brunt of the negotiation, and Rabin made his life hell. A month before Goldstein's massacre in Hebron, after intensive negotiations in the Swiss resort town of Davos in late January 1994, Peres thought he had ingeniously overcome all the obstacles to the implementation of the "Gaza-and-Jericho-First" phase of autonomy. He phoned Rabin in Jerusalem to report. But the Prime Minister blocked the deal – unhappy with the security arrangements. When Peres finally sowed it up in Bucharest and Cairo in late April, after the prolonged, post-Goldstein suspension of negotiations, the 15 pages of the DOP had grown to 19 and there were now six detailed maps, showing precise lines of redeployment, as well as provisions for joint patrols and liaison committees. But there were still one or two loose ends. The main problem was that Arafat felt he had been bullied, and he wanted one or two last-minute face-saving achievements. Well after midnight on 3 May, just hours before the planned signing in Egypt's capital, President Mubarak swept dramatically into the side-room assigned to the Israeli team in Cairo's Al-Itihad Palace. He put his arm around Rabin, took him aside and whispered, "You must give Arafat the Muasi area on the Gaza coast." Rabin, who had been unyielding, seeking to keep that area because of its proximity to Jewish settlements, agreed.

That should have done the trick. But it didn't. As a worldwide audience watched the 4 May signing ceremony – timed to coincide with Mubarak's 66th birthday – on live television, Rabin went to put his signature to the stack of documents only to discover that Arafat had not signed the maps on the Jericho area. The assembled dignitaries – Mubarak, Peres, Secretary of State Warren Christopher among them – seemed at one point close to coming to blows with Arafat right there on-stage. Rabin stood with his arms folded, refusing to proceed unless Arafat signed. Amid extraordinary scenes, the leaders trooped off-stage, where a behind-the-scenes tongue-lashing from Mubarak cowed Arafat into finally returning to put pen to paper. For Rabin, and Israeli viewers, here was a reminder of Arafat's potential deviousness. For Arafat, it was probably a pre-planned stunt, designed to show the Palestinian public that he was not meekly accepting Israeli dictates.

A few days later, Arafat appeared in a Johannesburg mosque and, in another attempt to show he had not given away too much in the negotiations with Israel, declared the Palestinians would continue their jihad until they liberated Jerusalem. Afterwards he claimed that by "jihad" he did not mean "holy war", but "sacred campaign". Rabin declared angrily that any "continuation of violence and terror contravened the letter... that brought about mutual recognition, and called the entire peace process into question".

Still Rabin stuck to his side of the bargain. On 13 May, Israeli forces pulled out of Jericho, and on 17 May they left two-thirds of Gaza, retaining the settlements where 4,500 Jews lived and the access roads around them. On 1 July, after dismantling his Tunis head-quarters, Arafat made a triumphal entry into Gaza. Four days later he addressed cheering crowds in Jericho. Rabin's policy adviser Kalman Gayer asked the Prime Minister if he trusted the PLO leader. "That's not important," Rabin replied. "What matters is what happens now."

As soon as the "Gaza-and-Jericho-First" deal was signed, King Hussein sprang back into action. On 19 May, Rabin and Hussein met secretly in London and hammered out the framework for a peace treaty. Rabin was determined to show that this time he could pull it off without Peres. He set up a negotiating team comprised of cabinet secretary Elyakim Rubinstein, a holdover from the Shamir days, Mossad deputy director Ephraim Halevy, and his military secretary Danny Yatom. They were all directly subordinate to the Prime Minister and worked on the Jordan negotiations from his office. Peres and the foreign ministry were kept in the dark.

The three leaders involved in the talks – Rabin, Hussein and Crown Prince Hassan – were committed heart and soul to an agreement. But the negotiators had a hard time agreeing on the details. More often than not when things got tough, Hassan was the man who came up with the "creative solutions". The talks usually took place at night at the Royal Palace in Aqaba. Hassan and his wife would stay up in a room near where the negotiators were sitting.

When problems arose, Rubinstein would go across to Hassan, and formulate an accommodation.

Though kept out of the political negotiations, Peres did handle the economic side of the blossoming relationship. On 20 July, he became the first Israeli minister ever to be openly received in Jordan, flying from Jerusalem to the Dead Sea Spa Hotel on the Jordanian side of the sea to discuss plans to develop joint water resources, a Red-Dead Sea canal, joining the electricity grids and turning the barren Aravah desert into the thriving industrial, farming and tourist centre the Israelis had dubbed Peace Valley. "The flight," Peres said in his lofty rhetoric, "took only 15 minutes, but it crossed a gulf of 46 years of hatred and war." During the journey, Peres had stood at the helicopter's open door surveying the land in a visionary pose. Rabin was livid. The Jordanian track was his, and he didn't want to see Peres stealing his thunder.

The following week, on 25 July, Rabin and Hussein met openly for the first time in a three-way summit with Bill Clinton in Washington. American officials worked long hours on a text for a final communiqué. The US ambassador to Israel, Martin Indyk, then a member of the American peace team, brought their handiwork to the Israelis to make sure it wasn't too effusive. "Don't worry," Rabin's aides told him, "we have something better." They showed him the text of an already agreed-on joint Israeli–Jordanian declaration of non-belligerency. Indyk read the document and announced delightedly, "What you have here is peace."

In a speech during the summit, naming all the officials who had helped create the conditions for the historic non-belligerency declaration, Rabin mentioned everyone except Peres. The snub was intended to underline that now Rabin was making peace without Peres, that he deserved recognition as a statesman in his own right.

The next step after non-belligerency was a full-fledged peace treaty, and Rabin and Hussein made a series of goodwill gestures to keep the momentum going. On 3 August, Hussein made the first peaceful overflight of Israel by a Jordanian, piloting the royal jet himself, and talking by radio to Rabin on the ground. Five days later, Israel and Jordan opened their first border crossing point. It was in the Aravah desert, just a few kilometres from the Red Sea coast and, after the ceremony, Rabin and the Israeli army's top brass were the King's guests for lunch at the Royal Palace in Aqaba.

Still, despite all the *bonhomie*, the officials negotiating the peace treaty were unable to solve lingering problems on the sharing of joint water resources and the precise delineation of the common border. Rabin and Hussein had to be called in to finish the job. They met at the Hashemiyah Palace on the evening of 16 October, and began working at 9 o'clock, going through the agreement paragraph by paragraph and solving problems as they arose. When the thorny border issue came up, they got down on their hands and knees to pore over a huge aerial photography map laid out on the floor. Together, they worked out the whole line from Eilat and Aqaba in the south to the point where the Israeli, Jordanian and Syrian borders converge in the north. In some areas they agreed on land exchanges; in several cases, they agreed that fields Israel was due to return to Jordanian sovereignty would continue to be used by the Israeli farmers who had been working them – an arrangement showing extraordinary goodwill. As for the water, it was decided that the Jordanians would get 50 million cubic metres a year more from Israel (equivalent to 8 per cent of Israel's annual consumption from the Jordan) – but would withdraw a demand for direct access to the precious Sea of Galilee – and that the two countries would raise $200 million for an ambitious dam and desalination scheme.

Rabin and Hussein worked until 4 a.m. Then they took a rest, while the officials wrote it all up. When they met again four hours later, it was all done, ready to be initialled. Rabin phoned President Ezer Weizman to give him the good news, and then he and Hussein held a joint press conference to announce their peace deal to the world. On 26 October, the treaty was signed at a border point on the Aravah desert that had been a minefield just a few days before. Clinton flew in to witness the deal. Rabin said it was time "to make the desert bloom", and Hussein promised "a warm peace" – unlike the cold peace with Egypt – that would change the quality of life in both countries.

It was after the peace deal with Jordan that relations between Rabin and Peres finally began to undergo a fundamental change. Rabin saw the Jordanian treaty as his achievement, and he felt easier now about coming to terms with Peres. But there was still a lingering rivalry over their relative places in history. Only a month before, in September, they had clashed bitterly over a ceremony in Oslo marking the anniversary of the signing of the Declaration of Principles with the Palestinians. Rabin had initially agreed to allow Peres to go alone. But when Peres invited 150 people, Rabin changed his mind and decided he would go along too, leaving Peres upstaged and angry.

There was a final flickering of tension too between Rabin and Peres over the Nobel Peace Prize. It had been rumoured for months that one of them was going to get it, and each was lobbying at the other's expense. In the end, showing Solomonic wisdom, the prize committee gave the award jointly to Rabin, Peres and Arafat. And with international accolades now coming thick and fast, the recognition helped the inveterate rivals realise just how successful they had been working together.

At last, they began to trust each other enough to become true friends. It was, as Rabin's adviser Kalman Gayer says, a very special kind of friendship. "It was never a case of going out for a drink together or inviting each other over for lunch. It was more a friendly alliance to change history." And in March 1995, Rabin paid Peres the ultimate compliment by giving him overall charge of the negotiations with the Palestinians on extending their self-rule from Gaza and Jericho to the rest of the West Bank – the crucial phase of the autonomy deal. Rabin himself would lead the fight against Islamic terror.

Both men faced tough tasks. By early 1995, Palestinian extremist violence was close to subverting the whole peace process. In October 1994, a suicide bomber had shocked Israel by striking in the heart of Tel Aviv, killing 22 civilians in a bus outside the fashionable Dizengoff shopping arcade. In January 1995, two other bombers killed 20 soldiers and a civilian at a busy bus station at Beit Lid, near Netanyah.

Opposition Likud leader Benjamin Netanyahu was quick to use the upsurge in terror to lambast the government's peace policies. Within an hour of the Dizengoff blast, he was on the scene telling the nation that the situation was now intolerable. Rabin countered that the opposition was "dancing on the blood" of the Israeli victims – using terrorism to make cheap political points. The hysterical reaction, he charged, only encouraged more bombings. Both the opposition and Hamas were trying to torpedo the peace process, and in this sense, said Rabin, they were collaborators. But calling the Likud "Hamas collaborators" was a rhetorical step too far, and caused a storm. "The Prime Minister," Netanyahu sneered, "must have fallen on his head." President Weizman, who was supposed to be above politics, added fuel to the flames. Appearing to back the opposition, he called on the government to "rethink" its peace-making with the Palestinians. Public support for the peace process, which had been polled at well over 60 per cent when the Declaration of Principles was signed, slipped relentlessly back toward 50 per cent.

Rabin, though, was determined to press ahead, and the way forward was to stop the fundamentalists – with Yasser Arafat's help. When Arafat phoned the Prime Minister to offer his condolences for the Beit Lid bombing, Rabin demanded stronger action against the radicals, warning that the autonomy process was now in real danger. Arafat took him seriously, and launched the first determined clampdown against the Gaza fundamentalists – arresting Islamic leaders, setting up military tribunals to jail militants, confiscating weapons.

Rabin, meanwhile, imposed another closure on Gaza and the West Bank – a move intended to stop would-be bombers crossing into Israel, but one that also again denied thousands of bona fide Palestininan workers access to their jobs. In the past, the Palestinians had tended to blame Israel for the economic hardship caused by the closure orders. Now, though, Arafat's clampdown delegitimised the fundamentalists. Hungry workers started blaming the bombers, and the Islamicists lost ground. Arafat's firm action this time went a long way toward finally convincing Rabin of his credibility as a worthy partner in the fight for peace.

Between March and September 1995, Peres met Arafat six times to discuss the peace process. They set up subcommittees to handle everything from military redeployment, to security, the phased transfer to the Palestinians of specific spheres of responsibility, and prisoner releases. Peres and Rabin were working in closer coordination and in far greater harmony than ever before. More suicide bombings – in Gaza in April, in Ramat Gan in July and in Jerusalem in August – caused further public outrage in Israel. But Rabin, Peres and Arafat had now gone well beyond the point of no return, and Rabin was satisfied that Arafat was doing all he could to contain the fundamentalists.

Peres and Arafat eventually finalised the 314-page agreement on extending self-rule to the West Bank on 24 September, after an intensive week-long session at the Egyptian resort of Taba. The negotiations had been extremely complex, mainly because of the need to provide security for 140,000 Jewish settlers. The Rabin–Peres solution was to divide the territory into three categories – A (the large towns, to come under Palestinian control), B (villages, under joint control) and C (Jewish settlements and all other territory, under Israeli control) – and to build a system of roads enabling the settlers to bypass major Palestinian population centres.

The signing of the agreement, dubbed "Oslo II", took place in Washington on 28 September 1995, two years and two weeks after the now-famous reluctant handshake on the White House lawn. This time both Rabin and Arafat were far more relaxed. Arafat affectionately patted Rabin on the back in full view of the TV cameras. And while Rabin never put a friendly hand on Arafat, he did show some warmth toward the PLO chief. Taking the podium after Arafat had delivered a lengthy address, Rabin observed that Jews were supposed to be great speechmakers. Having now listened to the Chairman's protracted oration, he said good-naturedly, he was beginning to wonder whether Arafat might have some Jewish blood. Along with Clinton and the other dignitaries, Arafat burst out laughing. It was, by a considerable distance, the highest compliment Rabin had ever paid him.

In many ways the second interim agreement was more significant than the first. It provided for Israeli withdrawal from seven West Bank towns and for Palestinian elections, and set in motion the machinery for ending Israel's 28-year-long military occupation. On 6 October, the Knesset approved the deal by the narrowest of margins, 61–59. Alex Goldfarb, a breakaway from the right-wing Tsomet party who had crossed to the government ranks and was made a deputy cabinet minister, embarrassed the coalition by refusing to say how he would vote until the very last minute. There were rumours that he had been promised a better government car in exchange for his "yes" vote.

Weizman was critical of the agreement. It had been negotiated too quickly, he said, and without sleep. In private conversations with Knesset members, the President implied that the parliamentary majority had not been large enough and that it had all hung on "Goldfarb's Mitsubishi". Rabin seethed. It was Weizman who had leaked the story of Rabin's pre-Six Day War breakdown to help Peres in the 1974 Labour leadership contest. Now, he was helping the opposition against a process Rabin saw as his crowning achievement. Rabin could make peace with the PLO, and even with Shimon Peres, but it seemed he could never reach a reconciliation with Ezer Weizman.

After the Knesset had approved the Oslo II accord, one major section of the peace puzzle had yet to be filled in: accords with Syria and its client-state Lebanon. Rabin saw peace with the two countries as a major strategic goal. But he and Syria's President Asad had got caught up in a stubborn game of "after you, sir", which they failed to break. Asad refused to engage in serious negotiations until Rabin committed himself to total withdrawal from the strategic Golan Heights, captured from Syria in 1967 – when Rabin was Israel's Chief of Staff, and Asad was Syria's Defence Minister. But before Rabin would contemplate such a commitment, he wanted to hear exactly what kind of peace relationship with Israel President Asad had in mind.

In early 1994, Israel and the United States made a major effort to break the deadlock. On 16 January, Clinton met Asad in Geneva – but failed to get new commitments on expelling the Palestinian rejectionist groups hosted in Damascus or on the nature of normalisation envisaged with Israel. Rabin, disappointed that little of substance had emerged from the Clinton–Asad summit, nevertheless launched a new strategy aimed at securing a breakthrough. The day after the Geneva summit, deputy Defence Minister Mordechai Gur was despatched to the Knesset to announce that if a peace treaty with Syria entailed a significant Golan withdrawal, the government would hold a national referendum for approval.

The signal to the Syrians was clear: Rabin was ready for a major territorial compromise, but in the context of a peace he could sell to the Israeli people. The referendum would enable Rabin to circumvent the Knesset, where he could not be sure of a majority for a Golan withdrawal. The move also placed a large burden on President Asad. Rabin was effectively telling him that, through Sadat-style public diplomacy, he would have to help win over a sceptical Israeli electorate if he wanted Israel to make concessions on the Golan.

To break the negotiating deadlock, Rabin proposed that the parties first focus on security arrangements. If they could reach agreement on a security regime, he reckoned, everything else would fall into place. Israel would be able to withdraw from the Golan, the Syrians would be able to contemplate full normalisation of their ties with Israel, and interlocking timetables for implementation could be worked out. Later that month, in a secret meeting in Washington, Israel's ambassador to the United States and chief negotiator with Syria, Itamar Rabinovich, put the new Israeli approach to his Syrian counterpart, Walid Mu'alem. The Syrian response was chilly. And as the year passed, and the next, it seemed that nothing could break the deadlock. The success of the peace deals with the Palestinians and with Jordan, a second Clinton–Asad summit in Damascus in October 1994, and even face-to-face talks on security arrangements between the Israeli and Syrian military Chiefs of Staff in December 1994 and June 1995, all failed to produce any tangible progress.

Asad suspected that Rabin was marking time until the scheduled election in 1996, avoiding promising a complete withdrawal from the Golan until he had received a renewed mandate from the voters. Rabin believed Asad was more interested in negotiations than in a peace agreement. That way he could get American and European acceptance and support for his harsh regime without having to pay the price of peace with Israel. In the summer and early autumn of 1995, American diplomats spoke of a "breakdown of trust" between the two leaders.

Nevertheless, Rabin's vision of Israel's future included accommodation with Syria as one of its central building blocks. One of the main reasons the cautious ex-general agreed to make peace with the PLO was his fear that the uncompromising Hamas fundamentalists would otherwise gain sway in the territories. In microcosm, this mirrored his view of the fundamentalist threat to the Middle East as a whole. He argued that if nothing were done to reverse the trend, the region could be engulfed by fundamentalism within five years, threatening not only Israel, but all the current Arab regimes. His major policy thrust, therefore, was towards reconciliation of all the old national foes - Israel, the Palestinians, Egypt, Jordan, and Lebanon and Syria - to create a united front against the common fundamentalist enemy. Ultimately, the pursuit of that vision would be left to Shimon Peres.

10

Israel Transformed

THE HUGE MUD-COLOURED helicopter lifted off slowly from the green-topped Knesset hill in Jerusalem and headed east. The land below switched swiftly from the bleak moonscape of the Judaean Desert to a narrow fertile valley bisected by a sluggish stream, and then again to wind-swept desert. Suddenly another stone-built capital, perched on hills, loomed, and the Israel Air Force helicopter glided in to land. Twenty minutes after leaving Jerusalem, Yitzhak Rabin and his party stepped out of the helicopter on to the grounds of King Hussein's Hashemiyah Palace, just outside Amman. An Israeli businessman – and former general – quipped: "If Amman's this close, how come we never conquered it?" At the palace, Rabin was royally welcomed by King Hussein. The two old friends enjoyed a smoke together, before joining the delegates to the Amman Economic Conference, the reason for Rabin's visit to the Jordanian capital at the end of October 1995.

The conference was dramatic evidence of the extent to which the peace process had reconciled much of the Arab world to Israel's existence and legitimacy. Along with the collapse of Soviet communism, it had also led to a dramatic improvement in Israel's standing elsewhere in the world. In 1975, when the UN General Assembly approved the infamous resolution equating Zionism with racism – the low point in Israel's international relations – 75 member-states voted in favour. At the time, that was more than the number of countries that had diplomatic relations with the Jewish state. By the time of the Madrid Conference in October 1991, Israel had ties with 91 countries. After that, the slow crawl of governments sending representatives to open missions in Israel turned into a stampede. By the end of that year, the General Assembly had voted to repeal the "Zionism equals racism" resolution. And four years later, by the end of 1995, Israel was able to boast relations with 155 states.

As the peace talks moved forward, more distant Arab states also felt more comfortable in maintaining ties or holding open contacts with Israel. Morocco and Tunisia in North Africa, and Oman, Qatar and Bahrain in the Persian Gulf, all hosted Israeli delegations in the framework of the multilateral peace talks on wider Middle East issues. Morocco and Tunisia, indeed, both opened liaison offices in Israel – effectively establishing low-level diplomatic ties. Strategically and economically, cementing the nascent diplomatic relations with the two Asian giants, China and India, was particularly important. In 1991, in the huge slice of the globe from the former East Germany in the west to Vladivostok in the east and India in the south, Israel had only two embassies – in Romania and Nepal – and a consulate in Bombay. By the end of 1995, there were Israeli diplomatic missions in all but five of the countries in the area. The peace process also allowed Israel to deepen ties with Japan, an economic super-power, which had always hung back before because of its dependence on Arab oil. It helped improve ties, too, albeit without the exchange of diplomatic envoys, with other Asian/Islamic countries like Indonesia. And in December 1993, Israel signed a breakthrough diplomatic agreement with the Vatican, following decades of total refusal on the part of the Holy See to establish relations.

The peace process also brought dramatic improvement in Israel's status in international organisations, where it ceased to serve as the whipping boy of Arab and Third World countries. Anti-Israel debates and resolutions steeply declined, and Israeli representatives started to win election to senior positions in United Nations agencies.

The Amman gathering put the seal of acceptance from Israel's former enemies on its regional role – and demonstrated the close link between foreign and economic policy for Israel. Rabin and Peres were acknowledged as leading figures. Rabin set the tone – pointing out that no one was dealing with the Israelis because of their winning smiles, but because everyone wanted to make money. Egypt, which had kept trade with Israel at a minimum since it began after the 1979 peace treaty, realised that it might be missing the economic bandwagon, and announced unexpectedly that it was expanding economic ties with Israel. Cairo offered Jerusalem a comprehensive free-trade agreement – and said it would be the first in a series of agreements that would eventually encompass all the countries in the region. Jordan also announced it was removing trade barriers with Israel. Qatar agreed to supply Israel with natural gas, and a memorandum of understanding was signed for a $5 billion deal, with the gas due to start flowing in Israeli pipelines by the year 2002. Lebanon, influenced by Syria, officially boycotted the Amman gathering. Yet Lebanese businessmen were there in force.

A few days before the conference, Palestinian fundamentalist leader Fathi Shkaki, head of the Islamic Jihad terror group, had been shot dead by anonymous assailants in Malta. Shkaki's organisation blamed Israel – and Israel did not deny the charge. In the past, such an incident could have torpedoed an Israel-Arab forum. This time it had no effect. Asked at the conference about the assassination, Egyptian Foreign Minister Amr Moussa replied: "Shkaki killed? What do you say? I didn't know. Anyway, it's none of my business."

In a speech to the conference, Rabin noted the progress since the first such Middle East economic gathering, a year earlier in Casablanca. In Morocco, the very fact of Israel's presence was the achievement, and painstaking work was required to overcome deep-rooted suspicion of Israeli intentions and translate ceremonial contacts into nitty-gritty business. "There were cynics who scoffed that after the final handshakes of the Casablanca conference, the dust would once again settle on the Middle East," Rabin told his Amman audience. "But the hundreds of representatives of large corporations and multinationals, which have invested in this area in the last year and which are present here today, are the proof that the process which was started in Casablanca was a success." During the same year, Israel and its neighbours had initiated dozens of development projects in such diverse fields as water, transportation, agriculture, environment and energy. These joint efforts were weaving a fabric of coexistence and co-operation, said Rabin, "a fabric resistant to the pressures, scepticism and outright sabotage which attempt to disrupt and derail the peace process."

The Amman conference was by no means the only sign of economic change as a result of peace. At the end of 1994, all six members of the Saudi-led Gulf Co-operation Council lifted the secondary and tertiary elements of the Arab boycott of Israel. While the six oil-rich states were not yet ready for a policy of open trade with Israel, they would no longer boycott firms doing business with the Jewish state, or other companies dealing with such firms. Major companies throughout the world could now trade with Israel without fear of significant Arab economic reprisal.

Japanese firms in particular had been afraid of the boycott. Peace set them free to make deals with Israel. Israeli exports to Japan had been stagnant in 1991, and dropped 4.1 per cent in 1992. Then the line on the graph began to climb dramatically: up 17.1 per cent in 1993, and 25.8 per cent the next year. At the end of 1994, Japanese firms were for the first time authorised by the Tokyo stock exchange to invest in the Tel Aviv stock market. Meanwhile, major foreign companies, such as L'Oréal and Philips, which had previously stayed out of the Israeli market, began co-operating with and investing in Israeli firms.

President Clinton was co-sponsor of the Amman conference, which the US saw as part of a multilateral effort to integrate the Middle East fully into world markets. Israel's role in this effort was described by US ambassador Martin Indyk, who took up his post in early 1995, in an article in *Ha'aretz* in September 1995. "One of America's largest and most successful financiers told me of an encounter with an Israeli and an Egyptian businessman who had come to him to seek backing for a joint venture. What impressed him more than their interesting business plan was the relationship between them. It was obvious to him that the Israeli understood his Arab partner much better than an American could. This is the essence of the new partnership that can be built between Israel and its Arab neighbours, a partnership for peace and prosperity... that pulls the Middle East into the global market of the twenty-first century." Israel's own booming economy, Indyk noted, still only represented a market of 5 million people. "So when American businesses look at Israel, they want to know not only whether they can make money in the short term, but also whether by establishing a base here they can open the door to a much larger Middle Eastern market of some 300 million down the road. For the first time, some of the larger American firms are concluding that the proposition is worth testing."

Such words about Israel were unimaginable during Yitzhak Rabin's first term as Prime Minister, when Israel had a struggling economy and was virtually a garrison state. But the Israel of the second Rabin administration was a vastly different economic entity. In 1975, Israel's gross national product was $12 billion – half of the combined GNPs of Egypt, Syria and Jordan. In 1995, the GNP was $85 billion, 50 per cent more than the combined GNPs of the three Arab neighbours.

In 1975, defence spending accounted for one-third of Israel's GNP and 15 per cent of its imports. In comparison, by 1995, defence spending accounted for 9 per cent of the GNP and 1.5 per cent of imports. In 1975 the GNP was $3,400 per capita, in 1995 it was $15,000 per capita – similar to that of Great Britain.

The change was hardly lost on Rabin, who was a hands-on Prime Minister economically. His picture of Israel's economic future was closely tied up with his peacemaking – as shown by his refusal to continue pouring money into settlements in the occupied territories – but extended into other areas as well. Dealing with what the Likud governments had neglected – integrating the hundreds of thousands of immigrants who began arriving in 1990 into Israeli society, tackling unemployment that had topped 10.5 per cent, improving education, modernising the country's road system and building a transportation and communications infrastructure that could support a modern economy – were campaign promises Rabin had every intention of keeping.

On 13 July 1992, when he was officially sworn in as Prime Minister, Rabin said his government would increase economic growth by "retooling the economy for open management, free of administrative restrictions and superfluous government involvement. There's too much paperwork, and not enough production." The speech confirmed what everyone already knew – that Labour had broken from its Socialist origins, from the idea of a state-controlled economy. "A free world demands a free economy," he declared. His only gesture to his party's roots was a promise – which he would later have trouble keeping – that state-owned firms would be sold off "in co-operation with the employees, so they will suffer no harm".

"Concentrating on the economy," says Ilan Flatto, a finance ministry official who became Rabin's economic adviser, "was a strategic decision. In the past, most Prime Ministers concentrated on affairs of state, and left the economy alone. Rabin decided that the economy should be as important a priority as peace. That meant involvement in all-important economic issues, industry and trans-portation, communications and trade. It involved learning a subject, having meetings about it and making decisions."

"We made strategic decisions that changed the budgetary map," says Avraham (Beige) Shochat, a long-time political ally who became Rabin's Finance Minister. "We started to invest heavily in infrastructure, in roads and railroads, sewage projects, industrial zones and tourism projects. We raised funding in education by 60 per cent in real terms, and in high-tech research and development."

Only two Prime Ministers before Rabin – David Ben-Gurion and Shimon Peres – had displayed an active interest in economics. Menachem Begin gave a string of finance ministers free rein – one reason, perhaps, that inflation climbed into triple digits during his period of office – and waited for Peres to bring it under control. When Begin retired, his successor, Shamir, showed a similar disinclination to fill his head with figures. Rabin, even before the 1992 election, had a different outlook. "He'd always give the example of the Soviet Union," says Dan Propper of the Osem food company, who served as president of the Manufacturers Association, the main body representing Israeli industry. " 'Moscow,' he'd say, 'had all that military power and all those missiles, but look what had happened to it in the end because of its economy.' "

Rabin was particularly irritated by "generalities" – he'd use the English word – and wanted to get down to the facts. "You could give him some data and he would remember all the figures, for a long time," says economic adviser Flatto. "When people forgot what had been decided, he would remember. He remembered decisions from his previous premiership."

Rabin's first major decision as Prime Minister was to cut back public construction, especially in the West Bank and the Gaza Strip. "On one hand it was a political decision," says Shochat, "not to invest more in Judaea and Samaria. But it was also a decision to let the private sector start to build. It took a year between the freeze and the start of construction by the free market, which was a problem. But it was a clear economic decision, and a clear political one."

His second move was to push ahead with privatisation, the sale of some of the more than 150 companies and businesses owned by the government. The cabinet, at its first meeting, formed two committees, both headed by Rabin – one on security, the second on privatisation. But still, the economic professionals at the finance ministry and the Bank of Israel were not sure whether Rabin would be an active chairman, or a symbolic one. "After a short time," says Jacob Frenkel, Governor of the Bank of Israel, "it was clear that Rabin was not merely interested, but that he was the engine of the privatisation committee." Yossi Nitzani, who headed the Government Corporations Authority in charge of much of the privatisation programme until early 1995, says: "Privatisation has no chance if the head of government does not take a direct role in it. That's why it worked in Argentina, Mexico and France, and certainly in Margaret Thatcher's England." During the two and a half years Nitzani worked with Rabin, more than $2 billion worth of government companies were sold in public offerings and private placements of corporate shares, or in direct sales to investors.

Nitzani says Rabin – despite his socialist background – "wanted to get the government out of business because it wasn't its job, and because he knew governments are not good at business. He once said he would give away some of the defence firms, Israel Aircraft Industries [aerospace], Israel Military Industries [arms and ammunition] and the Rafael Arms Development Authority, if only someone would take their debts."

Still, when privatisation slowed – as it did after the Tel Aviv stock exchange took a sharp downturn in 1994 – Rabin was unable or unwilling to get it rolling again. Several proposed stock offerings were delayed when it became clear that the sale price would be lower than what the government thought the assets were worth. Rabin, his advisers say, accepted that there were objective reasons for the delays, and never showed his famous impatience on this issue.

The Labour leader's free-market orientation also showed in debates on how trade liberalisation should proceed and on how to create jobs for the immigrants flooding the country. The Likud government had adopted a seven-year plan for tariff reduction, removing protection of local industries in relatively equal increments of about one-seventh a year. In 1992, Rabin was approached by local industrialists, especially in the wood and textile businesses, who urged him to extend their protection from foreign competition. The pressure was considerable, and not only from the industrialists. With unemployment high, says Frenkel, "it was very tempting politically to say, 'Let's go a little slower, let's not expose domestic industry quite so much.' Proposals were put on the table for public works programmes – something that for the economist is a clear no-no, for the politician a clear temptation."

Rabin turned down the proposal by Minister of Labour Ora Namir – one of his oldest political allies – for major public-works programmes. Unemployment and absorption would be dealt with by allowing expansion of the private sector, allowing economic growth to create jobs. The government would provide education, retraining, and infrastructure – but no public works. The move had a profound effect on the immigrants from the former Soviet Union, who had been pouring in since the collapse of Communism. Unemployment in late 1992 had reached a peak of 11 per cent nationwide; among the 300,000-plus new immigrants at the time, the jobless rate was double. Many immigrant professionals had been forced to take menial jobs – doctors cleaning streets, engineers sweeping floors.

In the three years that followed, the economy's annual growth was over 5.5 per cent. By late 1995, unemployment had dropped to below 7 per cent. Among the former Soviets – whose numbers had risen to 600,000 – joblessness had dropped even more sharply. Nevertheless, many immigrants were unhappy. "Rabin should have pushed more," says Natan Sharansky, the best-known immigrant leader, who in mid-1995 began forming a political movement based on immigration and social issues, to run in the 1996 Knesset elections. "I understand the idea of helping the economy, but 25 per cent of the immigrants are not properly absorbed, and there are another 1 million potential immigrants waiting in the former Soviet Union. He should have accelerated the process."

One of the reasons Sharansky admired Rabin was distinctly unusual: Rabin was practically the only Israeli politician who *didn't* attend a frantic welcome for Sharansky when he arrived in Israel in February 1986, after being freed from a Soviet prison. They only met three months later, when both spoke on the same programme. "Not only was he a politician who had not rushed to shake my hand and be photographed with me, but he arrived at the meeting without a tie. In fact, he was in sandals, without socks," says Sharansky. Sharansky describes another meeting, just before the 1992 elections, where he told Rabin: "It looks like you are going to win the election. And it will be largely because of the Russians, who are supporting you. I hope you won't forget them." Rabin raised one arm, and told Sharansky that "this is for security." Then he raised the other, adding, "this is for immigration. They are both parts of my Zionism."

The Russians did vote heavily for Labour. But over the next year, the pace of immigration was slower than anticipated and the government began shifting funds set aside for immigrants – particularly for housing – to other purposes. Sharansky and other immigrant leaders were upset that Labour was not living up to what they saw as its promises. In May 1993, almost a year after the elections, about 15,000 immigrants gathered in Jerusalem in what Sharansky calls the largest immigrant demonstration in Israeli history. Later Sharansky and his activists met with Rabin. "I understood that the way he dealt with immigrants, or did not deal with them, was nothing personal; he was too absorbed with other things. I talked to him about stopping the shifting of budgets, to spend more and not less on immigrant absorption. He told me, 'Talk to Beige Shochat.' You could see that he was absorbed with other things," says Sharansky. The impression was correct – secret negotiations with the Palestinians in Oslo had just started.

If Rabin didn't always know how to deal with immigrants, he did know how to handle visiting businesspeople. "Investors I brought to him were always amazed at his grasp of things. They'd say to me, 'Look at what kind of Prime Minister you have,'" says Dov Lautman, a businessman who was Rabin's special emissary for economic development. "He knew a lot of businesspeople from the past, from his experience as ambassador in Washington and as Defence Minister, and he knew how to talk turbines and technical systems."

But there were some major errors, such as his intervention – after a strike in 1994 by university professors nearly caused cancellation of the academic year – to sharply increase faculty pay scales. The hikes triggered a wave of salary increases among other public employees, put a heavy burden on the state budget and created strong inflationary pressures. His government also took heavy criticism for failing to release sufficient public land for housing; the land crunch made housing prices soar, also adding to inflation.

Perhaps worst of all was the government's ill-fated capital gains tax on stock-market profits, never taxed in Israel. Shochat first proposed – and succeeded in getting passed in the cabinet and the Knesset – a flat tax on all stock transactions where there was a "real" gain, after inflation had been taken into account. Investors and opposition politicians railed against the tax, arguing that it did not give investors any credits when they lost money on stock deals, and Shochat, with Rabin's backing, promised to amend the tax law after it went into effect. But it soon became clear that the computers of banks, which act as stockbrokers and handle a large portion of stock-market transactions, could not handle the new tax. Rabin, who had originally backed Shochat, switched course and forced him to drop the tax. The opposition had a field day condemning Rabin's "zig-zag".

Still, robust economic growth marked Rabin's years in office.

True, one cause was the peace process, rather than pure economic management; and true, another was immigration, a factor beyond the government's control. Rabin's premiership bore the unmistakable aura of success – Israel's stock had risen.

11

The Private Prime Minister

AS PRIME MINISTER, he was absorbed in his job day and night.
But Yitzhak Rabin's grandson Yonatan told a TV interviewer after
the assassination: "He was also a grandfather. Everyone would say,
'How does he have time for you?' And it was unbelievable how the
man didn't miss a single ceremony of mine or my sister Noa's. Not
one. Every school ceremony, every army ceremony... He got to
them all."

That wasn't surprising to Dalia Pelossof, Rabin's daughter and
Yonatan and Noa's mother, who says Rabin did the same thing
when she was young. "He didn't come to parent–teacher meetings
in school, he wasn't part of that," she told an interviewer. "But
when a need arose, most of all when we were sick, he was always
with us. He'd be called wherever he was, and he'd come... He'd
drop in for a few minutes to see me. He was a very, very concerned
father."

Dalia says her father always told her and her brother Yuval, "'Be
comfortable with yourselves. The moment you are comfortable with
yourself, and confident that you are doing the right thing, you can
go forward. And never mind what anyone says about you.' It's a
motto I always remembered, always followed."

Still, Rabin was never one for heart-to-heart talks with his
children. "Sometimes I thought it should be different, but that's the
way he was, and I accepted it... I always thought that he was busy
with so many big issues and so many important decisions, that who
was I to bother him with my nonsense? And I knew that Mom told
him everything. So I left Mom to decide what to tell him and what
not, to choose the right time. After all, she was with him all the
time."

Leah Rabin has described how Yitzhak would take over at night when their children were sick. "When one of the children didn't want to eat, I'd lose patience," she told an interviewer in 1992. "He'd say, 'Here, let me do it.' To our son, Yuval, he would tell the same story, about tanks, every time he fed him. With him, the boy would eat.

"He'd never raise his voice, or his hand, to one of the children. He'd always be loving and never put pressure on the children because of what he expected from them. I think that's the way to give children the feeling that they are loved in any situation, any time, even if they don't live up to all your expectations. That was Yitzhak's secret: the children never owed him anything."

Rabin's public image was one of gruff gravity, and most Israelis were surprised when, after his death, stories about his personal warmth began appearing in the media. Says Niva Lanir, "Friends would ask me how I could bear to work with him. They'd say he was 'autistic.' I'd really get angry."

Lanir was often at the Rabin home in the 1980s, "when there was no office staff, and it wasn't all 'Yes, Prime Minister'. I saw him with Leah and the children and grandchildren. He loved them dearly... I also came to appreciate the relationship between him and Leah. I liked being around them. And despite what people say about him, he was a man who loved people. When he felt close to someone, he knew how to express it."

Lanir gives two examples: when Rabin came to her hospital bedside just as she came out of an anaesthetic after an operation, and when he made a point of visiting her after her divorce. "I was going through a tough spell," she recalls. "One day he came to my apartment, and he said, 'Oy, I'm going to paint it for you.'" It became a private joke between the two. Looking ahead to Rabin's hoped-for return to the Prime Ministership, they laughed that they would put up a sign in his office: "Prime Minister, Also Does Odd Jobs and Repairs."

It's easy to see, nevertheless, how Rabin gained a reputation for being cold. He was never one for small talk, and getting him going, says one close associate, was like lighting damp matches. "You try lighting one, and throw it away, then another and another until something catches." When he did start, he would talk for half an hour – but always lecture, never engage in conversation. "Yitzhak was one of those people whose insight and intellectual grasp you discover in five minutes, and whose personal qualities take 15 years to come out," said Dov Goldstein in a post-assassination interview.

"He was a very modest person. When we were writing his memoirs ... I heard nothing more often than the question: 'Dov, I'm saying "I, I, I," all the time. Isn't that too much?' And I told him: 'Yitzhak, it's impossible to write an autobiography in the third person. It's just not done that way.'"

In the first person, in private, Rabin was very different from the military man who radiated authority. Eitan Haber, who knew him for 37 years and was his closest aide, says he exhibited "warmth, closeness, personal interest and understanding. In the last few months of his life, everyone asked to meet him privately, that's where they'd get their problems solved. Most popular of all were the meetings in his home in Tel Aviv, on Saturdays. Everyone wanted to meet him there, it was a status symbol."

For years Rabin maintained private connections with the families of soldiers who had been killed in action and with victims of terror attacks. Amos Eiran, director general of the Prime Minister's Office from 1974–7, says it was "something that dated back to his army days, part of his responsibility as a commander". Hints of those unpublicised contacts emerged over the years; Rabin included representatives of bereaved families in Israeli delegations to the signing of the agreements with the PLO and the peace treaty with Jordan. But it was only after his death that the full extent of his involvement – the personal visits and frequent telephone calls – became known.

Yehudah Wachsman met Rabin the day after his soldier son, Nahshon, was killed during an attempt to rescue him from his Hamas kidnappers in early October 1994. In a newspaper article after the assassination, Wachsman wrote that Rabin "was very reserved and patient. Again and again, he went over the considerations and the explanations of why there was no other way, other than the way it was done, to carry out the rescue operation. I was convinced that Yitzhak Rabin had done everything he could to save my son." Three weeks later, at Rabin's invitation, Wachsman attended the signing ceremony for the peace treaty with Jordan. And afterwards, the Prime Minister stayed in touch. "He telephoned on the Memorial Day for Israeli soldiers," Wachsman recalled. "He said we were always in his thoughts, that he very much identified with our emotions because he himself had experienced bereavement, in the loss of relatives and many friends who had fallen in Israel's wars." Rabin called again before the signing of the Oslo II peace agreement on the eve of the Jewish New Year, to convey Rosh Hashanah greetings to the Wachsmans. Rabin "was a very sensitive man", Wachsman felt, "but it seems to me that in most cases he didn't let his sensitivity overcome his common sense. He knew how to control his feelings."

Rabin was Defence Minister in 1987, when a Molotov cocktail was thrown into Abie Moses's car. Abie and Ofrah Moses and their three children were driving near their home in Alfei Menasheh, a bedroom community just across the Green Line between sovereign Israel and the West Bank. Ofrah Moses and her son Tal, 5, died of injuries suffered in the burning vehicle; Abie and two older children, 14-year-old Nir and Adi, 8, were badly burned, but survived. When he was discharged from the hospital, Abie Moses, a gas station operator, met Rabin. "He came to my house," recalls Moses, "and was very warm and caring. Later on, he would call up to ask about my family, how the children were doing in school, or later in the army. We met often, at least once every two months. On Rosh Hashanah he would always call me personally, not through a secretary. And when he could not get me at work he would call me at home."

There were also visits. Before Nir Moses went into the army, he was invited to Rabin's office and presented with a book by the Defence Minister. The Rabins attended Adi's bat mitzvah, and when they visited the Moses home, they'd stay for hours. "I'd offer him Indian dishes," says the Indian-born Moses, "but he always preferred regular, Israeli food." Rabin, Moses says, "was straight and genuine and didn't behave like other politicians, who say things they don't mean. I'd go to meet him at the airport after he'd return from important meetings abroad, with people like Clinton, and he'd leave his entourage to sit alone with me for 15 minutes, to drink coffee and talk." Rabin invited Moses to attend the September 1993 signing of the agreement with the PLO. Moses refused, because "I didn't want to be there with Yasser Arafat... But I told him that this accord was the right thing, that I want my son to have a broom rather than a gun."

Rabin the workaholic would start his day at 7 a.m. and, when he had spent the night at his Jerusalem residence, would be in his office in the government complex near the Knesset by 7.40, going home after 8 p.m. At night, he unwound in front of the TV, watching thrillers or sports, with a cheese sandwich and a whisky.

Rabin's drinking was often a subject of gossip. Dov Goldstein recalled that on one occasion during the 1992 election campaign he went to the Prime Minister's residence in Jerusalem to interview the incumbent, Yitzhak Shamir. Goldstein spent 20 minutes waiting in the company of Shamir's wife, Shulamit. "He drinks a lot, Rabin, doesn't he?" she asked him. "No," replied Goldstein, "he's a moderate drinker, like me. It doesn't impair his judgment." Goldstein also remembered waiting to meet with Rabin at the defence ministry one morning. A new secretary, who didn't know him, asked him what he'd like to drink. "I told her a whisky would be nice. She was indignant: 'We don't have things like that here.' In other words, I was the enemy. . ." Only when Rabin arrived did the two men have a whisky.

Rabin himself shared that sensitivity to the drinking rumours. Eitan Haber recalled a visit to America in the early '90s, when Rabin was an opposition Knesset member. After meeting American Jews at a palatial home in Arizona, Rabin and Haber returned to the local Holiday Inn for the night. It was late, and there was no one in the lobby, though hundreds of cars were in the car park. They went to their rooms, and then Haber went back downstairs and spotted a huge discotheque filled with people. He went to tell Rabin to come with him, that no one would see him get a drink in the middle of the desert. Rabin refused. The next morning, they were spotted – and vocally identified – by a couple of guests in the lobby. Rabin turned to Haber, and repeated dryly: "No one will recognise us here, in the middle of the desert."

On the other hand, Rabin was an unabashedly heavy smoker, going through 30 cigarettes a day. "He smoked so much," said Haber, "that we installed a device to absorb smoke at the entrance to his office. We hid it behind a plant. He never saw it, to his dying day." Everyone talked to Rabin about smoking, but he waved them away. At 73, he had no intention of stopping. "He would say that 'if I've got this far, cigarettes aren't going to kill me,'" said Haber.

Smoking wasn't the only Rabin habit that would make a doctor turn green. He wouldn't eat lunch unless invited to a meal as a speaker; he generally wolfed down food like a soldier in the field; he worked non-stop except for brief naps, with his shoes on, behind the closed doors of his office. But Rabin was proud of his stamina. "Yitzhak is built to pull a very heavy load," Leah said in 1992. "He can be active, non-stop, almost 18 hours a day." In a later interview, she described their morning routine: "Before Yitzhak goes to the office, we drink coffee together. I manage to leaf quickly through the papers, and call his attention to what I think will especially interest him. Generally, we have the same opinion in those morning talks over the newspapers. But on everything that has to do with the performance of ministers, or people who work with him – I don't see myself as someone who's able to judge. Where do I have the information to do that? But Yitzhak shares his worries with me..."

They also shared tennis on Saturday mornings at the Ramat Aviv Country Club near his home, a pursuit that must have made his doctors happier. Rabin's mixed doubles partner was Zionah Leshem, an architect; Leah Rabin played with Raphy Weiner, general manager of the Sheraton Plaza Hotel in Jerusalem. On the court, Rabin – who for years wore the same old pair of blue shorts – would think only about the game. "He told me that from Sundays to Fridays he was Prime Minister, but on Saturdays he was a tennis partner," says Weiner. "When we began playing, he'd sometimes yell out 'idiot' in the middle of a point, and I was too shy to ask if he was talking about me. Later on I asked, and he told me that he was yelling at himself. From then on, he yelled *idiot she'kemoni* – 'what an idiot I am.'"

Both Rabins played to win. "Leah wanted to beat him," says Weiner. "If we lost, she would be mad at me. They were a wonderful couple, but on the court there was murder in their eyes." Weiner says Rabin used to wipe away the sweat during a tennis game with his arm. "One day I bought him a wrist band and he thought it was the invention of the century." And Rabin was "never a minute late, and never cancelled without letting me know... If Anat, his secretary from the defence ministry, called at 6.30 a.m. on Saturday, I knew something bad had happened, even if it wasn't announced till later in the day."

Tennis and TV weren't his only leisure activities. His daughter and grandchildren say he was an enthusiastic amateur photographer, even though in later years he didn't have time for it. David Rubinger, the veteran *Time* magazine photographer in Israel, recalls that Rabin was always attentive to his photographic needs: "He would sometimes say things to me like 'Do you have enough light?' And once, on a flight after the Six Day War, Rubinger was in the midst of photographing Rabin, then Chief of Staff, asleep in a seat next to Defence Minister Moshe Dayan. "He suddenly woke up, reached for the camera and said, 'Give.' He took my Pentax, looked at it, and started shooting me." Rubinger, who had an extra Leica on hand, was able to snap a rare portrait of Rabin as camera enthusiast.

But photography prompted no passion for the fine arts. Weiner says that in 1993, before the Rabins went on a trip to Spain, "Leah told him that he would be going with her to the Prado. 'Where?' he asked, and she replied: 'Don't show everybody you know nothing about art.'"

Music produced more interest, perhaps because Leah Rabin worked harder on it, regularly taking him to concerts. Kalman Gayer recalls that he was once approached by violinist Shlomo Mintz and Amnon Weinstein, a master violin-maker, who wanted to see Rabin. "Weinstein was making a very special violin, to be used in concerts and master classes – not a violin for one artist, but one that would be used by many. They asked for my help in getting in to see Rabin, and I told them I had nothing to do with such things, that they should call the Prime Minister's Office direct." It was, Gayer says, June or July 1994, around the implementation of the Oslo I agreement setting up Palestinian self-rule in Gaza and Jericho. But Rabin found the time to see the musicians. Afterward, Mintz told Gayer that Rabin had signed the frame of the violin they'd brought him, and talked about music. "He told them about a concert Leonard Bernstein had given, at the end of the War of Independence, in Beersheba. Some of the audience of soldiers were in jeeps. And Rabin remembered the concert, he remembered what they had played, the entire programme." (After her husband's death, Leah Rabin became patron of the project, called the Rabin Peacemaker's Violin.)

Rabin, though, was no highbrow, whereas he did remember the names of TV and movie stars he'd seen on late-night cable, and had a passion for soccer that lingered on from his schooldays. "If I visited him on a day there was a match on TV, we'd always watch," says Gayer. "He was very up to date on details of the game, of the players and the stars. He was particularly interested if Brazil was playing an international match. It was surprising how much he knew about the game. He had so much on his mind, so much responsibility, but he still knew the names of soccer players."

Rabin's grandchildren, Noa, 18, and Yonatan, 21, say they always knew when he was about to make an important decision. He'd be at home, and they'd sit down to talk to him. He'd drum his fingers on the table or the arm of the chair while he seemed to be listening – and would not notice even when they imitated him by drumming their own fingers. They weren't the only ones to recognise when he was preoccupied. Amos Eiran visited the Rabin home in the summer of 1993, as the secret Oslo talks with the PLO were reaching a crucial stage. "In his face, in his manner, I saw that something was going on," Eiran recalls. "There was the weight of having to make an important decision. And when I got home, I told my family that Rabin had to decide on something, something very important."

Kalman Gayer says Rabin's ability to concentrate on a single issue, to the exclusion of others, "was both good and bad for him. Sometimes, when he was deeply engaged in some matter, he would pass by people, people he knew very well, and not notice them at all. He was so caught up in the details that he really didn't see them."

Old comrades from the army, and officers he knew from his days in the defence ministry, often came to visit him in later years. "There was a closeness between him and his old army chums, even though some were on the other side of the political fence," says Uri Dromi, Rabin's appointee as director of the Government Press Office. "All down the years, he maintained a curious relationship with men like Ariel Sharon and Rechavam Zeevy" – two former generals, fire-eating hawks on the far right of the Knesset, both of whom were appointed by Rabin as advisers on terrorism.

Moshe Levi, who was Chief of Staff when Rabin became Defence Minister in 1984, continued to meet him subsequently in two other capacities: as chairman of the government authority preparing to build the Trans-Israel Highway, Israel's first superhighway, and as head of the Anti-Drug Authority. But Levi says Rabin was always happy to discuss these less urgent topics too. "It always surprised me," says Levi, "when I'd come and say 'I want to talk about matters that are a little peripheral,' he'd get angry. 'Why do you say that,' he'd ask. 'I have to deal with those things too, and I do.'"

Another frequent visitor was Nachman Shai, who became head of the government authority responsible for commercial TV. Shai's last meeting with Rabin was in October 1995. "It was very characteristic of him, he knew what I was there to talk to him about. I spoke for one minute, he spoke for 30 seconds, and our urgent business was done. Then we had a free half-hour to chat. He talked about political violence, the attacks on him, his difficulty in dealing with all that."

In mid-October, Israel (Talik) Tal received a phone call from Rabin's secretary at the defence ministry. Tal had been head of the Armoured Corps when Rabin was Chief of Staff. "Rabin is going to the Armoured Corps exhibition at the Square, at the Kings of Israel Square, and he asked 'Why shouldn't Talik come along?'" Tal was quick to accept. "We got there, and visited every tent, every exhibit," says the ex-general. "It was an unscheduled visit, there were no right-wing demonstrators around. People crowded around him, they cheered and encouraged him. It was a real measure of what people thought about him, not something organised."

Three weeks later, after a rally in the same Square before another enthusiastic, if far larger, crowd of supporters, Rabin was to meet his death.

12

Leader of the Jewish People?

THE SIGNING OF the Oslo II agreement between Israel and the Palestinians, on 28 September 1995, brought to Washington, DC many of the leading figures of the North American Jewish community. In a closed-door meeting with some 200 top organisational leaders, philanthropists and intellectuals that same day at the Madison Hotel, Yitzhak Rabin made what was to be his last major speech to Diaspora leaders. He began by speaking, as expected, on the need for greater support among Diaspora Jewry for the peace process. He lashed out against right-wing Jewish groups and individuals in the United States who had carried their fight against the Oslo agreements into the corridors of Capitol Hill. "While Rabin spoke out against them bluntly and forcefully, this was pretty much what we had expected to hear," says Seymour Reich, a prominent New York lawyer and former director of the Conference of Presidents of Major American Jewish Organizations.

But after talking about the peace process for some 20 minutes, Rabin suddenly shifted direction and began discussing Israel's efforts to absorb the hundreds of thousands of Jews who had immigrated in recent years from the former Soviet Union. Noting that the absorption process was costing the Israeli government $3.5 billion a year, he strongly criticised the American Jewish community for donating only some $200 million annually in philanthropy to Israel, while increasingly focusing its charitable efforts on its own local Jewish communities. "You call this a partnership?" he asked the crowd with pointed sarcasm.

"A sort of collective gasp went through the hall at that point," says Leonard Fein, founder of *Moment* and a leading American Jewish liberal activist. "People were at first stunned, and then started casting embarrassed looks at each other and rolling their eyes. They had come to this meeting expecting to hear an upbeat assessment of the peace process, and suddenly Rabin was castigating them on another issue entirely." Many of those present felt, as did Seymour Reich, that "Rabin was out of line. He got carried away, and demonstrated what I thought was a callousness toward, or at least a lack of understanding of, the special emotional commitment American Jewry has with the whole issue of Soviet Jewry."

Yitzhak Rabin's final face-to-face encounter with the American Jewish leadership encapsulated his complex and sometimes contentious relationship with Diaspora Jewry. The Prime Minister of Israel has traditionally been expected to serve not only as head of his country, but as a leader – as *the* leader – of world Jewry. It is a role that David Ben-Gurion, Golda Meir and Menachem Begin, each in their own way, embraced, enhanced and even seemed to enjoy. The same cannot be said of Rabin. Even before the final years of his life, when some of the harshest opposition to his peace policies came from Jewish communities abroad, he had clashed with Diaspora Jewish leaders over issues of both style and substance. As the quintessential sabra, he was culturally miles apart from the Jews of the Diaspora. "In all the years I dealt with Rabin," says Harry Wall, director of the Anti-Defamation League's Israel office, "I never even once heard him use a Yiddish expression."

His blunt manner was even more pronounced outside the company of fellow Israelis, and his natural taciturnity accentuated when he had to speak English, a language he had only partially mastered. Many of the Diaspora Jews with whom Rabin dealt over the years came away with the impression that he was far more an Israeli than a Jew. "Rabin," says former American Jewish Committee president Alfred Moses, "was not interested in religion or the cultural side of the Jewish world. He wasn't a *nefesh yehudi* [Jewish soul]; he was a 'new man' disdainful of *yiddishkeit*, always the soldier and never comfortable in any other role, and this didn't change up till the end of his life."

Yet others who worked closely with Rabin paint a more complex portrait of his relationship to Jewish issues. "The centrality of the entire Jewish people was always a fundamental tenet of his thinking," contends Yehuda Avner, his former Diaspora affairs adviser. "It was important to him, even if he couldn't find the words to express it. Rabin was obviously not at all a philosophical or religious thinker. But toward the end of his life he did, for example, come to understand the vital importance of such issues as Jewish education."

Despite his sometimes contentious relationship with certain Diaspora Jewish leaders, there is no question that Rabin did value
Diaspora Jewry – or, more specifically, the US Jewish community.
This stemmed from both his genuine affection for all things American, and his realpolitik appreciation of its political influence. "My
encounters with American Jewry," wrote Rabin in his memoirs,
"provided some of the most exhilarating moments... the concern,
warmth, and love that America's Jews displayed for Israel gave me a
deep sense of pride and confidence... Israel – her triumphs and
setbacks, her achievements and failures – serves as a kind of 'index of
self-respect' for American Jewry."

Rabin himself embodied this "index of self-respect", and despite
his less-than-charming manner and limited communication skills, he
usually succeeded in making a positive impression among Jews
abroad. "American Jews loved that strong, soldierly side to Rabin,"
says Ruhama Hermon, who worked as his aide in Washington. "He
embodied the 'sabra pride' which Jews abroad love to see." Harry
Wall concurs: "Rabin was the tough new Israeli Jew, totally at ease
with himself. His rough, blunt manner didn't necessarily work against
him when he met with Diaspora Jews; in some ways it worked to his
advantage. We wanted him to be different from us – to be tougher,
less self-conscious – and he was. Ironically, the fact that he was in no
way typically 'Jewish', only made us prouder to be Jews."

Rabin clearly enjoyed playing this role. "He would recharge his
batteries by going a few times a year on speaking tours to the
American Jewish community," says Nachman Shai, who worked
with Rabin in the mid-1980s at the defence ministry. "I remember
how two days after he started the job of Defence Minister, he was
scheduled to address a delegation of UJA leaders in Jerusalem. I told
him, listen, you just started a new job, you have a lot to learn, you
don't have to do this. He shooed me away and said, Listen,
Nachman, these people didn't abandon me when I was a mere
Knesset member. They invited me all the time to appear, they
respected me, it was always, 'Mr Prime Minister'. They helped me
stay above water, the UJA and the Israel Bonds people. I owe them
this, and I can't let them down."

But while Rabin had affection for American Jewry in general –
and individually for such personal friends as Republican Party
strongman Max Fisher and Abe Pollin, the owner of the basketball
team, Washington Bullets – his relationship with the American
Jewish leadership was far different. His first extended encounter with

Diaspora Jewry came during his tenure as ambassador to the United States from 1968-73. His immediate predecessors in that position, Abba Eban and Abe Harman, both native English-speakers raised in Great Britain, had felt perfectly comfortable in consulting with and seeking the aid of the powerful American Jewish lobby. But right from the start, Rabin took a different approach. "Following a deeply ingrained pattern of Diaspora living," he wrote disparagingly in his memoirs, "some of the leaders of the American Jewish community exercised their influence by means of a *shtadlan* [court Jew], the traditional intermediary who had sought the favour of the ruling powers in Europe... I believed that the Israeli Embassy should assume the principal role of handling Israel's affairs at all political levels and that it was entitled to avail itself of the help of Jews and non-Jews alike as it saw fit."

Rabin's dissatisfaction with the American Jewish lobbyists grew during the years the Likud was in power. He was particularly disturbed by the activities of AIPAC (American Israel Public Affairs Committee) which, with the blessing of Menachem Begin and Yitzhak Shamir, had become increasingly aggressive in lobbying the Congress and the White House on Middle East-related issues. Often, this involved battles over arms sales to Arab countries, such as the Jewish lobby's unsuccessful effort in 1981 to block the Reagan administration's delivery of AWACS planes to Saudi Arabia. "Rabin felt it was a major mistake to oppose the administration so openly on sales like this," says one of his former aides, "especially when he didn't see them as posing any kind of significant threat to Israel's security."

Even worse from Rabin's standpoint was the AIPAC-led attempt in the early 1990s to obtain $10 billion in loan guarantees for Israel. Yitzhak Shamir desperately wanted the guarantees in order to ease the crushing financial burden of absorbing the Soviet immigrants. But President George Bush conditioned the guarantees on a halt to all Israeli settlement activity in the West Bank and Gaza, a price Shamir wouldn't pay. In the summer and autumn of 1991, as AIPAC and other Jewish groups stepped up the pressure on the White House to grant the loan guarantees unconditionally, Bush reacted sharply. In a press conference held on 12 September, he became the first President to openly attack the American Jewish lobby, decrying the "thousands of lobbyists descending on the Hill". This was exactly the kind of direct confrontation with the White House which Rabin abhorred, made doubly worse by its futility as Bush stood firm and refused to grant the guarantees. Ironically, the loan guarantees fiasco, which left a significant amount of egg on both AIPAC's and Shamir's face in the winter of 1991, became a notable factor in Rabin's electoral victory the following June.

As Rabin took office a month later, he immediately began changing the tenor of the Israel-Diaspora relationship. His first move was to decline to fill the long-standing position of Diaspora affairs adviser, an office he himself had instituted during his first premiership with the appointment of Yehuda Avner. The office had traditionally provided an address for Jewish organisations from abroad to express their concerns and try to gain access to the Prime Minister. Though the position was largely symbolic, Rabin's decision not to fill it sent a clear signal to the Diaspora leadership that their relationship with Jerusalem was now going to take on a different tone.

Just how different soon became crystal clear. On his first visit to the United States after taking office, in August 1992, Rabin met at the Madison Hotel with AIPAC director Tom Dine – widely viewed as the most effective lobbyist in Washington – and other senior officers in the organisation. The Prime Minister blasted them for having pushed too hard on the loan guarantees and against arms sales to Arab countries, poisoning the waters between the US administration and Israel. According to reports that surfaced after the meeting, Rabin told the AIPAC leaders: "You waged lost battles... you created too much antagonism... You caused damage to Israel." Rabin was particularly incensed at what he saw as AIPAC's attempts to lobby the executive branch, which he saw as directly interfering in Israel's diplomatic business. "Do not conduct my affairs with the administration," he ordered them.

"Rabin was basically telling the American Jewish leadership to drop dead in 1992," says Alfred Moses. Rabin supporter Abe Pollin, himself an AIPAC officer, puts a gentler spin on the conflict: "What he was upset about, and I thought deservedly so, was Jewish organisations putting themselves above the Israeli government. I tried to explain to him that our task was to support whoever was in power, be it Labour or Likud." Rabin's office later tried to soften the stomach punch the Prime Minister had delivered by issuing a token statement praising AIPAC, but the damage was clearly done. Responding to Rabin's attack, AIPAC spokeswoman Toby Dershowitz countered strongly, saying: "Rabin is too naive. He doesn't understand how Washington works, and he doesn't appreciate how important AIPAC is."

But while AIPAC publicly tried to shrug off Rabin's attack, the new Prime Minister had clearly ignited a fuse that would set off a series of explosions in the organisation during the next few years. When the Rabin government decided to enter the peace process with the PLO, it had a natural ally in AIPAC's Dine, who was known to have dovish leanings. But Dine's influence at AIPAC had always been balanced by a group of long-time senior board members – Robert Asher, Ed Levy, Jr. and Meyer Mitchell, all former AIPAC presidents – who held more right-wing views. As Dine tried to steer AIPAC closer to the Rabin government's line, his relationship with this group reportedly grew more tense. In the spring of 1993, Dine provided them with the ammunition for his ouster; he was quoted in *Piety and Power*, a book by Israeli journalist David Landau about religion and politics, as saying that ultra-Orthodox Jews had the image of being "smelly". Not surprisingly, the comment raised hackles among American Orthodox leaders, and by the summer the AIPAC board had forced Dine out of his job.

Although Rabin personally had never been pleased with Dine's high-pressure tactics or his lobbying of the executive, some members of his government – especially the Foreign Minister Shimon Peres – were not happy to see their main liberal backer in AIPAC step down. And just how much opposition remained in the organisation to Rabin's government became all too evident later that summer. In June, AIPAC vice president Harvey Friedman accompanied three congressmen to Jerusalem to meet deputy Foreign Minister Yossi Beilin. Afterward, Beilin told reporters he had been astonished to hear Friedman not only speak out against the Rabin government's avowed policy of territorial compromise, but in favour of the extreme right-wing policy of "transferring" – expelling – the Palestinians from the territories.

After learning of Beilin's remarks, Friedman told an interviewer from the *Washington Jewish Week* that the deputy Foreign Minister was a "little slimeball" who had twisted his words. Within days, it was now Friedman who was out of AIPAC. Clearly, the time had come for the organisation to come to grips with the reality of the Rabin government. "Labour coming to power pulled the rug out from under AIPAC," said Beilin after the Friedman incident. "We want US involvement in the peace process; their agenda was to keep the Americans out. We want peace based on compromise, and their agenda was to explain why compromise was impossible."

Following the Friedman fiasco, AIPAC – under the prodding of president Steven Grossman, a liberal Democratic Party activist – began to regain its footing. It backed the announcement of the initial Oslo agreement in September 1993. That winter, it made the new Palestine Authority an additional beneficiary of its campaign for foreign aid to Israel. And in Febuary 1994, it hired Neal Sher, a former Justice Department official with liberal views compatible with those of the Rabin government, to replace Tom Dine as executive director. In the summer of 1994, when asked about his previous conflicts with AIPAC, Rabin answered with uncharacteristic diplomacy: "Let's just say that problem was solved."

Unfortunately for Rabin, problems with other American Jewish organisations soon arose. The Oslo accords caught the American Jewish establishment by complete surprise. Suddenly, after years of vilifying Yasser Arafat and the PLO, it was being called upon to embrace the enemy. For left-wing groups like Americans for Peace Now, which had long advocated recognising the PLO, the Oslo pact was a vindication. For mainstream organisations like AIPAC and the umbrella Conference of Presidents of Major American Jewish Organizations, it required a sometimes painful shifting of priorities and personnel.

But Orthodox and right-wing organisations were not prepared to make any shift. The Oslo agreement generated new, unprecedented opposition to the Israeli government policy in the Diaspora. On 12 September 1993, the day before the landmark Israel–PLO Declaration of Principles was signed on the White House lawn, Israeli ambassador to the US Itamar Rabinovich was pelted with tomatoes at a New York synagogue amid cries of "Rabin is a traitor!" Suddenly, leading right-wing Jewish figures – such as *Commentary* editor Norman Podhoretz – who had for years been castigating left-wing groups like Americans for Peace Now for daring to criticise the Israeli government publicly, decided to take that route themselves and condemned Rabin's policies.

But most disturbing to Rabin was that some Jewish groups were willing to take the fight against his government directly to Washington. Leading the charge was Morton Klein, a Philadelphia businessman who in early 1994 became president of the Zionist Organization of America. While the ZOA had traditionally been affiliated with Likud positions, it had been considered a mainstream organisation which operated according to the consensual framework of the Conference of Presidents. As soon as Klein took over, the ZOA took a more aggressive approach toward fighting Rabin's peace policies, aided financially by the support of wealthy right-wing American Jews, and boosted ideologically by the Republican landslide in the November 1994 congressional elections.

The ZOA lobbied Congress to deny American foreign aid to the new Yasser Arafat-led Palestine Authority in the territories. With Klein's encouragement, New York Republican Senator Al D'Amato proposed a bill to ban the stationing of US troops on the Golan Heights as part of any Israeli–Syrian peace accord – even though no such idea had even been raised by either side. And Klein was among those who successfully pushed Senate Majority Leader Bob Dole to submit a bill mandating relocation of the American Embassy from Tel Aviv to Jerusalem by 1996 – just when talks on the final status of the city were set to begin within the Oslo framework.

Rabin had no choice but to appear publicly supportive – or at the very least indifferent – to the embassy bill, since it espoused a longstanding Israeli position. But "privately", says one source who consulted Rabin on the same issue, "he was disgusted over the way the whole embassy bill was handled. He saw no reason to push the bill through at a time when it would only complicate the negotiations with the Palestinians. It also put the Clinton administration in the difficult position of having to activate a clause in the bill enabling the President to postpone moving the embassy in the interests of national security. And the last thing Rabin ever wanted to do was embarrass the White House. This was exactly the kind of grandstanding by certain American Jewish leaders that Rabin despised."

In the last few months of Rabin's life, the opposition to him in certain quarters of the Diaspora reached a pitch no less fevered than in Israel. In the summer of 1994, an Orthodox Brooklyn rabbi, Abraham Hecht, gave an interview to Israel Television in which, referring to Rabin, he declared that any Jew who turned over parts of the Land of Israel to non-Jews had to die, according to religious law. Israel Television thought the interview was so inflammatory it decided not to air it – and finally did so only after Rabin's murder. Yet as harsh as the rhetoric against him grew, those close to Rabin say it was the politicking against his policies in Washington which upset him most of all. "It was unconscionable to him that some American Jews would openly petition the US government to oppose Israeli government policy," says Yehuda Avner. "This hurt him deeply."

While seeking support for the peace process occupied centre stage in Yitzhak Rabin's dealings with world Jewry in his final years, there were other Diaspora-related issues he dealt with during his second term as Prime Minister. One somewhat surprising cause taken up by Rabin in his last few years was the effort to free imprisoned Jewish-American spy Jonathan Pollard. Rabin had said almost nothing public on the subject since Pollard's arrest for espionage on Israel's behalf in 1984. To campaign for Pollard openly would have violated Rabin's cardinal rule of placing the strategic US–Israeli relationship above any other consideration. "I spoke to Rabin just before his first meeting as Prime Minister with George Bush in August '92," says Seymour Reich, "and I asked him to bring up the Pollard case. He declined, telling me there were too many other issues he wanted to press with Bush first, including Ron Arad [an Israeli Air Force navigator missing since being shot down over Lebanon in 1986] and the other Israeli MIAs. I responded by telling him that Pollard himself had come to believe that if he had been a sabra, and not a 'galut [exile] Jew', Israel would have made a much bigger effort to help him, and he would already be free."

Yet although Rabin refused to raise the Pollard affair with Bush, he did bring it up in meetings with Bill Clinton. In his last meeting with the President on 28 September 1995, he even linked Pollard to Israel's release of Palestinian prisoners as part of the Oslo accords, suggesting to the President that some of the Israeli public anger at granting freedom to Palestinians might be lessened if similar mercy were granted to Pollard. Clinton responded by not ruling out the possibility of granting executive clemency to Pollard, and Rabin later wrote a letter requesting Pollard's release, which Shimon Peres presented to Clinton on his first trip to Washington after the assassination.

Given Rabin's aversion to creating any friction with the American administration, his strong personal interest in the Pollard affair seems out of character. The true story of how deeply Rabin was involved in the Pollard affair may never come out. But Rabin was Defence Minister when Pollard was captured, and it was a defence ministry department, Lekem (the "scientific relations bureau"), that had recruited and operated him.

One American Jewish official who dealt with Rabin on the Pollard affair believes that "Rabin was motivated by his strong sense of personal responsibility in the Pollard case. He wasn't responding to Pollard as a Jew in trouble, but more as a sort of Israeli soldier who had been left out in the field."

This kind of thinking would certainly be more in line with the conventional image of Rabin as a man with an extremely narrow view of the Jewish world. "Rabin viewed the Diaspora, especially American Jewry, primarily as an important strategic asset for Israel," asserts one American Jewish leader. "He had no real interest in Diaspora issues, except when they touched directly on Israel. For example, I know of several occasions over the years when people came to him and asked him to speak out more strongly on the issue of Soviet Jewry, and he absolutely refused, because he did not want to do anything that would complicate US *détente* with the Soviet Union."

During his last years, Rabin did seem more interested in speaking out more on such Diaspora issues as anti-Semitism, assimilation and especially the need to support the continued immigration to Israel of Jews from the Soviet Union. But because Rabin almost never discussed his thoughts with even his closest aides, it is hard to assess whether this represented a genuine shift in his ideological outlook. "I don't believe that Rabin suddenly became more 'Jewish', or more concerned about the Jewish world outside," says one Jewish affairs activist. "More likely, he simply came to perceive that the Soviet immigrants, in terms of boosting the Israeli economy and providing the country with a massive infusion of brainpower, had become a genuine strategic asset for Israel."

Yet others assert that, especially in his last years, Rabin did demonstrate a growing interest in other areas of Jewish concern that had no direct connection to Israeli security. "In April of 1994," recalls Harry Wall, "I was part of a delegation with the World Jewish Congress that presented Rabin with a report on anti-Semitism around the world. To my surprise, Rabin started to engage us on the subject. Although, in his typical fashion, he asked very unemotional, technical questions about the exact number of anti-Semitic incidents in this or that country, it was the first time I can recall seeing him genuinely curious about the topic."

Rabin also seemed more interested in the issue of Jewish education, and began talking more about what Israel could do to maintain the Diaspora, rather than just vice versa. "Israel must co-operate in maintaining the Jewishness of the Jewish people," he told *The Jerusalem Report* in the summer of 1994, after returning from a tour of the former Soviet Union visibly impressed with the rebirth of the Jewish educational system there.

"Remember, Rabin was a man whose basic education about such

Jewish concepts as *kashrut* [dietary laws] and the Sabbath derived mainly from his years in the army," says the religiously observant Yehuda Avner. But in private conversation, says Avner, "Rabin began expressing concern over the huge assimilation rate of American Jewry – he even referred to it as a 'holocaust', which is not at all the kind of language you expected to hear from him. Jewish education had become an important issue to him; even if he himself did not emotionally relate to it, I think you could say Rabin had developed a 'strategic appreciation' of its importance to the survival of the Jewish people."

When Avner ended his term as ambassador to Australia in the autumn of 1995, Rabin called him up and asked him to once again take on the duties of Diaspora affairs adviser – perhaps finally recognising the need for a capable spokesman to convey his policies to Jews abroad. His first job was to draft the speech which Rabin was scheduled to give before the Council of Jewish Federations' General Assembly in Boston in mid-November.

"We began discussing it just two days before Rabin was killed," says Avner. "This speech would have been his unifying message to the Jewish world. It would have gone beyond the politics of the day, to repair the misunderstandings which had developed between Rabin and Diaspora Jewry over the past year by emphasising those issues on which a Jewish consensus still exists."

It was, of course, the speech Rabin never gave. Instead, on 10 December, a memorial rally in honour of the slain Prime Minister was held in New York's Madison Square Garden. It attracted a crowd of 15,000, the kind of turnout Rabin probably could not have drawn while alive.

Intended as a unity rally, it also underscored that the deep divisions in Diaspora Jewry over Rabin's peace policies had not been resolved with his death. Although the event had the backing of the Conference of Presidents, the ZOA boycotted it, in protest at the absence of a member of Rabin's political opposition from the speakers. In an attempt to mollify Orthodox groups, the organisers scotched a plan for Barbra Streisand to sing, since this would have violated a religious precept against women singing in public. Despite this, and despite the presence on the podium of Israel's Ashkenazi Chief Rabbi, Yisrael Lau, some Orthodox groups still refused to attend the event on political grounds.

In his speech that day at Madison Square Garden, Shimon Peres did not gloss over his predecessor's often stormy relationship with

Diaspora Jewry; "Rabin never tried to please you," Peres said, "he tried to lead you." Leah Rabin, who knew her husband's heart better than any other, delivered a more emotional address. "Yitzhak Rabin loved you," she told the thousands who came too late to appreciate the slain Jewish leader. Rabin himself would, of course, never have expressed himself so openly. It was, perhaps, only toward the end of his life that he even began to understand why he might feel that way about all the world's Jews.

13

Rise of the Radicals

"VISIONARIES HAVE SEEN their vision torn asunder before their eyes." In these words, a prominent ideologue summed up the mood on Israel's religious right in the months after Yitzhak Rabin's handshake with Yasser Arafat on the White House lawn.

The comment was made by Dan Be'eri, writing in the West Bank settler journal *Nekudah*. It describes a movement's goals in words connoting prophecy and religious truth. And it depicts the peace process not as a political defeat, but as an act of violation – akin, in the Hebrew, to a predator consuming its prey. In both respects, Be'eri's words are a telling portrayal of the passions sparked on the religious right by Rabin's diplomatic steps – passions that fuelled mass protests and that drove Yigal Amir and his alleged accomplices to plot the Prime Minister's death.

Rabin's peace policies were opposed by the entire Israeli right, and polls consistently showed that much of the public rejected them too. Secular politicians, including Benjamin Netanyahu, Ariel Sharon, and others further to the right, stridently declared that the agreement with the PLO was dangerous to Israel's security. But the activists who planned demonstrations against the government, who blocked roads and fought with police, and who called on soldiers to refuse any future orders to evacuate settlements, came almost exclusively from the ranks of Orthodox Zionists – religious settlers in the occupied territories, and their supporters within sovereign Israel. The Prime Minister, for his part, devoted some of his choice invective to the settlers.

Israel's Orthodox right is as much a religious movement – a particular, peculiar development in Judaism – as it is a political camp comprising Orthodox settler groups and most of the National Religious Party. Its beliefs posit that the End of Days is at hand, and that Jewish control of the Land of Israel is an essential step toward the final Redemption. Israel's agreement to give up control of parts of the Jewish homeland to Arabs threatened principles of faith and not only the country's security.

The ideology of most of the religious right is rooted in the dense writings of Avraham Yitzhak Kook, a Lithuanian-born rabbi who became a Zionist before the turn of the century and moved to the Holy Land in 1904. In the fevered politics of Eastern European Jewry in those years, Zionism was one of several secular movements – like Socialism – that rejected traditional religion as perpetuating Jewish suffering, and sought to replace it with a political programme. Most Orthodox rabbis, in turn, despised the Zionists as pork-eating heretics who defied God by trying to end the Jews' exile from their land before the arrival of the messiah promised by the prophets.

To justify his Zionism, Kook fused kabbalah (Jewish mysticism) and European-style nationalism into mystical messianism. For Kook, the fact that Jews were organising the return to their homeland was proof that the Divine redemption had actually begun. Secular Zionists, the pioneers who had begun immigrating from Europe to the Biblical homeland, farming the land and building new towns, were carrying out God's will – unknowingly, despite themselves – and would eventually return to religion.

Kook provided a basis for Orthodox Jews to join the national movement, co-operate with anti-religious pioneers, and regard both physical labour and modern education as religious obligations. His ideas draw on classic Jewish mysticism – yet they also affirm a nineteenth-century faith in human progress, and reflect the confident reading of "inevitable processes of history" popular among left-wing radicals of the time. To this day, Kook's writings are read by some religious Jews as a mandate for a liberal openness to the modern world.

In 1921, Kook was appointed the first Chief Rabbi of the Ashkenazi (Eastern European) community in British Mandatory Palestine; several years later he established his own yeshivah (rabbinic academy), Merkaz Harav, in Jerusalem. After his death in 1935, his place at the head of the yeshivah was taken by his only son, Rabbi Tzvi Yehudah Kook, who lived until 1982. The younger Kook emphasised the national rather than the universal side of his father's philosophy. He, and others influenced by his father, continued reading history as fulfilling a Divine script. After Israel's independence in 1948, the chief rabbis of the new state adopted a "Prayer for the State" that defined Israel as "the first flowering of our Redemption".

Meanwhile, religious Zionism developed into a significant minority within the Zionist movement. Orthodox Zionists, following the example of their secular compatriots, established a handful of Orthodox kibbutzim, a labour union and their own school system and youth movement, Bnei Akiva. In the Zionist leadership and then the new state, their political representatives (who eventually joined forces to form the National Religious Party) were perennial junior partners of the dominant Labour movement. But religious Zionists suffered a double inferiority complex: on the one hand ultra-Orthodox Jews, still opposed to Zionism, regarded them as second-rate in religious study and commitment. Yet as state-builders, they'd clearly played no more than a minor role. The young generation of "crocheted yarmulkes" – the distinctive skull-cap of religious Zionists – was regarded as well-behaved and rather harmless.

The Kooks' philosophy was not the only one within Orthodox Zionism, but as time passed, graduates of Merkaz Harav gained increasing influence in the religious schools and Bnei Akiva. The turning point came with Israel's sudden, startling, Rabin-engineered victory in the Six Day War. The triumph inspired euphoria among many Israelis, but for religious Zionists, and especially disciples of Tzvi Yehudah Kook, the joy was deeper: an obvious Divine miracle had occurred. The heart of the sacred land that God had promised Abraham – Hebron, the hills of Samaria, the Old City of Jerusalem – had been restored to Jewish rule. Indeed, Kook's students believed he had virtually prophesied the miracle; three weeks before the war, at an Israeli Independence Day celebration at his yeshivah, the rabbi had burst out: "Where's our Hebron? Have we forgotten her? Where's our Shechem [the Biblical name of Nablus], our Jericho?"

There could be no sign more clear than the victory that the messianic process was moving forward. Summing up the mood, Kook would later tell his students that they were not in the beginning but "the middle of Redemption. We're in the living room and not the entry hall." Another prominent rabbi wrote that the Land of Israel had been liberated from the *sitra ahra* – the kabbalistic name for the primordial evil – an argument that identified flesh-and-blood enemies with satanic forces.

Soon after the war, a disciple of Kook said in a meeting with Orthodox cabinet members: "I believe with a perfect faith that if the

Holy One, Blessed be He, gave us the land through obvious miracles, He'll never take it from us, for He does not perform a miracle in vain. The integrity of the Land of Israel isn't subject to the decisions of the government." More than a political statement, denying the government's *right* to pull back from the newly conquered territory, this was a statement of theological certainty: a denial of the government's *ability* to give up land. But the political implications were clear.

Ideologically, the pieces were already on the board, even if it would take another quarter-century before an Israeli government would actually decide to pull out of the West Bank and set the conflict with the messianists in motion.

The theological response to the Six Day War quickly became a programme for action – settling the newly "liberated" territories. Three months after the war, a group of Orthodox settlers – led by Hanan Porat, a young teacher at Merkaz Harav, later to become a National Religious Party Knesset member – re-established Kibbutz Kfar Etzion in the rocky Judaean Hills between Bethlehem and Hebron. Porat had spent the first five years of his life on the same site, at the original Kfar Etzion, which had been overrun by Arab forces on 13 May 1948, the day before the State of Israel was declared, after a long siege.

The founders of the old–new kibbutz received approval in advance from the then-Prime Minister Levi Eshkol. Not so the next settlement bid, by another student of Kook, Moshe Levinger, a thin, often dishevelled young rabbi. In the spring of 1968, over the Passover holiday, Levinger and 60 other settlers moved into the Park Hotel in Hebron and refused to leave. That effort eventually led to government approval for the establishment of Kiryat Arba, the Jewish town on the edge of Hebron that became the hotbed of settler extremism – and finally, in 1979, the springboard for several hundred Jews to settle inside Hebron. Levinger and the other settlers saw themselves as renewing the small Jewish community that had lived in the intensely Islamic city until 1929, when Arab rioters killed 67 Jews. A series of terror attacks on the settlers confirmed their view of the Arabs as a murderous threat, and relations between the two groups were always on the brink of explosion.

Just before Yitzhak Rabin became Prime Minister in 1974, Porat, Levinger and others formed Gush Emunim, which would force Rabin into one of his most embarrassing defeats. Rabin's policy rejected settling in the Samarian hills of the northern West Bank; he hoped to return that area, heavily populated by Arabs, to Arab rule in a peace treaty. From the summer of 1974 on, the leaders of Gush Emunim and other members of its Elon Moreh group led hundreds of supporters in a series of attempts to establish a Jewish settlement near Nablus. Each time, troops removed them – until in December 1975, unwilling to confront thousands of Gush Emunim backers gathered at an abandoned railroad station at Sebastia, Rabin agreed to let 30 families move into an army base in Samaria. The defeat left Rabin's policy on the West Bank's future – and his image as a leader – in shreds.

Gush Emunim, meanwhile, became the leading force in religious Zionism. Its leaders presented themselves as the true heirs of the early Zionist pioneers, willing to defy discomfort and danger to settle the land – and at the same time insisted that their religious vision was more complete than that of the ultra-Orthodox. The inferiority complex of the "crocheted skull-caps" was forgotten. The National Religious Party relinquished its traditional alliance with the Labour Party and steadily swung to the right, following the lead of Gush Emunim. In religious schools, rabbis trained in Merkaz Harav or *hesder* yeshivot – academies where young men alternated between army duty and religious study – preached the integrity of the Land of Israel as a principle of faith. The "Zionism of Redemption" – at once a political movement and religious sect – had an aura of triumphant confidence.

The right's rise to power in 1977 appeared another godsend. The Likud governments of Menachem Begin and Yitzhak Shamir were driven by the Revisionist Zionist ideology of Ze'ev Jabotinsky, which posited the historic right of the Jews to the entire Land of Israel. They were committed to permanent Israeli control over the West Bank and Gaza Strip, and settlement after settlement sprouted up, backed by generous government aid. Thousands of Gush Emunim supporters moved into the territories, which they referred to as Yesha – the Hebrew acronym for Judaea, Samaria and Gaza – meaning "salvation". Unsatisfied by Gush Emunim's settlement pace, the Likud also built large suburbs in the West Bank near Tel Aviv and Jerusalem, attracting Israelis with low-cost housing.

The alliance was shallower than it looked. The Likud's leaders were secular rightists, who cited historical and security reasons for claiming the West Bank and Gaza as Jewish. It's doubtful they understood, much less identified with, Gush Emunim's theology;

the writings of their thinkers, studded with Talmudic and kabbalistic terms, can be impenetrable for secular Israelis. Gush Emunim regarded Begin's agreement to return the entire Sinai Peninsula to Egypt, and his proposal for limited Palestinian autonomy in the West Bank, as an unacceptable surrender of full Jewish control over the homeland. Israeli troops had to evacuate Gush Emunim protesters by force from the Sinai town of Yamit to complete the pullout in 1982; Israeli papers were filled with photos of angry men in skull-caps struggling against young soldiers on rooftops.

Some Orthodox settlers, it turned out, had planned more radical action. In April 1984, the Shin Bet security service uncovered a 28-member Jewish underground – based in the settlements – that had carried out terror attacks on local Arabs in revenge for Palestinian terror. The conspirators included prominent Gush Emunim activists (one of whom was Dan Be'eri). Under interrogation, several revealed that they had gathered explosives to blow up the Muslim shrine of the Dome of the Rock in Jerusalem. A key goal had been shattering the peace with Egypt and stopping the withdrawal from Sinai.

The underground affair deeply divided the movement. Some leaders condemned the terrorists' actions; others, including Levinger, campaigned for their release from prison. When members of the underground were released, often after brief jail terms, some resumed public roles in the settlement movement. The most severe sentences – life imprisonment – went to three men who had attacked Hebron's Islamic College, murdering three students. But after a series of commutations by President Chaim Herzog – a Labourite – all were out of jail by 1990. It was a dangerous show of leniency toward perpetrators of nationalistic crime.

If the mainstream of the religious right had shown an ambiguous attitude toward violence, the followers of Meir Kahane positively sanctified it. An American-born Orthodox rabbi, Kahane moved to Israel in 1971, and developed a theology that stood normative Jewish belief on its head. Traditionally, for instance, a Jew who is honest in business, or resists anger, "sanctifies the Divine Name" – that is, shows others the purity of his religion and God. When a Jew is crude, dishonest, cruel, he "desecrates the Name". But for Kahane, God's reputation in the world was purely a function of Jewish might. If Jews were killed, he said, God looked weak; if they were strong, God's power was revealed. The "upturned Jewish fist" sanctified the Divine Name.

In *Forty Years*, published in 1893, Kahane laid out his messianic vision. The Holocaust, he said, had been the worst possible desecration of the Name, because Jews had been so weak. God had therefore created the State of Israel to prove His might. He had given the Jews 40 years, or "a few more, a few less", to prove themselves – to create a theocracy, "drive out the Arab... cleanse the Temple Mount" – before the End. If "the Jew" passed the test, messianic redemption would come peacefully; if not, it would be preceded by an "unnecessary, needless holocaust, more horrible than anything we have yet endured".

In 1990, Kahane was killed, and his disciples split into two groups – Kahane Chai, with a few dozen members in the settlement of Kfar Tapuah near Nablus, and Kach, centred in Kiryat Arba and Hebron, with several hundred members. Both groups were linked repeatedly to violence against Arabs. In far-right Kiryat Arba, Kahane's disciples fit in well; one, an American doctor named Baruch Goldstein, represented Kach for a time on the town council.

When Yitzhak Rabin returned to the Prime Minister's Office in June 1992, an estimated 105,000 Israelis lived in the occupied territories. Probably a quarter belonged to what Professor Ehud Sprinzak, a Hebrew University expert on the radical right, calls the "Gush Emunim culture" – living mainly in Orthodox communities of a few dozen or hundred families scattered between Arab towns of the West Bank mountain ridge. Though Gush Emunim had long since ceased functioning as an organisation, its graduates controlled many of the local Jewish governments, and the umbrella Council of Jewish Settlements in Judaea, Samaria and the Gaza District.

Not only had Rabin, proponent of territorial compromise, been elected Prime Minister. The far-right Tehiyah party, supported by many settlers, failed to re-enter the Knesset, and the National Religious Party, virtually for the first time, remained outside the ruling coalition – a symbol of a community suddenly marginalised. Still, settler leaders remained confident: too many Jews now lived beyond Israel's pre-1967 borders to turn the clock back. Rabin himself was regarded as a hawk in Labour. Settler rabbi Jonathan Blass, in a *Jerusalem Report* opinion article in July 1992, argued amazingly that "the underlying loyalty of the people to the Land of Israel was demonstrated... by the election results". Shamir, he said, had shown weakness by going to the Madrid peace conference, and "Rabin received the people's trust" by "espousing positions considerably more nationalistic and security-oriented than those of his party". The argument reflected Kook-style theology; even unknowingly, the Jewish soul was tied to the sacred land and redemption. Yisrael Harel, the pragmatic head of the Council of Settlements, later commented that "in the whole Labour camp, we were closest to Rabin. He wanted to keep the Jordan Valley [in the West Bank] and the Golan Heights. We assumed that what he wanted would be enough to keep the Arabs from agreeing."

In the autumn of 1992, the Rabin government froze all government-funded construction in the occupied territories, and required private contractors to get special approval to build — a move in line with promises to change spending priorities, but also emphasising willingness to trade land for peace. In some settlements, completed homes were left locked and empty. Yet the freeze was far less sweeping than it appeared, and the Jewish population of the West Bank kept climbing. Meanwhile, public negotiations between Israel and the Palestinians moved fitfully. In their well-groomed neighbourhoods on the West Bank's hills, settlers seethed over sporadic terror attacks. But the youthful enthusiasm of the early years of Gush Emunim had been replaced by middle-class solidity; the early charismatic leadership had lost its aura, and the settlers put their energy into maintaining their settlements.

At the end of August 1993 came the earthquake: the announcement of the Oslo accords. Palestinian autonomy in the West Bank and Gaza Strip was near. While the interim accord promised that settlements would remain in place, there was no guarantee that the final agreement would do the same. The right regarded the PLO's acceptance of peace as a tactical step alone, on the way to eliminating Israel in the future.

The opposition's response was shrill; from the start its leaders charged Rabin with endangering the country, and even with perfidy. Benjamin Netanyahu told Shimon Peres in a Knesset debate: "You are much worse than the British Prime Minister Neville Chamberlain, because Chamberlain threatened the security and freedom of another nation, while you are threatening the security and freedom of your own nation." A newspaper advertisement run by opposition parties — and approved by Netanyahu, according to Ha'aretz — said, "The people rise up against the treason of the Rabin government." Hanan Porat said ominously, "We're not prepared to continue playing by the rules of the democratic game. We're not prepared to obey the laws of the government."

On 7 September, as the White House signing ceremony drew closer, the right held its first mass protest against the Oslo accords. As night fell, a crowd estimated at anywhere from 50,000 to 200,000 flooded the streets around the government's offices in Jerusalem. The protesters rhythmically chanted "Rabin is a traitor," and tried to break through lines of baton-bearing policemen to reach the Prime Minister's Office, before listening to Netanyahu roar: "We can overcome Peres and Rabin."

The strident, angry demonstration set the tone for the mass protests that followed, at intervals of several months, over the next two years. In Harel's words "Likud politicians always appear, they share in the funding, but we – the Council of Settlements – do the organising. They don't have the ability." The protesters, overwhelmingly, were Orthodox. At that first protest, an additional boost came from the Chabad hasidic sect, the New York-based ultra-Orthodox Lubavitcher movement, then in the throes of its own messianic fervour and virulently opposed to territorial concessions. At later protests, the foot-soldiers would be almost entirely Orthodox Zionists – men and boys in crocheted yarmulkes, women and girls in long skirts – settlers, members and graduates of Bnei Akiva, and others from the religious right.

Netanyahu, hoping desperately to pressure the government into holding new elections, continued to appear before the frenzied crowds, ignoring moderates in his party who accused him of alienating centrist voters. The following July, for instance, an estimated 100,000 demonstrators crowded the centre of Jerusalem, drawn there by a campaign claiming that PLO leader Yasser Arafat was about to visit the capital. Netanyahu spoke from a balcony on Zion Square above a huge banner reading "Death to Arafat".

Rhetoric aside, the failure of the politicians to bring out rank-and-file secular right-wing voters to the streets could only increase the settlers' sense of isolation. Yet in the weeks after the White House signing, it seemed that the settlers themselves were also unable to mobilise a campaign of constant pressure on the government.

What did galvanise protests was Palestinian terror. On 29 October 1993, terrorists abducted Haim Mizrahi, a settler from Beit El, near Ramallah, murdered him, and burned his body. Hundreds of angry settlers from the area poured into nearby Arab villages on a Friday afternoon, hurling stones at houses, overturning cars, and shooting and wounding several residents. The rampage, settlers said afterward, had the approval of Beit El's rabbi, Zalman Melamed, one of the most respected clergymen in the settler community. According to one settler, Melamed "turned the whole thing off with one call on the walkie-talkie 20 minutes before the beginning of the Sabbath", lest the rules of the holy day be violated. The Council of Settlements organised a more calculated response the following Sunday morning, with activists simultaneously blocking dozens of roads, paralysing traffic throughout the West Bank for two hours.

The Mizrahi killing was followed within days by other Palestinian attacks on settlers. Near Hebron, gunmen opened fire on a car carrying Rabbi Haim Druckman, a *hesder* yeshivah head, former Knesset member and another central rabbi of the religious right. Druckman survived the attack, but his driver, Efraim Ayubi, was killed. In early December, terrorists killed Mordechai Lapid of Kiryat Arba and his 19-year-old son Shalom. Lapid, an early Jewish activist in the Soviet Union and member of the original Elon Moreh group, was known throughout the settler movement, and his death deepened the fear and anger that had been growing since the accord with the PLO.

At a memorial gathering for the Lapids in Kiryat Arba's Nir Yeshivah, one eulogy was delivered by Baruch Goldstein. "He called for vengeance," Dan Be'eri would later recall, "and expressed in great sorrow his pained view that because we were apathetic and had refrained from vengeance, we were guilty of their deaths – not on the practical level of deterrence, but on the metaphysical level, before heaven."

Goldstein's views were extreme. But in Kiryat Arba and the Jewish settlement in Hebron in particular, a siege atmosphere developed. Clashes between Jews and Arabs in Hebron were common. In one incident, Rabbi Levinger, his wife Miriam and other settlers reportedly went on a rampage in the town's open market, hurling stones and overturning stalls. In several cases, settlers shot at Arab cars or hurled stones at them, causing injuries. Elsewhere in the West Bank, three Arabs were shot and killed near the village of Tarkimiyah – presumably by Jews avenging the Lapids' deaths. The security forces failed to make any arrests in the case.

The Council of Settlements, for its part, called on Jews not to attack Arabs. As in the past, though, some leaders provided an equivocal response. Pinhas Wallerstein, head of the regional body of settlements north of Jerusalem, referred to the rampages in Hebron as no more than "unwise", saying: "If people feel they've been denied the minimum of elementary defence, it's no wonder they behave as if they have no choice but to defend themselves."

The Mizrahi killing was attributed to a renegade cell of Yasser Arafat's Fatah group. Otherwise, the escalating terror attacks were carried out by Palestinian opponents of the peace process, particularly the fundamentalist Hamas organisation. For the right, however, the distinction was largely irrelevant. Continued terrorism showed that the Oslo accords had not delivered peace with the Palestinians. What's more, the settlers believed, the government was failing to protect them. As Kiryat Arba's Mayor, Tzvi Katzover, said after one terror incident: "The common feeling today, which grows after every attack, is that the government has deliberately decided to abandon us and make life unbearable for us, with the hope that we'll leave voluntarily. We won't give anyone the pleasure." Further increasing fear was the prospect of Palestinian policemen – presumably members of Fatah, still seen by the right as a terror organisation – receiving arms and taking control of areas of the West Bank under autonomy.

The settlers, who had already lived with years of stone-throwing and worse attacks during the Intifada, had practical reason to be scared. Most commuted to work inside sovereign Israel, which meant driving through Arab areas; and many saw their children bused to school daily on the West Bank's roads.

The crisis, however, went beyond practical issues. The accords with the PLO created unbearable contradictions in the theology of the religious right. The sacred state, "the foundation of God's throne in the world", had agreed to give up sacred land – to enemies that at least some theologians had identified with the metaphysical forces of evil. And part of the holy people supported this step. As Rabbi Menahem Felix of Elon Moreh, a Gush Emunim founder, wrote in *Nekudah*: "Transferring rule over parts of the Land of Israel to gentile hands means bringing destruction upon the land... This time, it's not [the Roman emperor] Titus or Nebuchadnezzar but an Israeli administration that stands to destroy the land."

Within the same article, Felix offered two contradictory explanations – both commonly heard in the religious right. Israel had been established as a Jewish state, he said, but "the present regime did not have a Jewish majority in the Knesset to ratify the surrender to the PLO." Though it had reached power by "supposedly democratic means," the government had "lost legitimacy to rule the Jewish state." Implied here was not only a rejection of Israeli Arabs' rights as citizens, but also an assumption that the majority of the Jewish people retained its organic link to the land. At the same time, Felix argued that the agreement resulted from a spiritual crisis in the people, from "the desire to be freed from the burden of Jewish heritage... and the place of the Land of Israel in it." Soon after Felix's article appeared, *Ha'aretz* reported that the respected rabbi had left Elon Moreh's synagogue with a group of followers, rather than listen to the "Prayer for the State" – a demonstrative break with the old doctrine of the state's sacredness. (Felix's 19-year-old daughter Ofrah was killed in January 1995, when terrorists opened fire on her car north of Beit El in the northern West Bank. At her funeral, the Likud's Ariel Sharon told thousands of mourners that "leftists incite the Arabs of the West Bank against our living on our land. The government hopes the spirit of the settlers will break, so that they'll want to leave.")

In geographic terms, some *Nekudah* writers drew a line between the settlements and the secular Tel Aviv of "pubs, discotheques and beaches". Azriel Ariel, a young rabbi, urged settlers to retreat into their own communities and give up attempts to work with "the majority of the people, which has abandoned the nationalist tendency of its soul for shaky Western 'morality'." The Kooks' faith in secular Zionists, in other words, had been proven wrong.

One of the strongest challenges to the government's legitimacy came from Shlomo Goren, who had served as chief military chaplain from 1948 until 1971 and then Chief Rabbi of Israel from 1972 to 1983. Goren issued a ruling in December 1993 saying that Jewish religious law required soldiers to disobey any future orders to dismantle settlements. The ruling caused a public storm, and raised questions in the general public about the loyalty of Orthodox soldiers – further undermining the Orthodox–secular partnership.

Early on the morning of 25 February 1994, Baruch Goldstein rose, put on his army reservist's uniform, took his Galil assault rifle, and left his house for Hebron's Tomb of the Patriarchs to pray. When the Jewish service was over, Kiryat Arba's doctor entered another hall of the tomb, where Muslim services were in progress, and hid behind a column. Then he began shooting in all directions, using up one magazine after another, firing over 100 bullets. Within moments, 29 kneeling Arabs had been killed and scores injured. The shooting stopped only when several Arabs managed to strike him with iron bars and kill him.

Goldstein, it appears, hoped both to please heaven by reasserting

Jewish strength and to derail the peace process. "This wasn't momentary madness, but an act of despair, of a man who despaired because the majority surrendered Jewish destiny and honour," wrote Dan Be'eri in *Nekudah*. While some settler leaders simply condemned the massacre, others put the blame on the government for "abandoning the security" of Jews in the West Bank and Gaza. Goldstein's body was brought to Kiryat Arba's Nir Yeshivah, headed by two rabbis from the extreme wing of Gush Emunim, for eulogies before burial. One of Nir's rabbis, Dov Lior, would later call Goldstein "a martyr" like "the martyrs of the Holocaust". Shortly after the funeral, Nir's Public Relations director Gary Cooperberg sent a fax to newspapers saying that Goldstein's "desperate act of love for his people. . . will some day be recognised by all Jews as the turning point which brought redemption upon us". Goldstein's supporters later published a book praising him, *Barukh Hagever* – "Blessed Be the Man". A copy was acquired by a Bar-Ilan University law student, Yigal Amir.

Horrifying as the massacre was, it should not have been a surprise. Academics and journalists had warned of the danger of Jewish terror since the White House signing. For an extreme religious group, faced with the failure of prophecy and sudden social isolation, despair – and nihilistic action – was one likely response.

Yet speaking in the Knesset, Yitzhak Rabin confessed that he had not imagined such a crime in his worst dreams, and referred to Goldstein as "mentally ill". Danny Yatom, head of the army's Central Command, told the Shamgar Commission investigating the massacre that no one could have expected the "insane deed". As he testified, Yatom raised one hand beside his head and turned it, as if asking what had turned the switch in the doctor's mind.

One possible reason that Rabin was so taken by surprise was that he was an intensely secular man. He apparently had no understanding of the religious right's beliefs, and regarded it simply as a strident but marginal political group. After the Hebron killings, the government outlawed Kach and Kahane Chai, and jailed several key activists. Yet Rabin and the security forces apparently remained unprepared for violence from others on the extreme edge of the religious right. The massacre was not only a disaster in its own right, but a tragically missed warning.

In the two years following the Oslo accords, the public relationship between Rabin and the settlers was one of obvious antipathy. In large part, that was unavoidable: after a quarter of a century of Israel avoiding decisions about the future of the West Bank and Gaza Strip, Rabin had chosen a path that negated the idea of the integrity of the Land of Israel, and the settlers' efforts to hold it. But for the settlers, the Prime Minister's coldness toward them deepened the animosity -- and the minimal fanfare attending his personal contacts with settler victims of terrorism meant there was little to soften that sense. Says the Settler Council's Harel: "His sharp turn gave us a feeling of being sold out. If he had made any emotional gestures, maybe it would have softened the impact. But he never even admitted that he had changed... You have a guy you respect, and then you find out he's a different person. As much as you once respected him, now you'll feel the opposite."

Indeed, the Prime Minister made clear that he would not be moved by protests. In one comment, responding to demonstrations against a possible pullback on the Golan Heights, he said that he would carry through with his policies, and opponents could "spin like propellers". It was, essentially, a restatement of the well-known phrase used by the right while in power to dismiss protests: "The dogs bark and the caravan passes" – a macho declaration of determination.

On another occasion, speaking to reporters about the pullout from Gaza, Rabin spoke of the tiny, isolated community of Netzarim in the Strip. "If that's a settlement, I'm a ball bearing," he said. Settlers were soon angrily repeating that the Prime Minister had termed all of them "propellers" and "ball bearings". For those who had seen themselves as the Zionist vanguard, his disrespect could only increase frustration and anger.

In late 1993, Harel and two other leaders of the Council of Settlements held a secret meeting with Rabin to discuss security and other practical issues. When word of the meeting was leaked to the press, Harel was bitterly attacked by other settler leaders for sitting down with the Prime Minister. Meetings between Rabin and settler leaders continued. But both sides often made efforts to keep them out of the spotlight – indirectly adding to the sense of alienation.

The Oslo accords guaranteed that all settlements would stay put during the interim period, but said nothing about their permanent status. For many months, Rabin kept his own views on the final-status map to himself, unwilling to show his cards to the Palestinians. One result, though, was to leave settlers – not only those of Gush Emunim, but the secular suburbanites living near the pre-1967 border – uncertain and fearful about their prospects.

Speaking to the Knesset on 5 October 1995, in the debate on the Oslo II accord, Rabin did indicate his goals for the final-status agreement: The Jordan River would be "the security border of the state of Israel"; the border around Jerusalem would be moved to include the large settlements of Ma'aleh Adumim and Givat Ze'ev; and in other places, the border would be moved eastward from the pre-1967 lines to take in Jewish settlements. He also indicated that within the Palestinian entity, there would be "Jewish settlement blocs", which he apparently envisaged remaining under Israeli rule. Though revealing much more than he had in the past, Rabin still left much to the imagination – and fears – of the settlers.

As the negotiations between Israel and the PLO on autonomy in the West Bank dragged on, in July 1995 a group of 15 right-wing religious Zionist rabbis met to issue a ruling that would deeply divide the country – and their own followers. Led by Avraham Shapira, former Chief Rabbi of the country, the group announced that evacuating West Bank military bases threatened Jewish life, meaning that religious soldiers should refuse orders to take part in any such operation.

"A standing military camp is a Jewish settlement in every way. Uprooting and leaving it is equivalent to uprooting a settlement from the Land of Israel, which is forbidden," said the rabbis, who also included Haim Druckman and Nahum Rabinovitch, the once-moderate head of the *hesder* yeshivah in the settlement of Ma'aleh Adumim.

Shapira, following Shlomo Goren's lead, had ruled the year before that soldiers should refuse to evacuate settlements. And Rabinovitch had equated any orders to evict Jews from settlements to "Nazi orders". But the new ruling posed a much more immediate challenge, since the next stage of autonomy would require moving army bases.

Some of the rabbis' colleagues immediately rejected the ruling; prominent among them was Yoel Bin-Nun, a Gush Emunim veteran and long-time critic of extremism in the settler camp. Others defended it. "This is a minority Jewish government whose survival depends on the support of Arab Knesset members," said Rabbi Benny Elon, an activist in anti-government demonstrations. In that reasoning, Elon was also following Shapira's lead. In a stunning reversal of religious Zionism's original tenets, its followers were now being told to choose between loyalty to the Torah [Bible] and loyalty to the state.

Some clerics went even further. In a conversation with Yitzhak Frankenthal, a leader of the dovish religious group Netivot Shalom, Rabinovitch said that if the army planned to dismantle settlements, settlers would spread remote-control bombs around the area "as the Arabs do". Any soldiers who participated in such an operation, the rabbi said, "are sinners, absolute sinner".

Early in 1995, according to the daily *Ha'aretz*, three settler rabbis – Dov Lior and two others – wrote to some 40 prominent rabbis, asking whether Rabin and other government ministers could be considered accomplices to murder. "Would it not be appropriate," they asked, "to warn the Prime Minister and other ministers that if they continue to turn the residents of Yesha over to the rule of murderers, according to Jewish law it will be necessary to put them on trial and punish them according to the law of a *moser?*" That Hebrew term refers to a Jew who turns other Jews, or their property, over to an oppressor; theoretically, the punishment can be death. According to one of the rabbis involved, they received few responses, and decided to end the discussion on the instructions of Rabbi Shlomo Aviner, another prominent settler cleric.

Bin-Nun would later allege that some rabbinical authorities had ruled that Rabin was an "assailant" under Jewish law. "Assailant" – *rodef* – refers to a person pursuing another to kill him; Jewish law requires a bystander to stop the pursuer, by taking his life if necessary. Yet it remains unclear whether, before the night of 4 November, any rabbi had explicitly ruled that Yitzhak Rabin was a *rodef* – or had passed that opinion on to Yigal Amir.

On 5 October 1995, as the Knesset debated the Oslo II accord, right-wing demonstrators again filled central Jerusalem. Addressing the crowd, Benjamin Netanyahu attacked Rabin for basing his coalition's Knesset majority on Arab Knesset members whose children did not serve in the army and on two right-wing legislators who had crossed over to back the Prime Minister. This time, when the demonstrators responded by chanting "Traitors, traitors," Netanyahu asked them to stop. For Netanyahu's critics, that would be regarded as too little, too late.

The mood was heated up by other secular right-wing Knesset members. Rechavam Zeevy, leader of the far-right Moledet (Homeland) party, declared that "This is an insane government that has decided to commit national suicide." And the Likud's Ariel Sharon roared that the Rabin government had "collaborated with a terror organisation". Among the demonstrators, Kahanist activists – reportedly including Avishai Raviv, head of a shady radical group called Eyal (a Hebrew acronym for Jewish Fighting Organisation), friend of Yigal Amir, and a reported informer in the pay of the Shin Bet – passed out leaflets showing Rabin dressed in the uniform of a Nazi SS officer.

From Zion Square, tens of thousands marched to the Knesset. There, hundreds of protesters tried to break through police lines to reach the plaza in front of the building, hurling burning torches at the men in blue. Kach activists attacked Housing Minister Binyamin Ben-Eliezer's car with stones as he drove away from the building. Others found Rabin's empty car, and set to work smashing it. Never, it appeared, had Israeli politics come so close to an open battle.

The worst was yet to come.

14

God's Assassin

YIGAL AMIR WAS NOT a West Bank settler. He lived with his family in Neveh Amal, a neighbourhood of Herzliyah gradually pulling itself up out of poverty. But Amir deeply supported the settlers, fiercely endorsed the rabbinical injunctions against withdrawing from the West Bank, and contemptuously rejected the Rabin government's justifications of its peace policies. So, of course, did many hundreds of thousands of other Israelis. What made Amir different was that he was a doer. He didn't just talk, he acted.

Born on 23 May 1970, Amir was the second of the eight children of Shlomo and Geulah – he a Yemenite immigrant, soft-spoken, ineffectual, scraping out a living as a scribe of religious documents and as an occasional ritual slaughterer; she, the dominant figure in the household, strictly Orthodox, a strong, confident woman, but with a softer side – known as the neighbourhood's amateur social worker, a shoulder to cry on. One neighbour speaks of Geulah providing emotional support through a particularly traumatic divorce: "She made me feel calmer, helped me deal with it."

For many years, Yigal and his three brothers, four sisters and parents were squeezed into two rooms at 56 Borochov Street. Ever since he was a baby, Geulah had been supplementing the family income by running a kindergarten at home for neighbourhood children. At first, it attracted only a few tots, mainly from Orthodox families like the Amirs. But word spread. Geulah ran a firm, but attentive and even liberal kindergarten. And the numbers gradually rose. With the extra cash, the Amirs fixed up the yard, and added a second floor to their house, turning it into a spacious, red-roofed testament to the profits of honest labour.

Yigal was a quiet, unremarkable child. Self-sufficient, as children have to be in families of that size, and a bit of a loner. He studied for eight years at an ultra-Orthodox school, Agudat Yisrael Woolfson, about a kilometre from the house, and regularly accompanied Shlomo to the local Yemenite synagogue, Tiferet Tse'irim. "Most of the kids would be outside playing football," said Ofer Benvisti, a neighbour. "But Yigal would study or pray." "He didn't hang out with us," agreed Tsuri Mimon, who described himself as a childhood acquaintance. "He wasn't one of the guys."

At 14, Amir moved a little way out into the big world, travelling to Tel Aviv to the Yishuv Hehadash Yeshivah high school. Again this was an ultra-Orthodox, rather than a religious Zionist environment. Most of its graduates go on to full-time yeshivah study, avoiding military service. But Amir had the instincts of a fighter, and had set his heart on joining a combat unit. He found a programme that suited him perfectly. The five-year *hesder* arrangement was designed with young men just like Amir in mind, offering them a combination of army service and religious study. Amir alternated between service in the Golani combat unit, much of it on patrol in the fetid Gaza Strip or the tense Israeli security zone inside south Lebanon, and Torah study in the idyllic rural environment of Kerem B'Yavneh Yeshivah south of Tel Aviv. Fit and strong with a deceptively wiry physique, he was a dependable soldier – trusted, but not beloved, by his comrades. He was known for his readiness, unlike most soldiers, to actually volunteer for extra or arduous duty, when it would have been easier to duck the additional load. He was highly regarded by his commanders for the "thoroughness" with which he carried out house-to-house searches for suspected violent Palestinian activists in Gaza. And he was also known to be fanatically religious. "He always got to synagogue first," said his colleague Boaz Nagar, who also remembered him hectoring the other religious soldiers to get up for prayers, when they'd rather have grabbed some extra sleep. "He was stubborn as a mule," said Nagar, "didn't let us breathe." At Kerem B'Yavneh, his commitment became a virtual compulsion. Teachers remember a solitary, determined pupil who excelled in his studies and relished the long hours. "He was an outstanding student," says the yeshivah head, Mordechai Greenberg. "He wasn't involved in politics. He was no radical. Just a smart, pleasant kid." In short, Yigal Amir had grown up into just the young man his mother had wanted: as one of the disenchanted parents of a child at Geulah's kindergarten was to say later, "She educated her children to follow things through, to honour their commitments. If they believed in something, to see it through to the end."

After army service, many Israelis take a year off, to travel and see the world. When his *hesder* programme was completed, though, true to his work ethic, Amir opted for something more practical. He got a job for the summer of 1992 with the somewhat shadowy Liaison Bureau, an office supervised by the Prime Minister's Office that sends emissaries to the former Soviet Union, to teach Hebrew and carry out other less-publicised missions. After obtaining the requisite security clearances and training, Amir was dispatched to Riga for three months.

On his return, the following year, he enrolled at Bar-Ilan, a university outside Tel Aviv aimed at promoting excellence in both academia and religious Zionism, but with something of a reputation as a hotbed of right-wing political activism. Again, Amir made life hard for himself, signing up for an exhausting programme that combined law studies, some computer classes, and long hours too in the university *kolel* – the campus yeshivah where about 400 of the most dedicated Orthodox students spent any free time poring over religious texts.

Yigal Amir entered Bar-Ilan just weeks after the Rabin–Arafat handshake on the White House lawn. While opinion polls showed about two-thirds of Israelis backing what Rabin described as "a gamble for peace", Amir was not among them. Neither teachers nor friends remember the Amir of the pre-Bar-Ilan days being particularly outspoken about politics. His mother, incidentally, was running that very winter on a Labour ticket in an unsuccessful campaign for a town council seat in Herzliyah. But the combination of the right-wing environment at Bar-Ilan, the dramatic government steps to an agreement with the Palestinians, and his own compulsive nature wrought a change. "Only when he began studying here did he become active in right-wing organisations," says Yaron Yehoshua, who knew Amir as a child and is now a student leader at Bar-Ilan.

Amir became a man possessed. He struck up strong friendships with a small group of fellow students at the *kolel*, chiefly the former Kach activist Avishai Raviv, head of Eyal. And he went into action to counter the government. Whenever Islamic suicide bombers, bent on torpedoing the Israeli–Palestinian reconciliation, struck at Israeli targets, said Rabbi Aharon Katz, the deputy head of the *kolel*, "Amir became more activated, more energised."

Fellow students say a girlfriend might perhaps have provided an outlet for some of that energy. But Navah Holtzman, the 22-year-old love of Amir's life, broke up with him at the end of 1994 after a five-month relationship. Holtzman remembered a different Yigal Amir – "not the sort to shout or stand out" – but, still, not the man she wished to spend the rest of her life with. Soon after leaving Amir, she met and then married another Bar-Ilan student, Shmulik Rosenbaum, and the couple now live in the West Bank settlement of Alon Shvut.

The breakup pushed Amir into a new frenzy of right-wing activism, say student colleagues. He helped organise student protests on the pedestrian bridge to Bar-Ilan across the major Geha highway. On occasions, the protesters would come down from the bridge, and block the traffic by lying down in the road. He organised campus hunger strikes and protest tents. When settlers sought ways to subvert Rabin's declared freeze in West Bank building, he went out to help them – assisting in the establishment of the illegal settlement of Ma'aleh Yisrael, and in the summer of 1995 joining the settlers of Efrat, near Bethlehem, in a campaign of passive resistance to army evacuation from a symbolic new neighbourhood on a barren hilltop at the settlement's edge. He organised a demonstration of Bar-Ilan students outside the Ashkelon home of Knesset member Alex Gold-farb, who had defected from a right-wing party to support the Rabin coalition. Along with about 800 other army reservists, Amir also signed a statement declaring that he would refuse to participate in the West Bank pullout.

And, most significantly, he began organising weekends away for like-minded students, solidarity Sabbaths spent with the 450 settlers in the heart of Hebron, or the 30 families at Netzarim, to the north of the Gaza Strip. The most successful of those weekends was on the Sabbath between the Jewish New Year and the Day of Atonement, the weekend of Friday, 29 September 1995. In the days beforehand, Amir, Raviv and a few fellow enthusiasts had been energetically recruiting on the campus, urging students to spend that Shabbat in Hebron – to send an unmistakable message of defiance to the government, and backing for the settlers, as an immediate response to the festive 28 September White Housing signing of Oslo II. At 1 o'clock that Friday, when students gathered at the entrance to Bar-Ilan for the journey to Hebron, it was clear that the call had been answered. More than 500 people turned up, filling the eight buses to bursting point. Yaron Kaner, a journalist who was writing an investigative article on Avishai Raviv's Eyal movement, was one of those who went along. The sheer mass of people, he recalled, was a triumph of solidarity, but a nightmare of logistics. For one thing, there weren't enough beds in the various Jewish-held buildings in Hebron for the students to sleep in. Kaner himself could only find space on the roof of one of the settler buildings, in the Avraham Avinu complex and, coincidentally, spent that night under the stars together with Yigal and Hagai, Amir's look-alike older brother.

It was a weekend of prayers in the Tomb of the Patriarchs, and of lectures and workshops with Hebron settlers – hammering home a unanimous message of opposition to the peace process and concern for their own safety and future. Amir, says Kaner, was quite clearly the main organiser, standing up at meal times to read out the timetable. On the Friday night, during a meal after evening prayers at the Tomb, it was Amir who got up to welcome the group. "We're glad that all of you have come to spend the Sabbath in the city of our fathers, and to contribute not a little to strengthening the Jewish presence here," he told them. "Yes," he went on, "we invited 400 people and 540 came. And that has caused a few organisational problems. But please co-operate, so that everything can work well."

On the Sabbath morning, Rabbi Eliezer Waldman, co-head of the *hesder* yeshivah at Kiryat Arba, gave a sermon during the service in the Tomb. According to Kaner, the rabbi accused the government of working with the Arabs against the settlers, and stressed the Jews' historical and religious rights to the city. Later that day, some of the students went on armed "patrols" through the Arab streets of the town. According to some reports, Amir's patrol provoked something of a disturbance. A Palestinian photographer claimed his camera was smashed, and there was talk of Palestinian windscreens being shattered. But such minor clashes between Jews and Arabs in Hebron had long been almost routine, and no action was taken.

Exceptionally successful though the weekend had been, it was, for Amir, still deeply unsatisfactory. No amount of campus activism, no quantity of weekend solidarity trips, it was becoming clear, would be sufficient to halt the West Bank land handover. The opposition parties, led by the Likud, were performing well in the polls, and the betting among optimistic rightists was that Labour would probably fall from power at the next elections. But those elections were still more than a year away. And by then, if the autonomy timetable unfolded as planned, Yasser Arafat would have control of all the West Bank's big cities, bar a tiny Jewish enclave in Hebron, and much more of the West Bank besides.

As a dedicated scholar, Amir had spent hours studying Jewish texts dealing with the concepts of *din rodef* and *din moser* and debating with colleagues in the *kolel* and outside as to the applicability of these concepts to the leaders of the present government. One university friend, identifying himself only as A., gave an extraordinary interview to a Hebrew newspaper, describing a conversation on the issue involving Amir, himself, and several other friends. "He believed that Peres and Rabin merited *din rodef*," A. recalled, "and he used Maimonides [the medieval Jewish religious authority] to justify this, saying that since they were making peace with Arafat, handing over Israeli land, they were the equivalent of collaborators, abandoning Jews, and it was thus right to kill them. We all argued against him when he spoke like that. His interpretation was warped. I said to him, 'Okay, say you take a gun and shoot them. What have you achieved?'"

Amir's response, A. went on, was to say that "'Peres and Rabin are snakes. Cut off their heads, and the snake will lose its way. Poke out their eyes and they're in the dark. They must both be killed, because each eggs the other on. The state will be saved if someone gets up and eliminates them. There will be elections. Bibi [Netanyahu] will come to power.' That was the salvation Yigal wanted."

A. countered that "'only rabbis can give a ruling on this. Your approach has no backing.' He said, 'The rabbis are all cowards, all afraid to interpret Jewish law my way. Only I am properly interpreting Maimonides.'" Still, A. continued, "It was all theoretical, no one thought it would ever come to anything."

In fact, Amir meant every word that he said. Together with Hagai and their closest confidant, Dror Adani, a friend from Yigal's army days who'd also been a regular at the settler weekends, he had been stalking Rabin and Peres with increasing intensity throughout 1995. Hagai had stolen a considerable amount of *matériel* from the army; another of Yigal's friends from the Kerem B'Yavneh yeshivah, Eric Schwartz, now a commando in the Golani brigade, had allegedly got them some more, and they had built up a weapons cache at their Herzliyah home – explosives and hand-grenades hidden away close to where Geulah Amir's kindergarten tots played innocently each morning. Some of these explosives were earmarked for attacks on Arabs – on prisoners released in the course of the peace process, on leading Palestinian official Faisal Husseini, and on Arafat himself (one plan, said by Hagai to be extremely workable, was to shoot down the Palestinian leader's helicopter). But though considerable energy was devoted to the subject of attacking Palestinians, and though other Bar-Ilan students, allegedly including a 20-year-old fellow law student and West Bank settler named Margalit Har-Shefi, were co-opted to the project, Peres and especially Rabin remained the top priority.

Yigal Amir, Har-Shefi and Adani all reportedly sought rabbinic sanction for killing Rabin. Adani told investigators he found no rabbi willing to grant approval; Hagai Amir told a different story under interrogation, saying that one West Bank rabbi did tell Yigal and Adani that Rabin deserved to die. Har-Shefi, too, reportedly told her investigators that she received a rabbi's sanction, but refused to name the rabbi concerned. Meanwhile, the brothers and Adani debated how best to carry out the murder. They toyed with the idea of placing a bomb under Rabin's car, or a remote-controlled device on a route they knew he'd be taking. They discussed firing an anti-tank missile at the Rabin Cadillac, or pouring nitroglycerine into the plumbing at Rabin's home to trigger an explosion. Yigal and Hagai, who had served as a sniper in the army, made a scouting trip to Rabin's home in Ramat Aviv, assessing the best vantage points for possible sniper fire. Hagai had tried in vain to get issued with an M-16 rifle during one of his regular stints of reserve service, the idea being to fit a telescopic sight, and lie in wait on Rabin's street for the perfect moment. They even discussed blinding Rabin with a fire-bomb in a model aeroplane, or trying to obtain an interview with Rabin, purportedly for Yigal's law studies, and blowing him up with a booby-trapped microphone or tape recorder.

When all these plans came to nought, Yigal set off on more straightforward assassination missions: on 22 January 1995, he waited for Rabin at Yad Vashem, the holocaust memorial museum in Jerusalem, but the Prime Minister's visit was cancelled because two Islamic suicide bombers killed 21 people that day in a bombing at the Beit Lid intersection near Netanyah. Exactly three months later, he set off to kill Rabin again at the Mimouna folklore celebrations of Jews from North Africa at the Nof Yerushalayim hall, but was stopped by security guards from entering the building. And on 11 September, he planned to shoot Rabin at the inauguration of a highway interchange at Kfar Shmaryahu, near Amir's own home. But the ceremony was over by the time he arrived, and Rabin had gone on to his next engagement.

On the way to synagogue on Saturday, 4 November, Yigal and Hagai returned to their favourite subject, and specifically the chances of killing Rabin and escaping unharmed at that night's Tel Aviv

pro-peace rally. Hagai later acknowledged to the police, "I supported the plan to kill Rabin, but I wasn't prepared to die in the
process." And that's exactly what he thought would happen to any
would-be assassin amid the expected tight security that night. Hagai
claims he told his brother that the only way to get Rabin at the rally
would be with a sniper's rifle – which, despite his best efforts, he had
been unable to obtain. But Yigal was prepared to take the chance –
to try to kill Rabin even if it killed him. That evening in synagogue,
he prayed that, finally, he would be granted the opportunity to
assassinate the Prime Minister, and that his own life would be spared.

In his room once the Sabbath was over, he extracted his pistol
from among his most treasured possessions – which included a book
published in memory of Baruch Goldstein, and Frederick Forsyth's
methodical assassination thriller *The Day of the Jackal*. He had taken
out a gun licence two years earlier, falsely stating on his application
form that he lived in the West Bank, in order to establish the need
for self-defence required under Israel's gun-control regulations.
Now he loaded the 9-mm Baretta carefully, alternating hollowed-
out dumdum bullets, which Hagai had prepared, with ordinary
bullets, tucked the gun between his trousers and his right thigh, and
let himself out of the house.

An Egged bus took him to the junction of Arlosoroff and Ibn
Gvirol Streets, and from there he walked to the Kings of Israel
Square, removing his skull-cap *en route*. He wandered around the
stage area, but concluded that it would be impossible to get a clear
shot at Rabin from there. And then, fatefully, he found his way to
the ill-lit, improperly secured VIP car park beneath the stage, and
hung around in the shadows for perhaps as long as 40 minutes,
waiting for his moment. It was the ideal place from which to strike.
Micha Goldman, the deputy Education Minister, said later that there
were "at least 20 people" milling around down there who weren't
sporting the necessary security tags. Amir cut a casual figure, standing
with his hands in his pockets, or perching on a large, white, knee-
high concrete planter. The uniformed policemen who spotted Amir
assumed that he, like the other plain-clothes young men there, was a
detective or a Shin Bet agent. This time, he knew he would be able
to find his target.

Amir could, as he told his interrogators matter-of-factly afterwards, easily have shot Shimon Peres. As the only known filmed
evidence of the assassination, shot from a low rooftop opposite the
car park by an amateur cameraman named Ronni Kempler, shows

quite clearly, the Foreign Minister came down the stairs from the stage a short while ahead of Rabin, and paused in the car park to shake hands across a barricade with supporters, and to hold a brief conversation with Rabin's driver. Kempler's grainy footage shows Amir watching impassively, with a clear line of shot, from just metres away. Had Rabin not stopped midway down the stairs, to go back and thank the rally organisers, leaving Peres to go on without him, Amir might well have been able to execute the dual murder he had most dearly wanted, cutting the heads off both "snakes". As it was, he held his nerve and his fire, watched Peres drive away, and awaited his primary target.

When Rabin came down the stairs, and walked the few paces to his Cadillac, he passed right in front of Amir, standing between the stairs and the car just to the left of Rabin's path. Amir even joined in the mild applause for the Prime Minister, but as Rabin passed, Amir darted up the two or three paces to his back, slipping between a young media student who had been trying to interview Rabin and one of the Prime Ministerial bodyguards. His gun right up against Rabin's back, Amir fired three times – two dumdum bullets penetrating Rabin's lungs, the third striking a bodyguard. "I aimed for the centre of the back," Amir told interrogators later. "From that kind of range, you don't need to be any kind of shooting genius." Indeed, forensic evidence suggested that the pistol had actually been touching Rabin's suit when the first shot was fired. "Now I'm satisfied," Amir told his police interrogators later that evening, as the surgeons were fighting their losing battle to save Rabin's life. "I'd been planning to kill him for a long time."

Geulah Amir had been at a friend's house, watching TV, when the coverage of the assassination flashed on to the screen. Recognising her second-oldest child gripped in a police headlock, she wailed, "What has our son done?" and hurried home to husband Shlomo. "He's destroyed us, this boy," Shlomo Amir was quoted as telling a friend that night. "I don't understand who or how the mad idea to take a life got into his head. That's not what we taught him at home." When Shin Bet agents arrived that evening to search the house and question the parents, Shlomo told them, "Go check at Bar-Ilan. That's where he was brainwashed. Not at home."

In the days that followed, Shlomo and Geulah produced an anguished letter of regret and condolence for Leah Rabin, and Geulah gave television interviews plaintively begging forgiveness, insisting that they had no idea of what their sons had been up to, no idea that their home had been turned into a weapons cache, no idea where it had all gone so terribly wrong. At first, most of the parents at Geulah's kindergarten stood by her, but the discovery of explosives stashed at the house changed the minds of many. And after Hagai was arrested on 5 November, and Geulah attended a court hearing, blowing him kisses and muttering "liar" throughout a police investigator's testimony, more of the initial sympathy slipped away. Then Hagai himself reportedly told police interrogators he and Yigal had debated with their father the question of staging attacks on "left-wingers". Shlomo, said Hagai, "understood the idea". And in late December, under questioning, Shlomo Amir reportedly confirmed that Yigal and Hagai had discussed the need to kill Rabin in front of both parents at home. Yigal raised the issue "four or five times" in the months before the assassination, his father acknowledged. Geulah told investigators a different story, saying that she had seen Hagai tampering with bullets, but thought he was preparing ammunition for self-defence, and claimed never to have heard talk of killing Rabin.

As suspicions grew that the Amir parents and possibly siblings had some advance knowledge of the assassination plotting, the family began to close ranks around the jailed brothers. Having initially said she disowned Yigal, Geulah attended the opening of his trial on 19 December with Shlomo in tow, and was rewarded with a series of smiles and waves from the assassin. In letters from jail, Hagai was quoted as writing to his parents: "Yigal did a great deed. He did it in the name of God." And in mid-December, with her mother in the room, Yigal's sister Hadas, 15, gave a television interview to the BBC in which she expressed open support for the assassination. "Only Gali," she said, using Yigal's family nickname, "knew the meaning of 'to love your country, to love Israel, to do anything for your country'. He was the only one who had the guts to do it."

Hagai Amir and Adani continued to insist they knew nothing in advance of Yigal's specific plan to kill Rabin on 4 November, and Yigal was pleased to take solitary blame. At his various court hearings, he walked into court smiling broadly, and often used the minutes before the proceedings began to issue long monologues explaining his actions – evincing no remorse, no hint of self-doubt. His body language in court – his open-mouthed gum-chewing, and especially that semi-constant cocksure smile – revolted many Israelis. There were calls for him to be hidden away behind a screen. One newspaper, Ma'ariv, published a supplement that it said was dedicated to wiping the smile off Amir's face. But the assassin continued to act with the arrogant air of a man certain he had done no wrong, even filing a request for a day's leave from his isolation cell, in jail near Beersheba, to attend the December wedding of one of his sisters, Vardit. Needless to say, he was turned down.

In the hearings leading up to his indictment, Amir offered clear, simplistic justifications for the assassination – questioning the legitimacy of the government, rejecting the right of Israeli Arab citizens to play a role in Israeli democracy, highlighting what he saw as Rabin's contemptuous abandonment of the settlers, branding Arafat's Palestinians as unreformed terrorists. And, as he had done in his debates on campus before, he invoked Jewish religious law in support of the assassination.

In his first court appearance, before Judge Dan Arbel in Tel Aviv district court two days after the murder, he said it was "sad" that the Islamic suicide attacks had failed to unite the people of Israel against the peace process, and "fascinating" that the people were now united "because of me. I mean Rabin is already dead, so what unites them?" he wondered out loud. "Maybe he left a will that everyone has to condemn me at the same time? A whole nation ignored the fact that a Palestinian state is being set up here, with an army of terrorists we are going to have to fight. Everyone is shocked by the killing of a Prime Minister... who only felt responsible for the security of 98 per cent of the state and didn't give a damn about the other 2 per cent. A Prime Minister like that is not a Prime Minister for me. He was elected by Arabs, 20 per cent of his voters were Arabs. I was at that [Tel Aviv pro-peace] demonstration. Has anyone pointed out that 50 per cent of those there were Arabs? Should those Arabs determine my future in this state? If you are prepared for them to determine the future of the state, then put them in the security cabinet. What will you do when there are 2 million Arabs in the state? Give the state to the Arabs?

"I didn't do this to stop the peace process," he went on later, "because there is no such thing as the peace process. It's a war process. My aim was to shake up public opinion. People are indifferent to the fact that they are setting up a Palestinian state here, and an army of terrorists, who are being given weapons, not for purposes of peace. Anyone who really believes that the terrorists will protect us is wrong. And according to religious law, when a Jew gives up his land and his people to the enemy, one is obliged to kill him."

When the judge interrupted, to ask him which rabbi had explained Jewish law to him like that, Amir answered: "Nobody taught me that. I've been learning Talmud all my life, and I know all the details."

"But in the Ten Commandments it says, 'Thou shalt not kill,'" the judge persisted. "Where have you thrown the Ten Commandments?"

"The Ten Commandments haven't been abolished. In the Torah there are 613 commandments. There are commandments more important than 'Thou shalt not kill.' There's 'the saving of life'. If someone goes to kill another person, you are duty-bound to kill the attacker first."

Time and again in the weeks that followed, asked who had helped him, which rabbis had given him sanction for murder, Amir answered: "I acted alone. And maybe God worked with me." But to his interrogators, he had reportedly acknowledged that he had received unequivocal rabbinical sanction for the killing.

In either case, many of his explanations had sounded familiar to the Israeli public the first time he detailed them. For although he had taken opposition to the government to a horrific, unprecedented extreme, it was, terribly, a logical extreme. The months of right-wing political protest about the government's dependence on Arab votes for its majority, the routine, largely unopposed chants of "Rabin is a traitor" at opposition demonstrations, the rabbinical injunctions against the West Bank withdrawal and the "academic" rabbinical discussion of *din moser* – all of these had crystallised in the compulsive, aggressive mind of Yigal Amir. It was a murderous combination.

15

A Complete Collapse of Security

AT FIRST IT HAD seemed so straightforward. A lone gunman takes advantage of a split-second lapse in security to shoot dead the Israeli Prime Minister.

But in the first few weeks after the assassination, the plot seemed to thicken almost by the day. And the initial assessment that Yigal Amir had been able to hit his target because of a catastrophic, but one-in-a-million, momentary security breakdown gradually gave way to mounting evidence of a wholesale malfunctioning of much of the Israeli law enforcement and security network.

At the root of the failure was a fundamental misconception, shared by Yitzhak Rabin himself: no matter how bitter the differences over government peace policies, and how deep the rifts in Israeli society they were laying bare, no Jew would go so far as to kill a fellow Jew for political reasons – no Jewish Israeli citizens would ever stoop so low as to try to thwart the government by murdering its leaders.

It was, of course, a misconception that should have been shattered by a moment's objective analysis of even relatively recent Israeli history. Little more than a decade earlier, in February 1983, after all, just one such Jewish Israeli citizen, Yonah Avrushmi, had tossed a hand-grenade into the midst of a Peace Now rally in Jerusalem – held to demand the resignation of then Defence Minister Ariel Sharon for his role in the Sabra and Shatilla massacres in Lebanon – and killed a fellow Israeli, Emil Grunzweig. Here was proof positive that Jew would, could – indeed had – killed Jew because of ideological differences.

Even if memories failed to stretch back quite that far, then the February 1994 massacre in Hebron's Tomb of the Patriarchs should surely have exposed the absurdity of dismissing the Jewish threat.

Bent on destroying the peace process, Baruch Goldstein targeted innocent Arabs at prayer – true, not Jews. But could there really have been any doubt that, if the extreme right wing could produce someone capable of opening fire into the backs of kneeling worshipers in a house of prayer, eliminating one or two reviled secular Jewish figures would hardly be unthinkable?

Moreover, in the few weeks before the assassination, apart from the inflammatory rhetoric which had become the norm, right-wing radicals had repeatedly demonstrated their readiness to actually use violence: the attack on Housing Minister Binyamin Ben-Eliezer's car; the disturbance at the English-speakers' day-out at Wingate; the attempt to run pro-peace Environment Minister, Yossi Sarid, off the main Tel Aviv–Jerusalem highway; the attempts to assault Police Minister Moshe Shahal and Chief of Staff Amnon Lipkin-Shahak – the writing on the wall could hardly have been clearer.

And, it must be said, there were some fairly influential people reading it correctly. Chief among them was a man who, because of the restrictions of Israeli military censorship, was only identified by his Hebrew initial Kaf – the head of the Shin Bet security agency. In December 1995 the media violated censorship and published Kaf's name and photograph, revealing him to be Carmi Gilon. When Gilon was about to be appointed in early 1995, several leading right-wing activists issued strong objections, noting that his Haifa University master's thesis, and much of his field work in the Shin Bet, had focused on countering right-wing extremism. Such a man, they argued, was not the ideal figure to head the Shin Bet, which ought, surely, to be led by someone whose main expertise lay in the area that dominated the service's work: confronting Palestinian extremism.

With the advantage of his years of expertise, Gilon did recognise the danger signs of escalating right-wing tension. In the summer of 1995, he met, extraordinarily, both with Rabin and with opposition leader Netanyahu, and warned them of the urgent need to find a way of moderating the poisonous political climate, before it overflowed into real violence. He also met, again in a move almost without precedent, with a group of leading journalists, and told them the same thing.

Long before, back in January 1994, another voice had spoken out. But Professor Yehoshafat Harkabi, the incisive analyst who had been Israel's military intelligence chief in the 1950s, was by then a relatively marginal figure, and his warning was ignored even by those to whom he issued it. Seven months before he died of cancer, Harkabi predicted in an extensive interview with two researchers from Ben-Gurion University in the Negev that the internal argument over the eventual dismantling of West Bank settlements would be "so terrible" as to trigger assassination. "Rabin," he specified, "will not die a natural death. Not that I wish this on him, God forbid." Perhaps they discounted this as hyperbole; perhaps they feared to tempt fate. But when the researchers subsequently published extracts of that interview, they deleted the stark warning. The prophet of doom went unheard.

If Gilon was alert to the threat, perhaps even he didn't take it completely seriously. A few days after the Wingate incident, American secret service agents contacted their Shin Bet counterparts, seeking improved security arrangements for United States ambassador Martin Indyk. At a subsequent meeting, Gilon is understood to have reassured the Americans, telling them that while there was a real fear of a serious Jewish attack on Arabs or on Arab holy sites such as the mosques atop the Temple Mount, it was "not thought likely" that Israeli leaders, or foreign diplomats for that matter, would be targeted.

In any case, Gilon's sense of foreboding was all too evidently not communicated down the hierarchy through to the lower reaches of the organisation he controlled. Nor, evidently, did it permeate the offices of the justice ministry or the police. Unequivocal proof has been hard to come by that one or more of the rabbis with whom Yigal Amir and his co-planners were in contact gave a specific religious sanction for Rabin's assassination. But there can be no denying that the question was discussed by many of Israel's most prominent rabbinical authorities, no underestimating the impact on impressionable minds of rulings such as the rabbinic injunction to disobey West Bank withdrawal orders, no escaping the violent tone of rabbinical talk of laying remote-control bombs to thwart settlement evacuation. There is, in short, no avoiding the fact that some in the Israeli rabbinical community helped create an environment in which Amir had good cause to feel, at the very least, that he would not be unanimously damned for murdering the Prime Minister, indeed that there would be a good many ready to praise him, even publicly, as a new Jewish hero. And yet, as the climate of hostility escalated in the course of 1995, none of these rabbis – not the ones who called on soldiers to disobey army orders, not the ones who sought their colleagues' rulings on the applicability of *din moser* to

Rabin, not the ones who eulogised Baruch Goldstein, not even the one who advocated laying remote-control bombs – was so much as called in for questioning by the police or Shin Bet, much less indicted. The fundamentalist Jewish incitement went unchecked. The spiritual seeds of the assassination were freely sown.

Still, even given the lack of will to take on the spiritual fathers of the incitement, the Shin Bet – which enjoyed a somewhat inflated reputation as one of the world's finest intelligence agencies – should at least have been able to target those most likely to respond. People like Yigal Amir, for instance.

Far from being the anonymous figure described in the first shocked hours after the assassination, Amir was a well-known right-wing activist. Not only had several of his university friends heard Amir boast about his plans to kill Rabin, but one of them had also even passed on a warning to that effect, albeit under somewhat convoluted circumstances, to the Shin Bet. Hila Frank, who was studying for a master's degree at Bar-Ilan, befriended Amir in the spring of 1995. They met at one of the frequent demonstrations on the highway bridge, and friendship blossomed on some of the West Bank weekends they both attended. One day in June, they chanced to meet in a corridor on campus, and "in the course of our conversation," said Frank, a 23-year-old Haifa resident, "he suddenly blurted out that Rabin must be killed. Then Yigal said that he had already said *Vidui* [the Jewish confessional prayer said on the brink of death] – and that lit a red light for me."

That same evening, Frank met a good friend of hers, a former Bar-Ilan student named Shlomo Halevy, who knew Amir. Like Frank, Halevy was not disposed to take Amir's talk overly seriously, but he agreed to find a way to pass on a warning, without actually turning Amir in to the authorities. What Halevy did was to concoct a little fabrication. He contacted his former commander in the army's intelligence corps, and described a fictitious conversation he said he'd overheard in the public lavatory at Tel Aviv's central bus station, in which one man was telling another about his plans to kill Rabin. The intelligence officer immediately contacted the police, who in turn called in the Shin Bet. Halevy was summoned for questioning by Jerusalem police, and apparently elaborated some-what, saying he'd caught a glimpse of the potential assassin, whom he described as being short, of Yemenite appearance, and wearing a black skull-cap, and that he had learned from the conversation that the man was a student at Bar-Ilan. Halevy said later that he had been certain this information would be "enough for the security services to go on", but that if they had pressed him harder, he would have identified Amir fully. But the Shin Bet failed to extract a name, tried half-heartedly to follow up on what was merely one of hundreds of such warnings, and, coming up empty-handed, pigeonholed Halevy's evidence.

Astoundingly, however, Halevy was not the only person giving the Shin Bet intelligence information on Amir and his activities. Right-wing extremist Avishai Raviv persistently denied it, but it became widely accepted that he was in the employ of the Shin Bet, and that his Eyal group subsisted on Shin Bet funding – functioning as a kind of honey trap to attract extremists and facilitate their easy monitoring. The precise nature of Raviv's relationship with the Shin Bet remains a mystery. But there is reliable information indicating that, in the summer of 1995, Raviv was ordered by his Shin Bet controllers to compile a report for them on one of his campus colleagues: Yigal Amir.

Raviv came back with a document that highlighted Amir's extremist outlook, and suggested that he was capable of violent attacks on Arabs. There was, however, apparently no mention of Amir's oft-repeated threats to assassinate Rabin. It may be that Raviv was playing a double game, taking Shin Bet money in return for scraps of information, while maintaining a deeper loyalty to his extremist right-wing friends. Alternatively, it may be that Raviv was a scrupulous and conscientious Shin Bet operative, but was recognised as such by Amir, Hagai Amir and Dror Adani, who therefore took pains to exclude him from their planning. Or, finally, it may be that Raviv just wasn't good at his job, and never got wind of Amir's intentions. (Hagai told his interrogators that Raviv "agreed with us that Rabin should be killed", and that Yigal wanted to involve Raviv in the murder plans. But Hagai rejected Raviv because, he said, he felt Raviv was "not an appropriate person".)

Raviv's personal history – from a left-wing family background, to teenage propagandising in the service of Meir Kahane – is diverse enough to allow for all possibilities. But, in the final analysis, the questions of Raviv's loyalties and effectiveness are not all that relevant. What is relevant is that the Shin Bet had itself identified Amir as a potential danger, and received a report confirming that he posed a threat – but then, scandalously, failed to match that in-house information with the new warning filed by Shlomo Halevy, a correlating of information that would immediately have exposed Amir as assassin-in-waiting, and prevented the death of Rabin.

As for the security failures on the night of the assassination, the flawed conception – that Jews were not a threat – was again central to everything that went wrong. For days ahead, the various units of the Shin Bet, the police and other relevant parties, had been engaged in prolonged briefings for what, it was acknowledged, was a highly complex security operation. It was decided that about 1,000 security men from the various agencies would be deployed. The 13-storey City Hall, behind the stage at the Kings of Israel Square, would have all windows lit, to prevent a sniper aping Lee Harvey Oswald from a high, unobserved window. Expanded detachments of bodyguards would accompany Rabin and Peres. Escape routes were sketched out, in the event of an emergency.

But not once, at any of these briefings, nor in the briefings then passed on to the rank-and-file security operatives, was the possibility of a Jewish assassin so much as mentioned. The entire focus of the security operation was on countering the perceived threat from Palestinian fundamentalists – snipers, bombers, suicide bombers – especially in the wake of the previous week's assassination of Islamic Jihad leader Fathi Shkaki.

Security on the night was described by many of those there as "a joke". Several of the VIPs up on the main stage with Rabin were disturbed by the ease with which plainly unaccredited personnel gained access to what should have been a highly restricted zone. An amateur photographer with a fake press pass had no problem getting in. People dodged around the overworked security men at the side of the stage, personal passes were being thrown back and forth – the casual air reflected the feel-good atmosphere of the evening, but not the wider realities.

But it was in the parking area that the worst lapses occurred. Amir's presence, though unaccountable, was dismissed as irrelevant by Boaz Eran and Motti Serchi, two newly recruited policemen on duty in the car park that night, and doubtless dismissed too by the plain-clothes detectives deployed in the area. To cameraman Ronni Kempler, filming from above, Amir immediately looked suspicious, "like a potential murderer" he said later, and so he focused on Amir for long seconds of his film. But to the security personnel, Amir was plainly Jewish, and thus no cause for concern. The "sterile" area was not only infiltrated by Amir, but by at least 20 other people lacking the requisite security tags, according to eyewitnesses. The whole area was poorly lit, making it a gunman's paradise. Rabin's Cadillac was parked, ready for him, at least an hour before his departure, constituting a perfect marker for an assassin. Peres, leaving a few seconds before Rabin, was unaccountably allowed to linger for a short chat with Rabin's driver – standing exposed and vulnerable. Last-minute changes of plan may have left some security men unaware that Peres and Rabin were even leaving.

At the briefings, there had been talk of 10 bodyguards fanning out around Rabin as he moved around. But when Rabin came down the stairs, he had only five bodyguards close to him. One went a few paces ahead, to clear the route to the car. One stood to Rabin's right, and two to Rabin's left, where Amir was waiting. All four, captured for eternity in Kempler's amateur video, were looking ahead of them, toward the car; none was scanning the surrounding area. The fifth bodyguard – the man whose job it was to protect Rabin's back and watch the area behind him as the Prime Minister made his way to his car – turned back as Rabin walked from the bottom of the stairs to the car, reportedly responding to a request from Rabin to find out why Leah had been delayed a few seconds behind them. And thus it was that Amir was able to move from the Prime Minister's left and up behind him, untroubled and unnoticed. A bulletproof vest might have cushioned the impact of the shots. But Leah said later that the security agents had never suggested he wear one; and if they had, she acknowledged, he would doubtless have resisted the idea.

Even after the fatal bullets were fired, incompetence still reigned. Somebody – probably Amir himself – shouted that the shots were blanks. There was confusion as to whether Rabin had actually been harmed. Leah stood in shock for several seconds, alone and un-protected. As Rabin's driver, who unaccountably had not been briefed as to the best escape routes, sped toward the hospital via the only unblocked streets he could find, nobody in that vast security attachment had the presence of mind to call ahead, to warn the staff at Ichilov Hospital that the Prime Minister was coming in. And so, when the grey Cadillac finally pulled up, nobody was there to receive him.

Did that last display of incompetence make a terminal difference? Would immediate medical care – the nearest ambulance apparently tried to enter the car park the wrong way, across a retracting spiked metal barrier, and punctured all four tyres – or speedier progress to the operating table have saved Rabin's life? Two weeks after the assassination, a three-member state commission of inquiry, headed by the former Supreme Court Chief Justice Meir Shamgar, was charged with investigating the plethora of security failures that led to the assassination. It called in Shin Bet chiefs and agents, policemen, and eyewitnesses. And it called in Ichilov Hospital's Professor Gabi Barabash too, and asked him that final question. Choosing his words with the utmost care, Barabash acknowledged that, yes, "there is a question of, 'What if they had opened a more direct route [to the hospital for Rabin's driver].'" Barabash paused long and thought hard. "Even if he had arrived a couple of minutes earlier, it is unlikely that he would have lived. But the fact that we managed to revive him [Rabin]," he said at length, "leaves that question open."

Inevitably, as is the norm with high-profile political assassinations, new and more ludicrous conspiracy theories were hatched thick and fast – theories that, for the most part, run quickly aground when put up against the simple, incontrovertible fact that Amir was seen to pull the trigger, and has calmly and repeatedly declared since that he did so without the help or knowledge of anyone else. But there are two theories that deserve a mention. The first – initially propagated by Tel Aviv University historian Michael Har-Segor – holds that a conspiracy to kill Rabin extended deep into the Shin Bet, and that at least one of Rabin's bodyguards on 4 November was in on it, and helped facilitate the shooting. It was this bodyguard, the theory runs, who sowed confusion by shouting that the bullets were blanks. Yigal Amir was carefully selected to carry out the shooting, having had a file at the Shin Bet since 1992, when, it is claimed, he underwent a Shin Bet weapons and security training course before his trip to Latvia. Avishai Raviv, the theory goes, was deeply involved in the conspiracy, and helped incite Amir to murder, fuelling Amir's anti-Rabin sentiment day by day at Bar-Ilan. And after the assassination, the theory goes on, the traitorous bodyguard was executed by the agency. Amir himself asserted in one of his court appearances that a bodyguard had been killed. "Why don't you publish that they [the Shin Bet] liquidated one of Rabin's bodyguards?" he shouted to journalists on 3 December. The Israeli media did report the mysterious death of an Israeli security agent, named as Yoav Kuriel, and his secretive burial in the Yarkon military cemetery. But Israeli officials and Kuriel's family were quoted as denying that he had ever worked for the Shin Bet or had any connection with Rabin, and asserted that his death was an unrelated suicide. And Kempler's filmed evidence offers little support for the theory of a duplicitous bodyguard.

The second theory is more disturbing, particularly given the mounting evidence of the Shin Bet's involvement in Eyal and its employment of Raviv. According to this version of events, promulgated with almost desperate conviction by a handful of fringe right-wing activists, Shin Bet agents, far from being unaware of Yigal Amir's assassination plans, were on to him early – thanks to Raviv and/or other intelligence sources. So deeply had they penetrated Amir's inner circle, indeed, that they were able to substitute blanks for the bullets in Amir's gun. But Amir was one step ahead. He knew that the bullets had been switched. And so he replaced them again. That's why Amir, hoping to avoid being shot himself, shouted that the bullets were blanks as his gunfire exploded. And that's why the Shin Bet agents around Rabin weren't certain the Prime Minister was hurt, why nobody called ahead to Ichilov, why Leah Rabin was told something about a toy gun. This theory further holds that Raviv was responsible for sending a beeper message, received by several Israeli journalists immediately after Rabin was shot, that claimed responsibility on behalf of a right-wing extremist group, and stated: "We missed this time, but we won't next time." As a key part of the Shin Bet plot to entrap the extremist right, the theory runs, Raviv knew Amir was being allowed to get his shots in, but assumed that only blanks were fired, and that Rabin was thus unharmed.

It is, of course, tempting to dismiss this second theory out of hand, to argue that no responsible security service would take that kind of a chance with the Prime Minister's life. It is easy, furthermore, to see why the Israeli right wing would want to disseminate just such a theory, for it suggests that the Shin Bet deliberately sought to allow a right-wing extremist to be seen attempting to kill the Prime Minister, with all the negative political implications for the opposition cause.

But before putting it aside completely, perhaps it is worth noting the case of Eitan and Yehoyada Kahalani. These two brothers, residents of Kiryat Arba, were convicted in the Jerusalem District Court on 15 November – a coincidental week and a half after the Rabin assassination – of attempting to murder a young Palestinian, Ziyad Shami, in a February 1994 revenge killing for Palestinian extremist attacks. The two had stolen M-16 rifles from the Kiryat Arba settlement armoury, and laid in wait for Shami – a random victim – as he cycled home to his village, at Batir, near Hebron. But the Shin Bet knew of their plan from the start, and had tampered with their weapons – their guns wouldn't fire. They were taken into custody, and Shami cycled innocently home.

The "precedent" of the Kahalani brothers was enthusiastically recalled by conspiracy theory advocates in the weeks after the assassination. But the Shamgar Commission, its deliberations based not on self-serving speculation but on Kempler's film and the testimony of numerous witnesses, was reported in early December to have rejected all the conspiracy theories out of hand. Yitzhak Rabin had died because of a complete collapse of security. No sinister conspiracy. Just staggering incompetence. And before the Shamgar commission had even completed its deliberations, the head of Shin Bet, Carmi Gilon, had paid the price of that incompetence.

Gilon had offered to resign within days of the assassination, but had been urged by acting Prime Minister Shimon Peres to stay on and help rebuild the agency's shattered morale. On 5 January 1996, in a complex operation widely attributed to Shin Bet, the elusive bombmaker behind the Hamas suicide bus-bombings of the past two years, Yihiya Ayash, was killed in his Gaza hideout; a booby-trapped mobile phone he was using exploded and blew his head off. The death of Ayash – who had topped Shin Bet's wanted list for three years, and whom Rabin had personally ordered captured or eliminated – gave a welcome boost to the agency. Aware that the Shamgar Commission's findings would likely lead to his dismissal, and rather than waiting to be pushed, Gilon chose this moment to jump. On 7 January, he again submitted a letter of resignation to Peres. And this time it was accepted.

16

From Man to Myth

THE LOSS OF Yitzhak Rabin plunged Israel into a state of national despair. For outsiders, those with a more superficial understanding of the country and the region, the first question was how the Prime Minister's death would affect the delicate push toward Middle East peace. For them, it was some relief that the assassin was a Jew; had it been an Arab, they reasoned, the whole process would surely have ground to a halt.

But inside Israel, the fact that an Israeli Jew had pulled the trigger was the deepest cut of all. For this, clearly, was not the action of a deranged lunatic; Yigal Amir was a cool, calculating killer, who argued that he was doing the right thing for his people, and whose justifications for murder, if the truth were told, struck more than a faint chord in the hearts and minds of many thousands of his countryfolk.

That Rabin was struck down, of all places, at a rally dedicated to rooting out violence; that he fell just as he seemed to be embracing the Palestinian accords with full confidence for the first time; that his assassin was an ordinary, smart, yeshivah-educated ex-combat soldier – all these factors combined to produce an overwhelming sense of grief, not merely for the loss of Rabin himself, but for the irrevocable loss of national innocence. The last line had been crossed. If the Prime Minister could be gunned down by one of his own, then nothing was sacred anymore, nothing was stable or guaranteed. Israeli democracy itself was tottering. The notion that "national unity" would somehow always prevail was exposed as hollow.

There was, furthermore, something in Rabin's personality itself that seemed to magnify the loss to truly desperate proportions. In his absence, the contemptuous dismissal of settlers' complaints, the legendary irritability, the occasional disturbing sensation that here was a Prime Minister scrambling to react to events rather than planning for them – all these and other flaws were either forgotten, or somehow metamorphosed into virtues. Within hours of his death, Rabin was being elevated into a veritable national father figure, Mr Israel, guardian of security, embodiment of peace. And the outpouring of grief at the murder of such a figure was truly astounding.

Late into the night of 4 November, as Leah took her lingering leave of Yitzhak Rabin inside, thousands of Israelis flocked to Ichilov Hospital, to light memorial candles in his memory, and sing, over and over and over, bitter, tearful, plaintive renditions of that last "Song for Peace". At the Kings of Israel Square, tens of thousands who had earlier streamed home so uplifted by the rally, now flooded back, drawn by an appalled need to stand where they had stood before – when Rabin was alive and Israel was another country. There were similar scenes outside the Rabin home in Ramat Aviv, and the official residence in Jerusalem. Hurriedly improvised banners mourned the loss of "Our dead father", "Our beloved Yitzhak". Television broadcast through the night – a marathon of grief and horror. Come Sunday, many Israelis had lines under their eyes – from crying and lack of sleep. The country seemed quietened, numbed, uncertain and afraid.

In Jerusalem first thing on Sunday morning, a group of school-children picked up the vigil outside Rabin's residence. The railings and the pavement beneath them were caked with the wax of thousands of expired memorial candles. On Tel Aviv's Sheinkin Street, an eerie calm descended on the usually vibrant café society – everyone was buried in newspapers, their headlines screaming in unison: "Rabin assassinated".

In largely right-wing Jerusalem, where the city's walls and bill-boards were still plastered with posters announcing a memorial service for another slain Jewish leader – Meir Kahane, shot dead in New York five years before – opponents of the peace process were not letting Rabin's death still their voices. "Rabin is the one who more than anyone else caused this to happen," said one of a group of elderly people who regularly sat together in the fabled Café Atara. "He tried to give away land without a Jewish majority, and this drove some people to desperate acts."

For some, the news was still too difficult to absorb. "I heard it last night on duty and was in total shock," said soldier Meirav Shmueli. "A man like Rabin, so strong, murdered by a Jew, an Israeli, it's simply hard to believe." But for others, the act was, at least to a degree, understandable. "This guy who killed Rabin," said engineer Herzl Avitan, a Likud supporter, "wasn't some crazy guy, but a quality person, a soldier in Golani and a student at Bar-Ilan. Who knows how deep was the pain and anger he was feeling? You have to try to put yourself in his shoes."

When an argument broke out at a makeshift mourning-candle memorial set up at Zion Square in the city's centre, a face in the crowd yelled out: "Rabin was destroying the country, making the settlers feel like criminals!" "Shame on you, Rabin was a good man!" retorted another.

Twenty-two-year-old Shaike Kigal, wearing a crocheted skull-cap, stood in the Cardo shopping arcade, in the Old City's Jewish Quarter, collecting signatures and donations for the writing of a Torah scroll commemorating Jerusalem's 3,000th anniversary celebrations. "We have 72,000 signatures, and Rabin's was the first," he said. "I didn't agree with his policies, but the fact that a young guy who had almost the same life experience as me – the same family background and army service – and still could have shot him down in cold blood, that tells me something is seriously screwed up in this country."

At midday, Rabin's coffin, accompanied by eight generals, was driven the 60 kilometres from Tel Aviv to Jerusalem in an army truck. All along the route, traffic ground to a halt, people stood at attention. The grim convoy passed under several bridges over the main Tel Aviv–Jerusalem highway; on each, thousands crowded to catch a glimpse, their cars haphazardly halted. Before it began the long climb up the hills to Jerusalem, the convoy passed through Sha'ar Hagai, a last return to the point where Rabin's Palmah Harel Brigade fought its battles with Palestinian gunmen blocking the road to Jerusalem during the War of Independence.

At Bar-Ilan University, at about the same time, a memorial gathering was taking place. Students were sombre, some holding signs reading, simply: "We condemn." Faculty members talked about their horror at the murder, their disbelief that one of their own was responsible. At a press conference that followed, university president Shlomo Eckstein insisted that "We try to educate our students to love all Jews." There was, he said, a small crumb of comfort in the fact that Yoram Rubin, the Rabin bodyguard injured in the attack, was also a Bar-Ilan student, that the man who tried to save Rabin had also come from the university.

When Rabin's coffin arrived at the Knesset at 2 p.m., it was laid gently to rest on a raised bier in the broad forecourt of the parliament building – draped in a blue and white Israeli flag. Leah, son Yuval, daughter Dalia, and the Rabin grandchildren filed up, stood in tearful silence, then took seats at the side, Leah weeping, head bowed. Peres took her head gently in his hands as he passed, and embraced her tenderly. Supreme Court justices, the chief rabbis, ambassadors and other dignitaries paid their respects. Former military men-turned-Knesset members stood to attention in honour of their fallen comrade. And then an endless stream of ordinary Israelis – old and young, religious and secular, immigrant and veteran – began trickling past, carrying flowers, private messages, flags and countless candles. A long, blue line of policemen and several strands of rope kept the thousands a few metres away from the coffin itself. "Keep moving," said the uniformed officers, politely but firmly. "But he's my Prime Minister," objected an older woman, who wanted to photograph the bier. The policeman tried to move her on, and she lost her temper. "Why didn't you do that last night?" she asked. "Maybe then we wouldn't have to be here today."

As darkness fell on Jerusalem, a vast mass of people still waited to bid farewell. All through the night, hundreds of thousands converged on the Knesset from across the country. Even at 4 and 5 in the morning, it was impossible to get within hundreds of metres of the Knesset, never mind reach the coffin. As a chill breeze sprang up before dawn, young parents were frantically pushing toddlers in strollers up toward the parliament building, driven by an emotional compulsion to bid a personal farewell to the Prime Minister. All along the route up the hill to the Knesset, small, improvised memorials had been erected: dozens of candles placed to spell out the word "Why?" in Hebrew, or "Yitzhak"; photographs of Rabin affixed to rocks and surrounded by more candles.

A short drive away, in the section of the national cemetery on Mount Herzl reserved for the country's most prominent figures, Rabin's final resting place had been dug out, near the graves of former Prime Ministers Golda Meir and Levi Eshkol. Some of the grave-diggers, from the defence ministry's memorial unit, had cried as they shovelled away the earth. "It's an appalling feeling, digging the Prime Minister's grave," said Aharon Hamamy. "But that is our job. We are doing this to give Rabin the last respects that he is due. Our hands are shaking. Our hearts are breaking."

Outside Rabin's house in Ramat Aviv, thousands of youngsters spent the night in candle-lit mourning. "It encourages me, my children and my grandchildren that you are honouring Yitzhak in this wonderful way," Leah came out to tell them. "Yitzhak would have been very moved to see you here. This is where the demonstrators stood, and screamed 'Traitor' and 'Murderer' at him. It's a shame you didn't come then. But you're here now and that encourages us. Thank you for coming. I appreciate it, and I love you on his behalf."

By Monday morning, amid growing recriminations over the security failures that had left Rabin vulnerable, a massive 10,000-strong contingent of Israeli security personnel – 10 times the number that had been deployed in Tel Aviv 36 hours earlier – was gearing up to try to do a better job of protecting the dozens of international leaders who had flown in for the funeral. Here, unmistakably, was proof of the change in Israel's status in the region wrought during the three and a half years of Rabin's Prime Ministership.

King Hussein, who had watched his grandfather die of an assassin's bullet on Jerusalem's Temple Mount 44 years before, and narrowly escaped death that day himself, returned to the city where Rabin the soldier had taken full control, to mourn Rabin the peacemaker, the leader who had become an ally. Hosni Mubarak, who had refused so many of his good friend Rabin's entreaties to visit in the past, came now to mark his passing. Who better than Mubarak, who inherited power after the assassination of Anwar Sadat in 1981 and had only weeks before narrowly escaped the assassin's bullets on a trip to Ethiopia, could understand the trauma, the pain, the need for friends to stand up and be counted?

Yasser Arafat badly wanted to come. He had been having dinner with the visiting Portuguese Prime Minister Mario Suares when the American consul in Jerusalem, Edward Abington, the State Department's "ambassador to the Palestinians", phoned to tell him that Rabin had been murdered, and was sobbing so uncontrollably that he had to whisper to the consul, "Call me back in 10 minutes." Now Arafat spoke imploringly to Peres and to Leah Rabin. Yitzhak would have wanted me there, he argued. We had become real partners in the peace of the brave. Remember how he joked about me, after that long speech I made in Washington for Oslo II, when he said he was beginning to wonder if maybe I was close to being Jewish? But Arafat remained too controversial, too divisive a figure, when the pressing need was for internal Israeli reconciliation, for national healing. So security considerations were invoked and Arafat stayed at home in Gaza – taking care to ensure he was filmed watching the funeral respectfully on television, and sending a delegation of senior officials to represent him instead. (Later, on 9 November, Arafat paid a secret late-night condolence call to the Rabin home – his first visit to Israel. He sat bareheaded in the living room, drinking tea with Leah and the family, telling her that "we lost a great man".)

Also there, on that sad, silent Jerusalem hillside in the bright, early-winter sunlight, were the splendidly robed Information Minister and officials from Qatar, and the Foreign Minister and officials from Oman, where Rabin had been due to visit later in the month. The Prime Minister of Morocco was there; his King had sent a personal telegram. To stand at Rabin's graveside was to recognise that Israel was slowly taking its place among the nations of the Middle East, and to lament that it took his death to bring that change into the public consciousness.

At 2 p.m., when a two-minute siren sounded, all of Israel – or virtually all – stood in silence, taking its leave of Rabin, crippled by the two bullets that had left a vacuum at its core. At the cemetery, Leah stood, clad in black, with her family at her side, and the family of nations around her. Representatives from more than 80 countries – royalty from Britain's Prince Charles to Holland's Queen Beatrix, heads of state and of government from Australia to Turkey. Reading in his newspaper that the Albanian President would be attending, Cyprus's President Alexis Galnos, who'd met Rabin two years before, decided he'd better change his plans and attend. Estonia was swearing in a new government the next day, but President Lennart Meri left them to it, sending a formal seal of approval by fax from President Weizman's residence. Eduard Shevardnadze, re-elected President of Georgia the previous day, forsook his own celebrations and flew to Israel.

There were 11 speeches in all. Stilted, if heartfelt eulogies from Russian Prime Minister Viktor Chernomyrdin, from UN Secretary General Boutros Boutros-Ghalli, and from Spain's Prime Minister Felipe Gonzalez, representing the European Union. And an ill-conceived address from Weizman, a man perhaps still coming to terms with his own guilt feelings, wondering whether he should have been more supportive of Rabin's policies, whether in trying to somehow pull together a divided people, he had provided a measure of legitimacy for Rabin's most extreme opponents. Weizman conspicuously failed to use the funeral to endorse the Palestinian accords, instead merely noting Rabin's own "immense pride" at the breakthroughs, and talking casually of the many hours the two had spent alone together – "We ate some good food, drank some good drinks." Had Rabin been there, Yediot Aharonot's star columnist Nahum Barnea asserted, probably rightly, in the following day's paper, he would have dismissed the address "with a wave of his hand. Not serious. . . not presidential."

From the other seven speakers, though, a fitting tribute to Rabin – and to the policies he was pursuing – emerged. Mubarak, in his limited English, praised Rabin's vision, described his death as "a severe blow to our noble cause", and argued that only by redoubling peace efforts could "those traitorous hands hostile toward our goal" be thwarted and Rabin's memory properly honoured. But it was King Hussein who set the emotional tone for the event. Two nights earlier, he had telephoned Israel's ambassador in Jordan, Shimon Shamir, every 10 minutes for frantic updates on Rabin's condition. Now he began, typically, from the heart: "I never thought that the moment would come like this, when I would grieve the loss of a brother, a colleague and a friend, a man, a soldier who met us on the opposite side of a divide, who we respected as he respected us. A man I came to know because I realised, as he did, that we had to cross over the divide." Now Hussein spoke as though Rabin were still at his side, sighing that "I have never been used to standing, except with you next to me, speaking of peace, speaking about dreams and hopes for generations to come... Never in all my thoughts would it occur to me that my first visit to Jerusalem in response to your invitation, the invitation of the Speaker of the Knesset, the invitation of the President of Israel, would be on such an occasion."

His voice quiet but firm, the King then issued a challenge, to the people who believed in coexistence, to Arabs, to Jews, to stand up and be counted – whatever the price. "You lived as a soldier," he said of Rabin, "you died as a soldier for peace. And I believe it is time for all of us to come out openly and speak of peace. Not here today, but for all the times to come. We belong to the camp of peace. We believe that our one God wishes us to live in peace and wishes peace upon us... Let's not keep silent. Let our voices rise high to speak of our commitment to peace for all times to come, and let us tell those who live in darkness, who are the enemies of light, 'This is where we stand. This is our camp.'"

Hussein recalled his grandfather, gunned down at Jerusalem's Al-Aqsa Mosque, another who paid the ultimate price for peace. And, then, the King offered a prayer of his own, that "when my time comes, I hope it will be like my grandfather's, and like Yitzhak Rabin's". For after all, he said, "So many live and so many inevitably die. This is the will of God. This is the way of the world. But those who are fortunate and lucky in life are those who leave something behind. And you are such a man, my friend."

Late on 4 November, Shimon Peres had demonstrated his personal anguish at having had to inherit the Prime Ministership under circumstances too nightmarish to have ever been conceivable. Emerging from a crisis cabinet meeting held at the defence ministry in Tel Aviv, the offices where Rabin probably felt most at home, Peres had briefed the world's media to the effect that his colleagues had unanimously elected him acting Prime Minister, but had managed to do so without actually uttering his own name. The next morning, he had been at work in the Prime Minister's Office almost from the crack of dawn, but had concentrated on reassuring Rabin's staff that their jobs were safe – "I know you've lost a father," he told them – and had honoured his predecessor's memory by forbearing from so much as sitting in Rabin's chair, conducting business, instead, from the office sofa. Now, again, Peres showed his sensitivity, delivering a speech of grace, affection and, above all, of respect for a man who for years was his nemesis, but who had become almost his second half. "I didn't know that those would be our last hours together," he said of the Saturday night rally, but "I felt as if a special grace had descended on you, and suddenly you could breathe freely at the sight of the sea of friends who came to support your way and cheer you. You reached the summit, broke through the clouds, and from there you could view the new tomorrow. The view that was promised to the youth of Israel. Yitzhak, youngest of Israel's generals. Yitzhak, the greatest trailblazer of peace...

"You did not leave us a will," Peres concluded, "but you left us a legacy which we will follow firmly and faithfully. The nation weeps, but these are also tears of unity and resolve."

Shimon Sheves, the close family friend who had worked with Rabin through long years in opposition politics as well as after Rabin was restored to the Prime Ministership, spoke bitterly of the "abominable, murderous hand" that had put an end to Rabin's life. On the Saturday night, learning that Rabin was dead, he had told a television interviewer, "For me, the country is finished." And now the bitterness was still tangible. "I cannot accept that all of us," he said, "are standing here beside your casket... You fell on a night filled with optimism. You fell on a night full of joy and solidarity. You fell on a night in which you brought the support of the nation for your path, the road to peace, to a peak."

Now Eitan Haber came forward – the man who, for so many years, had written Rabin's speeches for him, taking the microphone himself to speak to Rabin. "Yitzhak," he said, "this is the last speech." Lightening the mood a welcome fraction, he pointed out, "Yitzhak, you know you had a thousand good qualities, a thousand advantages, you were great – yet singing was not your strong point. You were off key just a little bit during the song." Then Haber delivered the *coup de grâce*, tiptoeing along the borders of good taste to produce what many would come to remember as the symbol of Rabin's death. He recalled that, when the "Song for Peace" was over, Rabin folded his lyric sheet neatly away in his jacket. "In the hospital, after the doctors and nurses had cried, they handed me the paper which they found in your jacket pocket." And now, Haber produced the page itself, protected in a clear plastic folder, its lines stained blood red. "I want to read some of the words from the paper," said Haber, "but it is difficult for me. Your blood, your blood, Yitzhak, covers the printed words. Your blood on the page of the 'Song for Peace'. This is the blood which ran out of your body in the final moments of your life, and on to the paper between the lines and the words." And then Haber read again the lyrics to the song, the final song:

> Let the sun rise, and give the morning light
> The purest prayer will not bring back
> He whose candle was snuffed out and was buried in the dust
> A bitter cry won't wake him, won't bring him back
> Nobody will return us from the dead dark pit
> Here, neither the victory cheer nor songs of prayer will help
> So sing only a song for peace
> Do not whisper a prayer
> Better sing a song for peace
> With a great shout.

Gut-wrenching though Haber's address was, it was not the emotional centrepiece of the funeral. That was provided by Noa Ben-Artzi, Rabin's 18-year-old granddaughter, in a tearful, heart-breaking outburst. Where others had spoken of Rabin the leader, Rabin the peacemaker, Rabin the general, Noa addressed herself to Rabin the grandfather. "I know we are talking in terms of a national tragedy," she said, "but how can you try to comfort an entire people or include in it your personal pain, when Grandma doesn't stop crying, and we are mute, feeling only the enormous void that is left by your absence?" Failing to halt the tears, she continued, "Grandfather, you were, and still are, our hero. I want you to know that in all I have ever done, I have always seen you before my eyes. Your esteem and love accompanied us in every step and on every path, and we lived in the light of your values. You never neglected anyone. And now you have been neglected – you, my eternal hero – cold and lonely. And I can do nothing to save you, you who are so wonderful. People greater than I have already eulogised you. But none of them had my good fortune to feel the caress of your warm, soft hands and the warm embrace that was just for us... I have no feelings of revenge, because my pain and loss are so big, too big. The ground has slipped away from under our feet, and we are trying, somehow, to sit in this empty space that has been left behind... Having no choice, I part from you, a hero, and ask that you rest in peace, that you think about us and miss us, because we here, down below, love you so much. To the angels in heaven that are accompanying you now, I ask that they watch over you, that they guard you well. Because you deserve such a guard. We will love you, Grandpa, always."

Across the globe, on television broadcasts that night, where Rabin's funeral led the news, it was, more often than not, Noa's speech that was highlighted – despite the fact that, as she said, greater, or at least far more famous people than she, had spoken, and despite the fact that most of them had spoken English, while she had stuck to Hebrew. In Israel, especially, Noa's was the speech that stilled the nation, that chilled the spine, that set the tears rolling. And it was her depiction of Rabin the gentle grandfather that helped push what seemed to be the entire generation of Israel's teenagers into the streets, to surround Rabin's home in solidarity with Leah, to maintain a vigil, day after day, at the scene of the crime, to stream past the fresh grave on Mount Herzl.

There was one more speaker, that day on the hill, the man who, along with Hussein, Rabin probably saw as his closest friend among the suited ranks of international statesmen. President Clinton had flown in on Air Force One along with his wife, ex-presidents Carter and Bush, and dozens of top officials and politicians from Capitol Hill. And, a black skull-cap standing out on his grey hair, the head of the world's only superpower delivered a speech that showed a personal commitment to Rabin, and to Israel, that went some way toward restoring a sense of stability and solidity after those first terrible hours of shock. He ranged through Rabin's career mixing admiration with humour. He noted Rabin's preference for deeds rather than words, recalling Rabin's opening line at the Oslo II ceremony on 28 September: "'First the good news. I am the last speaker.'" But he also stressed Rabin's understanding of symbolism. And just as Rabin, in Washington, had urged his audience to take note of the presence on-stage of peace partners who until recently were enemies, so Clinton urged the viewing world to take stock of the notables gathered for the funeral. "Look at the leaders from all over the Middle East and around the world who have journeyed here today for Yitzhak Rabin and for peace," he urged. "It is he who has brought us together again here, in word and deed, for peace. Now it falls to all of us who love peace, and all of us who loved him, to carry on the struggle to which he gave life and for which he gave his life."

Perhaps, having grown up in the shadow of John F. Kennedy's assassination, Clinton understood better than many the sense of loss and fear that Israel was experiencing. For now he turned directly to the Israelis and told them, "Even in your hour of darkness, his spirit lives on, and so you must not lose your spirit. Look at what you have accomplished, making a once-barren desert bloom, building a thriving democracy in a hostile terrain, winning battles and wars, and now winning the peace, which is the only enduring victory. Your Prime Minister was a martyr for peace, but he was a victim of hate. Surely, we must learn from his martyrdom that if people cannot let go of the hatred of their enemies, they risk sowing the seeds of hatred among themselves. I ask you, the people of Israel, on behalf of my own nation, that knows its own long litany of loss from Abraham Lincoln to President Kennedy to Martin Luther King, do not let that happen to you. In the Knesset, in your homes, in your places of worship, stay the righteous course." And if you stay that course, he concluded, "neither will America forsake you. May our hearts find a measure of comfort, and our souls the eternal touch of hope."

As Clinton began to step away from the microphone, he paused, then came forward again, with a last, fond farewell. "Shalom, *haver*," he half-whispered. "Peace, my friend."

When all the words had been said, the mourners walked slowly behind Rabin's coffin as it was carried to its final resting place, then lowered gently into the ground. Now covered in black cloth, the casket disappeared from sight, with Leah, standing at the foot of the grave – Dalia to her left, Yuval to her right – eyes hidden behind her sunglasses, fingers interlocked in front of her, staring rigidly, relentlessly downwards. Leah and her family stayed by the grave for another full hour and a half. "I can't go home and leave him here," she said, over and over. But when Shlomo Lahat, co-organiser of that last rally, came hesitantly towards her, she greeted him fiercely. "I've heard that you've been crying," she said. "But you shouldn't feel guilty. It was destined to be. It could have happened anywhere." "He enjoyed it so much," said Lahat. "Suddenly he realised that they loved him. And then it was over."

In the days and weeks that followed, Israel emerged, slowly and hesitantly, from the paralysis of Rabin's loss. It was a different Israel – a country of shattered illusions, no longer professing itself a light unto the nations, destined to bleed long years from the wounds of Yigal Amir's gunfire. It was an Israel in which extremists were already showing they had learned little from the assassination, and in which many figures even in the mainstream had taken the easy way out – blaming others, rather than re-examining their own actions.

But perhaps most crucially, it was an Israel with its most painful division – the rift over relinquishing the West Bank to Palestinian rule – brutally exposed. The assassination had forced all Israelis to face the fateful question that had hung in the air since Rabin shook hands with Yasser Arafat: did they feel a greater commitment to democracy, or to their positions on the issues of peace and territory? The answer to that question, in the wake of the first attempt to destroy democratic rule in Israel, would determine whether the country could be made whole again.

The question was particularly sharp for the right – and all the more so for the religious right, or those rabbis and their followers who had made Jewish rule over the entire land promised by God to Abraham a primary obsession – to the detriment of the sanctity of human life and the Orthodox partnership with secular Jews in the Jewish state. And astoundingly, even as Israel sought to recover from the trauma of Rabin's killing, it was by no means clear that those rabbis were ready to step back from the abyss.

For half the country or more, Rabin's death could best be given meaning by the redoubled pursuit of his peace policies. At a memorial assembly eight days after his death, in the same Tel Aviv square where he had been gunned down, Leah, addressing the largest public gathering in Israel's history, exhorted Shimon Peres "to lead the people of Israel to peace... in the spirit of Yitzhak". Some Israelis in the centre, in at least an initial response to Rabin's assassination, also indicated a desire to identify with the fallen leader and put aside criticisms of the peace process. A poll by the *Yediot Aharonot* daily, taken during the week of mourning, showed a massive 74 per cent support for implementing the Oslo II accord.

But for the remainder of the electorate, the continued pursuit of Rabin's policies could only exacerbate the internal divisions. Their opposition to turning the West Bank over to the Palestinians – be it because they didn't trust Arafat, because they felt Israel should never compromise with the Arabs, because they feared for their security or, most passionately, because they believed that no secular Israeli government had the right to give up land promised by God to the Children of Israel – was neither deepened nor lightened by the assassination. It remained as heartfelt as it had been before.

Where there was a real change of tone, it was often led by the youth. Within the 50,000-strong Bnei Akiva movement, for example, high-school-age leaders sought ways to emphasise the positive combination of Zionism, democracy and Torah – and highlight the sanctity of Jewish life. The Sabbath after the murder, meetings centred on studying a saying by Gush Emunim's late spiritual leader, Rabbi Tzvi Yehudah Kook, warning that "No one should decide... that he has the complete truth and complete justice."

Encouragingly, at Amir's old yeshivah Kerem B'Yavneh, Rabbi Mordechai Greenberg acknowledged: "We've been doing a lot of soul-searching. Our ideology isn't going to change – we'll continue to teach the Torah, the centrality of the Land of Israel, and the connection between the Land of Israel and Redemption. What will change is how we express our views. We must think more of the views of others. If half the people are not ready for the whole of the Land of Israel, we can't fight them."

But there were less encouraging signs too. While most religious Zionist leaders issued public condemnations of the assassination, there was no strong sense of a radical reordering of priorities taking place in the religious Zionist camp. Rabbi Yoel Bin-Nun, the rabbi from Ofrah who had asserted that one or more rabbis had given explicit sanction for Rabin's assassination, received death threats from the extreme right, spent weeks with a bodyguard in constant tow, and was repeatedly criticised by rabbinical colleagues. Rabbis

Dov Lior and Nahum Rabinovitch, called in for police questioning in connection with Bin-Nun's allegations, received staunch public support from those same colleagues. When Rabinovitch was quoted on Israel Radio as having said before the killing that "turning in a comrade to gentiles in a way that endangers his life, and handing over Jewish property, whoever does such a thing must pay with his life", he issued only a grudging statement of regret, saying he apologised if any of the "harsh comments" he had made "out of pain" could have led to unfortunate consequences.

Within a week of the assassination, yeshivah head Rabbi Haim Druckman spoke at a Jerusalem gathering purportedly convened for the purpose of religious Zionist soul-searching. Druckman began by attacking left-wing criticism of the religious Zionist camp, continued by asserting that "we are not guilty... we educated according to true values", and concluded by repeating the slogan, "It's impossible to go on with the Oslo process without consensus." Another speaker, the settler rabbi Menahem Felix, attacked the government's legitimacy for all the world as though the murder had never taken place. "We must continue to oppose the government, which rests on support from the haters of Israel," he said – referring to the coalition's reliance on Arab Knesset members. "I don't think we have to retract one truth – that the Land of Israel is ours, and giving it up will bring destruction."

Among most politicians, on the left and in the mainstream right, by contrast, the assassination did seem to have underlined the need to strengthen democracy by moderating the tone of debate and eliminating the verbal brutality that had become the norm. Where previously he had addressed rallies despite their presence, the Likud's Netanyahu now publicly dissociated himself from the extremists, declaring that he wanted neither their votes nor their support. On 13 November, Peres did what Rabin had refused to do, and met Netanyahu to agree that political disputes would henceforth be kept "within the bounds of restraint and civility". Codes of political ethics were drawn up, designed to exclude extremist sentiments from legitimate political debate. Though quick to complain that the left was using Rabin's assassination as a pretext for delegitimising all right-wing opposition, Netanyahu also set a statesman-like tone early on, by pledging to seek no political profit from Rabin's death, and so to support Peres in forming the next government. "In democracies," he preached, "power is transferred through elections, not murder."

Most ordinary Israelis – those who supported Rabin's policies, and those who didn't – seemed to have been shocked into somehow gentler behaviour: speaking more quietly, interrupting less often, even driving more carefully, and removing the more inciteful anti-Rabin-style stickers from their cars (replacing them with the tender "Shalom, *haver*" farewell coined by President Clinton, or by "No to violence" stickers that carried Rabin's face).

Sadly, though, the climate of violence among the government's extreme enemies remained. Within hours of the assassination, graffiti scrawled on Jerusalem walls warned that "Peres is next" – a threat repeated in several anonymous phone calls over the following weeks. At Bar-Ilan, one student celebrated Rabin's death in a message sent over the Internet. A mere week after the murder, another student – a young Orthodox woman – was telling Israel TV there was no escaping the fact that "Rabin was a traitor" – and intimating that he had received the appropriate punishment. Two ultra-Orthodox men were arrested after spitting on Rabin's grave, and apparently preparing to urinate on it.

More than a week after the killing, Attorney General Michael Ben-Yair warned that Rabin's killing "has removed a psychological barrier among that part of the public that has developed an extreme, fanatical and dangerous world view. And this will facilitate another murder. For these people, the assassination constitutes a success. Therefore there is a certainty, not just a likelihood, of another assassination." And that stark warning appeared to have all too sound a basis. Kahanist circles overtly celebrated the murder. In early December, left-wing Meretz party leader Shulamit Aloni received a package in her mail at the Knesset. Inside was a bullet and the warning: "Your place is in the heavens." Micha Regev, deputy commander of a reserve combat brigade and a former student at Merkaz Harav Yeshivah, was one of several people to express the concern that if religious Zionism could produce one extremist gunman like Amir, there was no reason to believe there would not be more.

Determined to succeed where last time they had so utterly failed, Israeli legal and security authorities instituted a wide range of measures cracking down on the extreme right-wing – issuing indictments for long-forgotten alleged infringements, enforcing restriction-of-movement orders on known activists with more tenacity than before, excluding American Kahanists from the country – and stepped up security around Peres and other potential targets to unprecedented levels. Yet for some on the far right, these steps merely provided another front for attacking the government.

Ya'akov Novick, head of the Ma'amatz group that organised many right-wing demonstrations, accused the government of trying to turn Israel into the Russia of old, where a person knew "that there was only one way to achieve change, through underground activity. The government is moving toward dictatorship. That will lead to civil war." In a press release issued the day after Rabin's funeral, Ruth and Nadia Matar, leaders of the settler Women in Green movement, accused the government of initiating "a sacrilegious reign of terror" to suppress dissent. This was followed by a stream of vicious press releases attacking Peres personally, asserting that "to be the kingpin again... was worth everything to him", and describing the peace process as a "hoax on the Jewish people". Nadia Matar, a mother of three from the settlement of Efrat between Bethlehem and Hebron, insisted that "we never carried placards branding Rabin a traitor or a murderer or showing him in SS uniform", and defended anti-government rhetoric she acknowledged was crude. "But the more people feel threatened, the more the Oslo accords are pushed without a huge majority, the more you have to scream *Gevalt* [Help!]."

When the allegations surfaced that Raviv was a Shin Bet agent, and that Eyal had enjoyed Shin Bet funding, the extreme right intensified its counterattack. In interviews in the first few days after the assassination, Leah Rabin had pinned blame directly on Netanyahu, accusing him and others in the mainstream right of fomenting a climate conducive to political assassination by continuing to appear at the rallies where Rabin was denounced as a traitor. It had been hard for her to shake Netanyahu's hand when he paid his respects at the Knesset, she said. His condolences, she had told him, were "too late". Now, though, some on the far right demanded an apology from Leah Rabin, as though the Shin Bet's appalling performance in some way exculpated the extremists, as though the Shin Bet, not Yigal Amir, had pulled the trigger.

To regional, indeed international relief, the smooth transition of power to Peres ensured that the peace process continued on schedule, and sometimes even ahead of it. Peres accelerated the pullout from Jenin in mid-November, and oversaw the withdrawal from all other West Bank cities, except Hebron, by the end of 1995, leading to the successful Palestinian elections of 20 January 1996. He also launched a determined effort to achieve a speedy peace accord with Syria – speaking in characteristically visionary tones of putting an end to all Middle East wars by simultaneously reaching peace treaties not only with Syria and Lebanon, but also with Saudi Arabia, Morocco, Tunisia and other Arab states.

But while Peres tried to build new international bridges, the crucial questions for Israel were internal, and specifically whether a society rocked by the murder would be able to deal with the new crises, waiting inevitably around the next corner. The wave of sympathy that had opinion polls showing Peres twice as popular as Netanyahu would surely dissipate the moment Islamic extremists resumed their suicide bombing campaign. And even if the bombers were kept relatively quiet, and if improved internal security and a new sense of restraint kept Israel's extremists from repeating Amir's horrific act, the divisions would not go away. If the soul-searching were not carried through thoroughly, if Israelis on both sides of the divide could not acknowledge that they all contributed to a climate of such hostility that political assassination became a logical extreme, then the faint glimmers of hope would be shut out.

For Leah Rabin, on her own after 47 years of marriage, the overwhelming evidence of national mourning created at least a degree of optimism. At the memorial gathering in the former Kings of Israel Square – now renamed Yitzhak Rabin Square – she had spoken of her confidence that the assassination would shake up the "silent majority", and help ensure the successful completion of the peace process. She took that same message of optimism to New York in early December, insisting at the packed Madison Square Garden tribute to Rabin on 10 December that "peace will come". In the first dark weeks after the assassination, she found some solace in writing a daily letter to her late husband – knowing he couldn't read her news on the impact his death was having, but drawing comfort herself from telling him.

Speaking while emptying out Rabin's office drawers a few days after the murder, Eitan Haber recalled that the Prime Minister believed himself to be "absolutely" invincible. He never felt threatened by right-wing violence. But equally, he really had felt alone in the face of all the incitement. So that last rally, said Haber, lifted Rabin to a personal high. "If I can take any comfort," said the man who had first met Rabin 37 years before – an army private trembling before his general – "it is that he died at his peak. You'd have to be some kind of genius director to conceive a finale like that: tens of thousands singing with him and in his honour, sending him such warmth. The hug with Shimon Peres. And then, the murder."

17

An Unfinished Mission

HE WAS 73 YEARS, eight months and three days old when he was murdered. But the tragedy of Yitzhak Rabin's assassination was that, chain-smoking, whisky-liking septuagenarian though he was, the Prime Minister was fit, strong and, according to those colleagues who knew him best, eagerly contemplating five more years in office.

In his final major television interview, on Israel TV three days before his death, he jokingly ducked his interviewers' repeated efforts to pin him down on whether he intended to seek another term, but there was no mistaking his seriousness in rejecting their mild suggestions that he might be too old for another stint in the hot seat. According to Eitan Haber, Rabin used to "brag all the time that he was in better shape than those much younger than him. He regarded himself as a young man." And he functioned at a young man's pace, putting in marathon work days. "He worked as though he felt he had to justify his salary the whole time," Haber said. "If we asked him to schedule his arrival on a visit to a foreign city a day early, to give him time to overcome the jet lag, he would say, 'Are you crazy? Think of the cost to Israel.'"

His closest aides have no doubt that Rabin intended not merely to stand for re-election in Israel's 1996 general elections, but that he was confident of winning and seeing through a full term in office. And top of his agenda in the next term would have been making peace with Syria. Although the peace treaty with Egypt had been strengthened during his three and a half years of Prime Ministership, although peace with Jordan had proved even warmer than he had dared hope, and although Arafat seemed to be reining in the Palestinian Islamic radicals with increasing success, Rabin regarded his job as only half done, and he desperately wanted to see it through to its conclusion. "Obviously, he was going to run again, and complete the term," says Uri Dromi, the director of the Government Press Office under Rabin who was often at the Prime Minister's side. "Rabin didn't quit in the middle of anything."

In death, President Clinton spoke of Rabin as "a martyr for peace" – but it is unlikely that Rabin would appreciate going down in history in those terms. Rabin was nobody's martyr. And rightful and natural though it was that his contribution to peacemaking rapidly came to be regarded as his legacy, Rabin himself would have wanted as much stress laid on his concern for Israeli security. A soldier to his dying day, even after almost three decades out of uniform, security was his watchword as he moved along the road to peace, serving as the filter through which he evaluated every clause of every agreement to which he affixed his signature. Crucially, he believed fervently that only a strong, secure Israel could make peace. "In these days of crying and mourning," said Haber shortly after the assassination, "it is only natural that the emphasis has been placed more on his peacemaking. But if Yitzhak Rabin were to come down from heaven now, he would say, 'Folks, first security.'"

After a rivalry that had lasted half a lifetime, Rabin in his last few months had come to see Shimon Peres as his genuine peacemaking cohort. What Haber called the late-blooming "love affair" was a consequence of each realising that the other brought crucial qualities to the partnership. Rabin, his colleagues say, had come to respect Peres for proving – through the Oslo process with the Palestinians – that his own suspicions could be misplaced, his cautions exaggerated, that negotiating avenues he would have instinctively dismissed as dead ends could be worth exploring.

But that said, Rabin was always aware of the need to slow Peres down, to "bring Peres back down to earth", as one former Rabin confidant puts it. Close Rabin aides have no doubt that, in pursuing his self-proclaimed task of completing Rabin's mission, Peres in the aftermath of the assassination was taking steps that Rabin would have avoided, instituting policies he would have shunned.

To illustrate Rabin's restraining influence on the man who came to succeed him, a close colleague recalled the events of 4 July 1995. That morning, Peres travelled to Gaza for talks with Arafat aimed at finalising the much-delayed Oslo II accord on expanding Palestinian self-rule in the West Bank. The two men resolved to stay at the negotiating table until a final draft had been worked out, and stay they did, right through the day, until white smoke emerged in the early evening. At 8 p.m., Israel Television led its nightly bulletin with the news that the deal was done, and that a lavish White House ceremony was scheduled for two weeks' hence, timed to give a boost to an international conference of donors to the Palestine Authority, scheduled for Washington at about the same time.

It being 4 July, American ambassador Martin Indyk was hosting a US Independence party at his Herzliyah residence that evening, attended by Rabin and most of the Israeli establishment. When the news came through of the Peres–Arafat success, it naturally became the chief item of conversation. But while the guests enthused at the breakthrough, and the American diplomats smiled their congratulations, a small coterie of Rabin's most senior aides seemed immune to the celebration. Asked why, Eitan Haber explained flatly: "There is no Oslo II accord. The deal has not been done. There'll be no White House signing ceremony this month."

And so it proved. It took from 4 July to 28 September for the Peres–Arafat Oslo II "accord" to become the eventual, White House-signed Rabin–Arafat Oslo II accord. More than 12 weeks during which, despite Palestinian impatience, domestic disquiet and American pressure, Rabin went over every clause of the document, insisting on innumerable changes to almost every aspect of the deal – examining it and altering it through his security filter.

The irony, after an assassination whose perpetrator says he was acting to protect Israel from policies he perceived as irresponsible, dangerous and rash, is that, without Rabin, that unique filter has been removed. With the Oslo II deal signed and sealed in late September, Peres in the months after the murder was merely implementing an accord with which Rabin was satisfied – overseeing the phased military withdrawal from West Bank cities, towns and villages, handing over power to Arafat within the provisions of a detailed treaty. But in pushing forward toward a peace accord with Syria, Peres was moving into territory uncharted by Rabin – and those who worked with him, speaking privately, say they believe the late Prime Minister would have acted very differently.

For a start, Rabin had told his aides that he had virtually ruled out the chances of reaching even a framework peace treaty with Syria before the elections scheduled for October 1996. He saw no urgent need for an accord: the Israel–Syria border had been quiet since the 1973 war; without Soviet support, Syria had no forseeable war option; and the two or three dozen losses a year in Lebanon, though painful, were minimal compared to, say, the carnage on the roads. He did not consider a deal with Syria to be a particular electoral asset

– understanding the electorate well enough to know that adjusting to a peace partnership with Arafat was hard enough, and forcing an accommodation with Asad down their throats as well might induce ballot-box sickness. And he wanted to see the Oslo II timetable unfolding successfully before turning to other business. His paramount fear was of another upsurge in suicide bombings and other acts of Islamic extremism – an upsurge he knew full well could cost Labour an election victory – and he did not want to be distracted. The only line that jarred in his otherwise upbeat speech at the White House signing of Oslo II was the warning to Arafat to "prevent terrorism from triumphing over peace... Otherwise we will fight it by ourselves."

Watching Peres rush toward the laudable, but not necessarily urgent, goal of peace with Syria, Rabin's aides say, the late Prime Minister would have been aghast at the sheer haste; he would have instinctively rejected the fawning, almost desperate advances made by Peres to Asad; he would flatly have opposed Peres's gambit of involving the Americans in the negotiations as full mediators – preferring to hammer out a treaty face-to-face; and, security obsession to the fore, he would have been disturbed by Peres's readiness to negotiate all aspects of an accord simultaneously, insisting instead that security arrangements for an Israeli withdrawal from the Golan Heights be agreed on first, before other elements of a treaty were tackled.

"Rabin was ready to sanction an Israeli pullout from the entire Golan Heights," says one close aide emphatically. "But it would have been a protracted process. He often recalled that the peace treaty with Egypt took three or four years to be fully implemented, and he would note that a deal with Syria would be infinitely more complicated and so would require maybe a decade to unfold." Indeed, Rabin himself told *The Jerusalem Report* in a July 1994 interview that while he wanted to make peace with Syria, and was prepared "to make painful compromises", he was in no great hurry. "We've been on the Golan Heights for 27 years, and we can happily stay there for another 27," he said. "It took four and a half years after Sadat's visit to Jerusalem before we began to withdraw from the Sinai... Asad has not been to Jerusalem yet."

The close aide believes that Rabin would have "insisted on Syrian troop withdrawals way back toward Damascus, on satellite and other intelligence to ensure Israel knew what the Syrian military was up to, and on a series of 'international trip wires' between the Syrian forces and the Golan to prevent any chance of surprise attack. With those arrangements in place, he would even have been willing to forgo a land-based early-warning station on the Golan. But it would have been an extremely lengthy process, nothing like the headlong dash Peres has embarked on."

Uri Dromi notes that "Rabin, unlike Peres, never belittled the Syrian military threat. He never spoke of Syrian arms being scrap-metal, or obsolete. And he had seen what a few dozen Scuds could do to the country, psychologically, during the Gulf War, when although there was only one direct casualty, all of Israel was shaken. So he knew the devastation that, say, biologically armed Scuds fired from Syria could do. While Peres believes that once peace is achieved, all the security guarantees will fall into place, Rabin felt that the security aspects of an accord had to be dealt with first. He viewed everything through a security prism."

Rabin's aides are ready to confirm his readiness in principle to give up the whole Golan, a stance that would have caused consider-able controversy had he professed it publicly, only on condition of being quoted anonymously. They attach the same condition when revealing another stance, again never publicly espoused by Rabin: his indifference to the establishment of a Palestinian state in the West Bank and Gaza Strip. "The truth is that Rabin wasn't really all that bothered about what he considered 'the semantics'," says one close confidant. "He recognised that, in any case, Oslo II effectively marked the creation of a Palestinian state. The Palestinians have a flag, an anthem, coins, stamps, passports, a president. That adds up to a state, and it didn't unduly concern him. His aim was to restore Palestinian self-respect to a degree that would ensure the accord was implemented and honoured."

As for the "final-status" issues – the central elements of permanent peace with the Palestinians like the delineation of borders, the question of returning Palestinian refugees, the fate of Jewish settle-ments in the territories, and the ultimate status of Jerusalem – the aides say Rabin was in no hurry to resolve them, again preferring to defer discussion for as long as possible, to see first how Oslo II was turning out. Although the agreed timetable provided for an opening of final-status talks in May 1996, Rabin would have manoeuvred to ensure that nothing was debated seriously until after the October elections, his aides say.

Rabin knew that, when the final-status talks began in earnest, the differences would initially appear unbridgeable. Says Dromi: "He knew the Palestinians would say they wanted an independent state, with Jerusalem as its capital, the removal of all settlements from the West Bank and Gaza, and the return of all refugees. Israel would say no to the state, forget Jerusalem, we're keeping the settlements, and there'll be no return for refugees. In the end, obviously, there would have to be compromises." The Prime Minister had taken no final position on the refugee question, but on other issues a blueprint was taking shape. In his 5 October 1995, speech to the Knesset, presenting the Oslo II accord for approval, he had set out his vision of the West Bank's final status. Anticipating an expanded Jerusalem extending into the West Bank, the retention of the Jordan Valley settlements, and the "attaching" to Israel of other settlement blocs, he derided opposition claims that he had set Israel on the path back to its 1967 borders.

All this sounded like a maximalist, "opening" negotiating position – certain to infuriate the Palestinians, designed to calm as many Israeli sceptics as possible in the short-term, and liable to result ultimately in a negotiated compromise. But although Haber has acknowledged that Rabin had little sympathy for the West Bank settlers – he regarded them as "a deliberately placed obstacle to peace" – the Prime Minister's closest aide has noted that Rabin had secured peace with Jordan "without uprooting so much as a clothes-line", and clearly believes Rabin would have sought to maintain Israeli rule over as many of the settlements as possible.

As for Jerusalem, Rabin was always publicly adamant that there could be no undermining of Israeli sovereignty throughout the city. He deliberately chose the Casablanca economic conference of 1994 – an unprecedented, highly sensitive gathering of Arab and Israeli leaders – to hammer home his pledge that that the capital would never be redivided. And in private his position was no different. Dromi says that on Jerusalem, Rabin was unmovable. "On many issues, he was the archetypal pragmatist, mechanical in his dispassionate evaluation of what stance best served Israel's security interests. But on Jerusalem – because he was born there; fought for the city while still in his twenties, sending teenagers to their deaths; then fought for it again in 1967 and emerged victorious – on Jerusalem there was an emotional perspective. I don't believe he would ever have sanctioned a substantial compromise on the city's status." He was, however, say his aides, prepared to consider some kind of "municipal autonomy" for the Palestinians, perhaps a borough system, and he had no strong objection to institutions like the Palestinian headquarters at the Orient House in East Jerusalem.

Speaking to the people who knew Rabin best, it becomes clear that final policy positions were not taken years or even months in advance. And while some critics would argue that this was symptomatic of a leadership responding to developments rather than shaping them, Rabin loyalists claim that it was, rather, a positive sign of Prime Ministerial pragmatism – the need to maintain flexible positions so as to be able to move ahead according to the dictates of a changing situation.

And nothing better illustrated the readiness of the 1990s' Rabin to change and reassess than his fascinating relationship with Yasser Arafat. At the start of the autonomy process, Rabin had, to put it mildly, a deep emotional resistance to the Palestinian leader. He had no problems shaking hands with Egyptian or Jordanian leaders – nor would he have had with the Syrians – because these were people he had confronted on the battlefields, general to general. Indeed, over the years, he had been more than happy to enter easygoing conversations with, for example, Mohammad Abdulghani al-Gamassy, the Egyptian general who led his forces across the Suez Canal in 1973, discussing aspects of the crossing with him.

But Arafat had never been a conventional military enemy. And for years, Rabin had despised the man and his methods. Even in the new realities, he simply could not bring himself to relax in the company of a man responsible for the killing of women and children – anathema for a soldier – a man who, to Rabin, had crossed the border into barbarism. He understood the Palestinian frustration and pain, he even understood that Arafat had little alternative to terrorism to pursue his goals. But that rational understanding could not overcome the emotional antipathy.

So when, on 13 September 1993, before the hundreds on the White House lawn and the hundreds of millions watching on television around the world, Rabin hesitated at the sight of Arafat's outstretched hand, the reluctance was heartfelt, the psychological barrier utterly real. Rabin had known in advance that Arafat would want to shake hands, and that Clinton would want to ensure a handshake. He had reconciled himself to it. Haber had even sent a message to the Americans saying that a handshake was acceptable, but that Arafat's standard kisses and hugs were not. And yet, Dromi recalls that on the plane to the United States for the ceremony, Rabin eschewed his customary habit of grabbing some sleep, and paced about, smoking, evidently in a turbulent state. And when the moment of truth arrived on the White House lawn, it took Clinton's gentle pressure at his elbow to overcome Rabin's hesitancy.

Two years later, when Oslo II was signed at the White House amid more modest festivities, the body language gave expression to how the relationship had improved. True, it was Arafat who patted Rabin on the back when the deal had been signed and sealed and the two men were leaving the East Room. But two years earlier, Arafat would never have dared. And if he had, Rabin would have winced and tried to escape the Chairman's clutches. Now, in the lighthearted atmosphere at the ceremony, the backslapping seemed almost natural.

Haber has said that Rabin never came to trust Arafat completely, but he had learned to respect him. In the early days of Arafat's rule in Gaza, Rabin had spoken dismissively of Arafat's system of patronage, derided the importing of Palestinian policemen from abroad, and joked cynically about Arafat's signature being required to get so much as a telephone installed in Gaza. But he had gradually become impressed by Arafat's ability to maintain the support of the majority of his people, impressed by his facility for survival, and most important of all, increasingly impressed by his ability to counter Islamic extremism – the barometer of the peace accords.

"He began talking differently about Arafat," says Dromi, "reminding himself and others that when Israel controlled Gaza, it had also failed to halt terrorism 100 per cent. The fact was that his intelligence reports were showing him that Arafat, under tough circumstances, was doing, if not his best, then certainly a lot, to fight terrorism." Rabin also came to admire the people who were working with Arafat – the urbane pragmatists who had led the Oslo negotiations like Abu Ala, Abu Mazen and Nabil Sha'ath. But impressive though these aides were, Rabin also knew that Arafat was the key – that Arafat was the only credible Palestinian partner, and that, having honoured his pledge to renounce terrorism, Arafat was proving that the "gamble for peace" paid off.

Interestingly, though Asad was by far the more implacable, and more dangerous enemy, Rabin's attitude to the Syrian President was far more straightforward. The two, of course, never met – though Rabin repeatedly, publicly and privately, sought face-to-face contacts. But, assessing the Syrian dictator in terms of past experience, Rabin felt that he could trust Asad, that he was "a man of his word", that he would honour any accord that was reached. Rabin appreciated the fact that Asad had ensured quiet on the Israel–Syrian border for more than two decades, and even admitted a grudging admiration for the manoeuvring that had enabled Syria to establish virtual hegemony in Lebanon. Still, Uri Dromi says that faith in Asad's word as his bond was jarred by the Syrian President's failure, despite an explicit commitment to the Americans, to resume talks between delegations of military negotiators in the summer of 1995. That failure, says Dromi, raised doubts in Rabin's minds about the nature of Asad's purported strategic choice of peace, and contributed to his pessimism about the chances of speedy progress toward an accord.

Rabin was also aware, through the briefings of the various American peace mediators, that Asad nurtured a healthy respect, if not a fear, of him. According to American diplomats involved in Israeli–Syrian mediation over the years, Rabin understood that Asad, a dictator who had never negotiated with anyone on an equal footing – and who had rarely even set foot outside the Middle East – was intimidated by the prospect of sitting down across a negotiating table with the former general whose troops had trounced the Syrian forces at every confrontation. Significantly for the future, perhaps, Asad had no such psychological problem with Peres.

Though Rabin was not convinced that peace with Syria was an immediate priority, it was certainly a goal to which he aspired – not only to complete what Peres has called "the circle of peace" around Israel, but to strengthen the secular front against the spread of Iranian-inspired Islamic extremism, "Khomeinism without Khomeini" as he described it. He also recognised the economic benefits for Israel from comprehensive peace and consequent Middle East stability, saw the markets gradually opening up in countries like Indonesia, Malaysia and some of the Persian Gulf states, and knew that the economy could truly soar once complete peace was achieved. In essence, he saw peace progress and economic progress working in tandem, and wanted to ensure the smooth development of both.

Belying the conventional wisdom that he was "always a soldier, and never a politician", Rabin also devoted considerable time and thought to internal domestic political issues – marshalling his forces with a certain cunning in an effort to maximise Labour's chances of winning the next elections. Those around him have little doubt that, among the immediate potential heirs, Haim Ramon was his favourite, but he had a close relationship with, and respect too, for ex-Chief of Staff Ehud Barak, and he deployed these two rising stars with great care.

Ramon's dramatic breakaway from Labour in February 1994 to compete for and win control of the Histadrut labour federation, say some who claim to be in the know, was co-ordinated with Rabin, who recognised that the grey Labour establishment then running the union was incapable of instituting long-overdue reforms. He anticipated Ramon transforming the Histadrut into a vibrant, attractive, corruption-free organisation – which would prove a Labour vote-winner come 1996. Others, including Uri Dromi, say Rabin would never have sanctioned so premeditated a strike on his own party – "he would have felt too duplicitous" – but that he swiftly reconciled himself to the potential advantages of Ramon's breakaway.

Similarly, when Rabin brought Barak into his cabinet in July 1995, he assigned him not to his natural home, the defence ministry, but to the interior ministry, a crucial posting in the run up to elections, given the ministry's central role in allocating municipal funding – for sewerage, building, recreation and more – and its consequent potential for alienating or attracting voters.

In short, as one of Rabin's close colleagues puts it, "He gave his two potential successors mechanisms for broadening Labour's electoral base – and for simultaneously building their own power bases." The short-term aim was that, in their separate areas, Ramon and Barak would help assure Labour's 1996 victory; the long-term expectation was that, toward the end of Rabin's next term in office, they would compete for the Labour leadership, on the basis of their respective achievements.

Rabin shared an almost instinctive understanding with Ramon – the man with whom he spent his last afternoon on 4 November. He didn't feel quite the same warmth toward Barak – he didn't like the way Barak, when deputy Chief of Staff, had managed to avoid direct involvement in handling the Intifada; took note of Barak's conspicuous abstention when Oslo II was first presented to the cabinet for a preliminary vote in August 1995; and thought that Barak's desire for personal popularity was a flaw in a potential national leader. "Whisper it gently," says a Rabin aide with a smile, "but Barak reminded him just a little of Peres."

But perhaps the man whom Rabin trusted and respected the most was Amnon Lipkin-Shahak, Barak's successor as Chief of Staff, with whom he had a virtual father and son relationship. It was a bond that began to develop when, while serving as head of military intelligence, Shahak was diagnosed with leukaemia. Rabin, as Defence Minister, was under pressure to order Shahak to take leave, but accepted Shahak's request to stay on at his post while he fought the illness. Rabin stood by his man, and Shahak made a full recovery. During the talks on the Gaza-and-Jericho section of the Oslo accords in 1993 and 1994, Rabin delegated much of the negotiation to Shahak, and was rewarded when Shahak established a strong, productive rapport with Nabil Sha'ath and his other Palestinian counterparts, and acted consistently in good faith with Rabin.

Says Dromi, "Rabin saw himself most closely in Shahak." He trusted him utterly. And he would have hoped to see him taking a senior government position when his time as Chief of Staff was over. Rabin's only reservation about Shahak was the fear that, if anything, he was too straight to make a complete politician. His hope was to nurture Shahak, to help groom him for eventual leadership.

Rabin was unusual among Israeli leaders in having begun to prepare the ground for his own succession. "The cemeteries are full of people who thought they could not be replaced," he observed in one interview with *The Jerusalem Report*. But he never lived to see how the succession battle turned out. He never even got to fight it out against Benjamin Netanyahu, a rival he constantly belittled, for the 1996 elections. He never saw the careful preparations he had made for the West Bank withdrawal translated into a relatively smooth and successful pullout. He never got to the final-status talks with the Palestinians, never had the chance to prove that his ultimate vision was of an Israel larger and more secure than it had been within its 1967 borders. And he never came face to face with Asad over the last pieces of the Middle East peace jigsaw. Yitzhak Rabin, a man who made an inestimable contribution to Israel, was stopped in his tracks – mission unfinished – by a cold-hearted killer who claimed to have God on his side. And, in an instant, Israel was changed forever.

Afterword: Echoes of the Past

IN THE JEWISH MIND, history is never far from the present. For two millennia, Jews in exile prayed for the restoration of Israel to its ancestral homeland and Biblical glory. And these prayers continue unabated, even as the dream of Jewish sovereignty and the gathering of the exiles has been made real, however imperfectly. "Take us back, O Lord, to Yourself, and let us come back," Jews chant, after reading each weekly portion of the Torah. "Renew our days as of old." The words are the prophet Jeremiah's, in the Book of Lamentations, written after the destruction of the First Temple in 586 BCE.

The story of Israel's ancient triumphs has been both the inspiration and scourge of modern Zionism. Jews would repossess the Promised Land, become farmers and soldiers again on their own soil, and speak a Hebrew language not spoken in its country of origin – or anywhere else outside the synagogue and seminary – since antiquity. But not everything from the days of old is worth renewing.

Dror Adani, indicted along with Yigal Amir as a conspirator in Yitzhak Rabin's assassination, told police investigators about a Sabbath retreat that Amir and other young right-wing activists held with West Bank settlers. Amir at that meeting argued that the political situation in Israel under the Rabin government was comparable to the Biblical story of Pinhas the son of Eleazar son of Aaron the High Priest (Numbers ch. 25), who slew a certain Zimri (who had brazenly consorted with a Midianite harlot), thereby stemming God's wrath and ending a plague that had killed 24,000 Israelites. For this, Pinhas was granted a Divine "pact of friendship" and "pact of priesthood" for his descendants for all time.

Indeed following the assassination, some apologists for Amir – aware or not of his chilling analogy at that West Bank meeting –

cited the tale of Pinhas and Zimri as justification of internecine murder in cases of national emergency. That the situations were ludicrously incomparable, that a literal extrapolation is antithetical to the spirit of traditional Judaism, was lost on individuals bent on viewing the Jewish state as the messianic embryo of a new Jewish kingdom of old.

As usual in the Bible, one may find an opposite model to the Pinhas story, if one is so inclined. Directly after the destruction of the First Temple, the Babylonian-appointed Jewish governor of Judaea, Gedaliah son of Ahikam, was assassinated by Ishmael son of Nethaniah (II Kings ch. 25, Jeremiah ch. 41), who considered him a traitor. The event is commemorated to this day by the Fast of Gedaliah, observed on the third day of the Hebrew month of Tishrei, the day following Rosh Hashanah. "It is surprising," commented one modern scholar, that the murder of Gedaliah, "a Babylonian puppet," was marked as early as the Second Temple period by a ritual day of mourning. But perhaps not surprising at all. One might argue that this nearly forgotten fast was intended to etch indelibly in the Jewish national consciousness the unacceptability of political murder.

It was a lesson easily forgotten. In the centuries preceding the destruction of Jerusalem by the Romans in 70 CE, the Jewish commonwealth was riven by deadly infighting. The beloved holiday of Hanukkah commemorates the victory of the zealous Hasmoneans not only over the Seleucid Greeks, but over their fellow Jews, chiefly upper-class types and intellectuals who welcomed the worldly culture of Hellenism. The less extreme of such Jewish Hellenisers sought not to become Greeks, but to reform Judaism and "drag the little temple-state", in the wry words of the historian Paul Johnson, "into the modern age". Countless generations of Jewish children have been inspired by the dazzling tale of Mattathias, father of the Maccabees, who slew an idol-worshipping Jew in the Modi'in marketplace, raised his sword high and proclaimed: "Whoever is with the Lord, come with me!" But civil strife bedevilled the Hasmonean dynasty, the Jewish monarchy allied with Rome that was established by Simon the Maccabee. In the time of his grandson Alexander Yannai, in the early first century BCE, a civil war raged that, according to the ancient historian Josephus, cost 50,000 Jewish lives.

Pharisees, Sadducees, Zealots — these labels linger, however vaguely, in the popular historical memory of Second Temple times. Less familiar are the Sicarii, the extremist assassins, named for their trademark curved dagger – *sica* in Latin – who made a habit of murdering Jews they considered ideologically deficient, usually at public celebrations. Some scholars believe that Judas Iscariot, the very symbol of betrayal and back-stabbing, was so named because he was one of the Sicarii. In 67 CE, while the Roman army was squelching the Great Revolt in the Galilee, the Zealots and their more moderate opponents were already slaying one another in Jerusalem. Three years later, the Temple went up in flames, and three more after that, 960 Jews committed suicide at the mountaintop fortress of Masada. It was a tragedy unparalleled in its significance for Jewish history until, arguably, the Holocaust. And why did it happen? According to the Talmud, the vast treasury of Jewish learning compiled in the early centuries of the Common Era, the Second Temple was destroyed by the Romans only "because of baseless hatred" among Jews – an offence equal in gravity to "idolatry, immorality, and bloodshed" combined (Talmud, Tractate Yoma 9b).

It would take nearly 19 centuries for the viability of a Jewish sovereign state to be tested again. Until the era of Jewish emancipation following the French Revolution, Jewish power was confined to the community, and the religious authority of Orthodox rabbis determined the behavioural and ideological parameters of Jewish life in the Diaspora. On occasion, Jewish informers – known as *malshinim* or *mosrim* – informed on Jews to hostile authorities, or conspired with gentiles to seize Jewish property, and were condemned to death under Jewish law. In thirteenth-century Barcelona, a young Jewish aristocrat and troublemaker named Vidalon de Porta was publicly bled to death after King Pedro III had compelled two of Catalonia's leading rabbis, Rabbi Solomon ibn Adret (known as the Rashba) and Rabbi Jonah Gerondi, to determine whether De Porta was a *moser*, which they ruled he was. In fourteenth-century Strasbourg, a Jew was placed in a sack and drowned in the river, having been convicted by a rabbinic court of enabling some Christian noblemen to rob wealthy Jews. To suggest that medieval cases are legitimate precedents for Yigal Amir's murder of Yitzhak Rabin is manifestly absurd.

In the year 1640, after rejecting Jewish ritual and expressing doubt that the Law of Moses was divinely ordained, the Portuguese-born Jewish free-thinker Uriel da Costa sought to rejoin the Amsterdam Jewish community he had previously criticised as overly rigid. To do so he was compelled to recant his views in public, submit to 39 lashes, and lie down on the floor so that the congregation could walk on him. In 1656, the same Amsterdam community excommunicated the philosopher Baruch Spinoza, who argued that after the destruction of the Temple, Jews were no longer bound by the laws of the Torah. Spinoza left the Jewish community, but did not embrace any other faith, and is regarded by historians as a prototype of the modern secular Jew.

By the nineteenth century, opposition to Orthodoxy had become widespread. Reform Judaism flowered in Germany and America, legions of Jews abandoned the strict practice of religious ritual, and many turned their energies to such secular ideologies as socialism and Zionism. The power of Orthodox leaders to maintain religious conformity within the Jewish fold had been shattered. Yet when the first Zionist pioneers came to settle in Palestine in the 1880s, they found they had been preceded by Orthodox and ultra-Orthodox Jews who had trickled back to the ancient homeland from European and Muslim countries over the centuries, not because they anticipated the creation of a Jewish state, but because they wished to fulfill the religious commandment of settling in the Holy Land.

It suited the Orthodox Jews of nineteenth-century Palestine, known as the Old Yishuv, to be living under the non-Jewish regime of the Ottoman Turks. In general they were deeply uncomfortable with the political agenda of the secular Zionists, considering them to be interlopers who had taken into their own heretical hands the role of the messiah who would arrive, when the Almighty was good and ready, to reverse the global scattering of the Jews and re-establish a Jewish polity in the ancient homeland. Indeed, many believed that if Jewish sovereignty were restored against God's will, dire consequences would ensue – another destruction.

Consider the case of Eliezer Ben-Yehuda, famous lexicographer and father of the Hebrew language revival, who arrived in Jerusalem in 1881 and began vigorously promoting the speaking of Hebrew as a means to promoting Jewish nationhood. Before long he was excommunicated by the ultra-Orthodox, who rejected the use of the holy tongue for day-to-day discourse. His enemies eventually persuaded the Ottoman authorities that Ben-Yehuda's muckraking Hebrew-language newspaper *Hatzvi* – which opposed financial handouts from the Diaspora to Palestinian Jews and aggressively supported Jewish self-sufficiency – had preached sedition against the regime, and he was briefly jailed. Even today, at Ben-Yehuda's house on Jerusalem's stately Ethiopia Street, you can find four little holes in the stone, instead of the commemorative plaque that was placed there by the city and removed, again and again, by ultra-Orthodox Jews.

The battle between Ben-Yehuda and the ultra-Orthodox may be viewed as the opening salvo of the secular–religious culture war in Israel that underlay the Rabin assassination and whose future course may well determine the country's destiny. In the Rabin assassination, that ongoing struggle merged with an intense conflict between left and right in the Zionist movement that preceded and anticipated the bitter contemporary argument over what to do with the territories conquered in the Six Day War.

In 1933, the brilliant young Labour Zionist leader Chaim Arloso-roff was shot dead on the beach in Tel Aviv while strolling there with his wife. Arlosoroff, as head of the Jewish Agency's political department, had been denounced by the right-wing Revisionist Zionists for negotiating with the Nazis to bring German Jews and their property to Palestine. A Revisionist named Abraham Stavsky was convicted of the murder by a British Mandatory court and sentenced to be hanged, but his sentence was later overturned, and it was said, but not proven, that two young Arabs had killed Arlosoroff. (A counter-theory says that the revisionists had disguised themselves as Arabs.) Chief Rabbi Avraham Yitzhak Kook was among those who denounced the prosecution of Stavsky as a blood libel. In the 1980s, the Begin government established a commission of inquiry into the Arlosoroff case, and concluded, controversially, that Stavsky was not to blame – but failed to determine who was.

The affair, wrote historian Howard Sachar, fuelled the "lethal fratricidal hatred" between David Ben-Gurion's Labour leftists and right-wingers under Revisionist leader Vladimir (Ze'ev) Jabotinsky and later his disciple Menachem Begin. (Ben-Gurion was known to refer to his rival as "Vladimir Hitler".) Years later, that animosity reached a tragic pinnacle with the *Altalena* episode in June 1948. Ben-Gurion believed that Begin's extremist Irgun had endangered the establishment of the state by terrorising the British. After independence, the Prime Minister refused to allow the ship *Altalena*, carrying arms for Irgun units that had yet to be integrated into the new state's army, to land. The Prime Minister opposed the continued existence of politically linked militias and feared that the Irgun might use the guns not against the Arabs but against the infant Labour government. One of the men who perished on it was, ironically, Abraham Stavsky.

Ten days after Rabin's assassination, during Ted Koppel's boisterous "Town Meeting" on the TV show "Nightline", broadcast to untold millions around the world from the Jerusalem Theatre, a left-wing Israeli panellist remarked that "the bullets always fly from right to left". At which were heard shouts from among the many Jewish settlers and other right-wingers in the theatre audience: "*Altalena! Altalena!*"

The murder of Rabin was not, in fact, the first political assassination in the State of Israel's short history. In March 1957, Rudolph Kastner, a government official and Labour Party insider, was gunned down in front of his Tel Aviv home by three young men, and later died of his wounds. Two years earlier, in a complex and dramatic libel trial, an Israeli court had held that Kastner, as chairman of the Jewish Rescue Committee in Budapest in 1944, had collaborated with the Nazis – "sold his soul to the devil" in the judge's inflammatory words – by negotiating with Adolf Eichmann for the lives of Hungarian Jews and providing the SS with a list of 1,685 Hungarian Jews who were in fact saved. Kastner's killers, who had accumulated large stockpiles of arms, were right-wing extremists and admirers of the outlawed Stern Gang, to which one of them – a former Shin Bet agent – had belonged. Indeed the Shin Bet domestic security agency, which had provided protection for Kastner, removed it mysteriously only days before the murder. At the time Kastner was killed, the libel case was under appeal, and he was posthumously vindicated of the charge of collaboration. There were calls for reform of the Shin Bet, which were not heeded. The killers' sentences were later commuted by President Zalman Shazar.

Comparing the Kastner case to the Dreyfus affair – the arrest and trial of the assimilated Jewish captain on false charges of spying for Germany just over a hundred years ago – Israeli author and journalist Amos Elon wrote in late 1995, just prior to the Rabin assassination: "All the cultural codes of the new Israeli society, its neuroses, prejudices, stereotypes and illusions – self-righteous and otherwise – were focused in this sensational trial and the surrounding public debate as under a magnifying glass." And indeed the very nature of Jewish identity was at stake. What were Jews: fighters or hagglers? Diaspora creatures, willing to negotiate with satanic anti-Semites, or new men and women, fierce Israelis, determined to rid the Jewish people of their foes forever? During the Kastner trial, Shmuel Tamir, attorney for the accused libeller Malkiel Gruenwald and himself a former Jerusalem commander of the Irgun, fuelled the fantasy that if only the Irgun and Stern Gang – and not the Jewish Agency, which evolved into the Labour government – had been running Jewish operations in wartime Europe, things would have turned out better. And was not this same Labour government, in the 1950s, powerless to stop the fedayeen, the Arab terrorists infiltrating Israel's borders and threatening its existence?

It is fairly stunning, even eerie, to contemplate the parallels between the Kastner case and the Rabin assassination, but then again the Rabin tragedy abounds in historical resonance. At the close of the 30-day mourning period, Rabbi David Hartman, the Orthodox educator and philosopher, gave a public lecture in Jerusalem on the subject of "Building a Decent Society on Jewish Principles". The State of Israel, he said, is composed of Jews thrown together after 2,000 years, harbouring radically different perceptions of Jewish history. What many of them share is the traditional Jewish penchant for apocalyptic thinking, for feeling that the world is always about to come to an end. What else to expect of a forever-persecuted, traumatised nation whose physical existence throughout history has never really been secure?

Whatever one's point of view, Hartman continued, the way to avoid disaster is clear: It is *your* way. For hard-line Orthodox Jews, for example, who believe that settling the Greater Land of Israel is a supreme Divine commandment, anyone who would give some of it to the Palestinians in the name of peace and security will bring about the Jewish nation's destruction instead. A "traumatised conscious-ness", argued Hartman, will not admit any justice or legitimacy to the enemy's point of view. "This," he concluded, "is the disease that brought about the assassination of Rabin."

If so, it is a disease whose germ goes back to the deserts of the Israelites, to the burning parapets of ancient Jerusalem, to a man being whipped in a synagogue in Amsterdam, to another man being shot in Tel Aviv. But can it be cured?

Rabin was not Zimri and the Arabs are not Midianites, any more than Israel is medieval Barcelona or, for that matter, the Warsaw ghetto. But what people believe has everything to do with which stories they prefer to retell. The principal challenge for contemporary Jews, in Israel and elsewhere, is to contemplate the possibility that Zionism has, in fact, constituted a transcendent historical revolution for the Jews. For Jews to cease being the victims of one another, they must come to realise that their isolation from the gentiles and their destiny as victims of anti-Semitism may not be an inevitability for all time.

The State of Israel is not the reincarnation of the ancient, theocratic Jewish commonwealths; nor is Saddam Hussein's Iraq, for all his posturing, a replay of the glory that was Babylon; nor does the restoration of Bethlehem and Nablus to Arab rule reprise the exploits of Saladin, who drove the Crusaders out of Palestine. Instead, as it approaches its 50th birthday, Israel offers up the real prospect of a safe and prosperous haven for Jews in their native territory, within a reasonably pacified Middle East.

At the same time, many Orthodox Jews fear the so-called "Americanisation" of Israel, its transformation into a modern, civil consumer society, a neo-Hellenised secular democracy in which Jewish values will be overrun by cable television, Tower Records, and McDonald's hamburgers. Many secular Jews are angered in turn by the continuance – owing to domestic political calculations going back to Ben-Gurion's time – of an Orthodox hegemony, through the established Chief Rabbinate, over many aspects of private life in Israel, including marriage, divorce, conversion and burial.

If King Hussein of Jordan could eulogise Yitzhak Rabin in Jerusalem, if Yasser Arafat could pay a condolence call on Rabin's widow, the time surely seems ripe for Israeli Jews to learn to talk to each other. Many Israelis, including many in the modern Orthodox camp, renewed their call after Rabin's murder for a separation of religion and state in Israel. The ability of Orthodox rabbis to coerce secular Jews into conformity was bad enough in Uriel da Costa's time; today it perpetuates a crippling climate of resentment and polarisation that inhibits communication among Jews.

The irreligious Rabin, as the veteran Israeli educator Gidon Elad – a secular kibbutznik – wrote in December 1995, in a highly penetrating piece in the *Ha'aretz* newspaper, was tragically unable "to internalise the feeling of great disaster that existed in religious settler circles. The political aspect of their struggle was and remains the external dimension of their struggle." Indeed, with a few exceptions, virtually no one among the Labour leadership "knows how to speak with them in their language; and to speak their language includes the ability to challenge them in their language".

In the early twentieth century, such towering intellectual figures of secular Zionism as the poet Hayyim Nahman Bialik, the essayist Ahad Ha'am, and the philosopher Martin Buber forged a modern Jewish culture that "rebelled, out of empathy, against the world of

Jewish tradition from which they came". Modern secular Israelis must be taught by their educators, Elad said, "to speak Jewish" – "a Jewish language, I say, which has no connection with Orthodox life-experience. Even the secular among us must know, internalise, and create in the Jewish language."

To make this argument is not to suggest that Rabin brought about his own demise. It is, rather, a way of pleading for the good health of the Jewish future. The outpouring of grief for Rabin unleashed a great wave of spirituality and improvised religious ritual, especially among young Israelis, that if properly channelled, and combined with long-overdue educational reforms, can provide the basis for a new era of Jewish dialogue. Only if all Israelis can converse intelligently – and critically – with their rich and problematic Jewish past, will they be able to talk productively, and respectfully, with one another.

Appendix: Milestones 1922-1995

1922   Yitzhak Rabin born 1 March in Jerusalem to Russian-born parents, Nehemiah and Rosa Rubitzov.

1940   Graduates Kadoorie Agricultural School.

1941   Enlists in the Palmah, an underground Labour Zionist commando unit. Participates in World War II Allied raid into French Vichy-controlled Lebanon.

1945   As deputy commander of a Palmah operation, helps liberate 200 illegal immigrants from the British Atlit detention camp.

1947   Appointed deputy commander of the Palmah, under Yigal Allon.

1948   Commands the Harel Brigade in Operation Nahshon, which opens the road to besieged Jerusalem during Israel's War of Independence. The brigade captures the Jerusalem neigh-bourhoods of Sheikh Jarrah and Katamon. As operations chief on southern front, oversees conquest of Negev and Eilat. After declaration of the State of Israel, commands the Palmah operation ending in sinking of the *Altalena*, a ship carrying arms for the dissident Irgun Zvai Leumi. On 23 August, marries Leah Schlossberg.

1950   Named Israel Defence Forces head of operations, under Chief of Staff Yigael Yadin.

1953   Graduates from the Royal Staff College in Britain, and is promoted to major general in the IDF.

1956   Appointed commanding officer of the Northern Command.

1959   Named head of the IDF's General Staff branch.

1961 Appointed deputy Chief of Staff.

1964 Becomes IDF's seventh Chief of Staff.

1967 Leads Israel's forces in the Six Day War that erupts on 5 June and ends with a victorious Israel newly in control of East Jerusalem, the West Bank, the Gaza Strip, the Sinai Peninsula and the Golan Heights.

1968 Having left the army, is appointed ambassador to the United States.

1973 Returns to Israel and is elected to the Knesset as a member of the Labour Party. Appointed Minister of Labour by Prime Minister Golda Meir.

1974 Selected by Labour as Prime Minister to succeed Golda Meir, who steps down in the bitter aftermath of the 1973 Yom Kippur War.

1975 Signs interim peace agreement with Egypt.

1976 Authorises 4 July raid on Entebbe, Uganda, during which Israeli commandos rescue more than 100 Jews from a plane hijacked by Palestinians.

1977 Resigns as Prime Minister over illegal US bank account. Foreign Minister Shimon Peres assumes leadership of Labour, which loses election to right-wing Likud.

1979 Publishes autobiography, *The Rabin Memoirs*.

1984 Returns to government, serving for six years as Defence Minister in Labour–Likud coalitions.

1985 Presents proposal to government for IDF withdrawal from Lebanon and the creation of a security zone along Israel's northern border.

1987 Visiting the United States at the outbreak of the Intifada in December, is blamed for the slow reaction of the army to the uprising.

1988 Allegedly orders troops to break the bones of Palestinians in an effort to quash Intifada rioting.

1989 Publishes a programme for phased negotiations with the Palestinians, which is accepted by the government and forms the basis of the Madrid conference and the peace process that follows.

1992   Having replaced Peres as party leader, leads Labour to victory in the June election on a campaign promising to intensify peace efforts. Becomes Prime Minister on 13 July.

1993   Authorises secret negotiations with the PLO starting in January, which eventually lead to the Oslo peace accord. Shakes hands reluctantly with PLO Chairman Yasser Arafat at the White House on 13 September, sealing their joint Declaration of Principles – the framework accord providing for the phased granting of autonomy to the Palestinians of the West Bank and Gaza Strip.

1994   Signs Oslo I accord in Cairo on 4 May, granting self-rule to the Palestinians of Gaza and Jericho. Joins Jordan's King Hussein in Washington on 24 July to sign a declaration ending the 46-year state of war. Formal Israel-Jordan peace treaty signed 26 October. Awarded the Nobel Peace Prize with Arafat and Peres.

1995   Signs Oslo II agreement with Arafat at the White House on 28 September, expanding Palestinian self-rule in the West Bank. Assassinated after a peace rally in Tel Aviv on 4 November aged 73.

Notes

1: From Triumph to Tragedy – Eyewitness reporting from the final, fatal Tel Aviv rally was provided by *The Jerusalem Report*'s own Sharon Ashley and Peter Hirschberg. Other material describing the day of Rabin's death was gathered from coverage in the Israeli Hebrew-language daily newspapers – *Ha'aretz, Davar Rishon, Yediot Aharonot* and *Ma'ariv* – as well as from Israeli state television and the commercial Channel 2, and from witness testimony to the Shamgar Commission of inquiry into the killing. Rabin's driver, Menahem Damti, gave his account of the Prime Minister's final minutes in an interview with Channel 2 soon after the killing. Ronni Kempler's amateur video, filmed from the low, flat rooftop above the car park, captured the moment when Amir darted up to Rabin's back and opened fire. In charting the intensification of right-wing protest to Rabin's policies, reference was made to material published in *The Jerusalem Report* in the months before the assassination. The authors also interviewed Jean Frydman, co-organiser of the pro-peace rally; Raphy Weiner, Leah Rabin's tennis partner; and Rabin's good friend and one-time aide Niva Lanir.

2: Schooled in Battle – The authors interviewed Rabin's younger sister Rachel; Shabtai Reveth, who was at school with him: Uzi Narkiss, who served under him in the Palmah and the Israel Defence Forces: Niva Lanir (see above) and Ilana Tsur, director of a 1994 Israel Television documentary on the *Altalena* affair. Use was also made of Robert Slater's biography, *Rabin of Israel* (Robson Books, 1977), and Rabin's own *The Rabin Memoirs*, (Weidenfeld & Nicolson, 1979).

3: The Path to Victory – In addition to Central Command chief Narkiss, the authors interviewed Yeshayahu Gavish, who headed the Southern Command during the Six Day War; Israel Tal, the former head of the IDF's armoured corps; Mordechai Bar-On, chief army education officer during Rabin's term as Chief of Staff; Ruhama Hermon, who headed Rabin's office during this period; and Michael Elkins, the BBC's Israel correspondent at the time of the 1967 war and the first journalist to report Israel's assault on the Egyptian air force. The authors also relied on the Rabin and Slater books as well as *The Road to War: The Origin and Aftermath of the Arab–Israeli conflict*, by Walter Laqueur (Weidenfeld & Nicolson, 1969); *A History of the Israeli Army*, by Ze'ev Schiff (Straight Arrow Books, 1974); *Battling for Peace* by Shimon Peres (Weidenfeld & Nicolson, 1995); Encyclopedia Judaica (Keter Publishing House, Jerusalem); and *The Political Dictionary of the State of Israel*, edited by Susan Hattis Rolef (Jerusalem Publishing House, 1993).

4: An Unlikely Ambassador – Apart from the Rabin and Slater books, other invaluable written sources were *Personal Witness* by Abba Eban (G. P. Putnam's, 1990); *Decade of Decisions* by William Quandt (University of California, 1977); *My Life* by Golda Meir (G.P. Putnam's); and *The Arab–Israeli Wars* by Chaim Herzog (Random House). The authors also interviewed former Rabin embassy aide and adviser on Diaspora affairs Yehuda Avner; Paul Berger, a member of the Jewish Agency board of governors: former Israel Embassy aide Amos Eiran; former

Washington Post correspondent Yuval Elitzur; US philanthropist Max Fisher; columnist and *Moment* magazine founder Leonard Fein; former foreign ministry director general Mordechai Gazit; former Rabin personal assistant Hermon; former American Jewish Committee president Alfred Moses; Rabin's close friend Abe Pollin; former defence ministry adviser Nachman Shai; former US Undersecretary of State Joseph Sisco; and others who spoke on condition of anonymity.

5: Instant Prime Minister – The authors interviewed Dan Pattir, media adviser to Rabin and later Begin; Eiran, who was director general of the Prime Minister's Office during Rabin's first term; Yehuda Ben-Meir, at the time a leader of the National Religious Party's Young Guard and later deputy Foreign Minister; and Prof. Shlomo Avineri, of the Hebrew University of Jerusalem, director general of the foreign ministry during part of Rabin's first term.

6: The Long Road Back – The authors interviewed deputy Education Minister Micha Goldman; Dov Goldstein, the former *Ma'ariv* writer and editor, and Rabin ghostwriter; former IDF Chief of Staff Moshe Levi; former defence ministry adviser Shai; Lanir (see above) and eternal defence ministry senior aide Haim Yisraeli. Written sources included both the Rabin and Slater books, and *Israel's Lebanon War* by Ehud Ya'ari and Ze'ev Schiff (Simon & Schuster, 1984).

7: Fighting the Intifada – The authors interviewed Dan Shomron, Chief of Staff during the Intifada years; Amram Mitzna, head of the Central Command during the Intifada; Ze'ev Schiff, co-author of *Intifada* (Simon & Schuster, 1989) and a leading defence analyst; and Sari Nusseibeh, a Palestinian leader and political thinker. Additional insights came from Ehud Ya'ari, co-author of *Intifada*, Arab affairs editor for Israel TV and an associate editor of *The Jerusalem Report*.

8: Second Chance at the Top – Considerable material on Rabin's return to power was drawn from the pages of *The Jerusalem Report* magazine, including interviews with Rabin, Peres and other senior officials, and reportage from the campaign trail. The authors also interviewed Gad Ben-An and Oded Ben-Ami, both one-time spokesmen for Rabin; Rabin's bureau chief Eitan Haber; and his adviser Kalman Gayer. Use was also made of Robert Slater's biography and David Landau's *Piety and Power* (Secker & Warburg, 1993).

9: Making Peace – *The Jerusalem Report*'s own coverage was integral to this chapter. The authors also interviewed Uri Savir, director-general of the foreign ministry; Yossi Beilin, minister in the Prime Minister's Office; Shlomo Gur, a Beilin adviser; and other sources cited above. Published sources included *Gaza First* by Jane Corbin (Bloomsbury, 1994), *Battling for Peace* by Shimon Peres (Weidenfeld and Nicolson, 1995) and *Through Secret Channels* by Mahmoud Abbas (Garnet Publishing, 1995).

10: Israel Transformed – The authors interviewed Amir Hayek, director of the Israel Export Institute; Yossi Nitzani, former director of the Government Corporations Authority; Finance Minister Avraham Shochat; Prof. Jacob Frenkel, Governor of the Bank of Israel; Minister of Industry and Trade Micha Harish; Ilan Flatto, Rabin's economic adviser; Dan Propper, head of the Israel Manufacturers Association; Ya'acov Levy, deputy director general for communications at the foreign ministry; Dov Lautman, Rabin's special envoy on industrial development; and Ohad Ben-Efrat, an official at the Bank of Israel.

11: The Private Prime Minister – Interviews were conducted with Lanir, who was Rabin's campaign spokesperson in 1981 and 1984 and also organised the Labour party memorial for Rabin after his death; Weiner, general manager of Jerusalem's Sheraton Plaza hotel; Yehuda Ben-Meir, Dan Pattir, Amos Eiran and Kalman Gayer – all cited above. Clippings from *Yediot Aharonot, Ma'ariv* and *Ha'aretz* were also invaluable.

12: Leader of the Jewish People? – Invaluable information in Yitzhak Rabin's relationship with AIPAC and his conflicts with the Zionist Organization of America was gleaned from articles in *The Jerusalem Report* by the magazine's Washington correspondent, Jonathan Broder. Further information on the American reaction to Rabin's peace policies came from the work of the magazine's Vince Beiser in New York. Also quoted is an interview with Rabin by *The Report*'s editor-in-chief Hirsh Goodman, which appeared in July 1994. Among those who spoke to the authors about their dealings with Rabin on Diaspora relations were former adviser Avner; Harry Wall, director of the Israel office of the Anti-Defamation League; Neal Sher, executive director of AIPAC; Lenny Davis, director of AIPAC's Israel office; Leonard Fein; Avi Becker, director of the World Jewish Congress's Israel office; former Rabin aide Hermon; Rabin's close American friends Abe Pollin and Max Fisher; Rabin's former defence ministry adviser Shai; former American Jewish Committee president Moses: and Seymour Reich, former director of the Conference of Presidents of Major American Jewish Organizations. Other material was provided by Israeli and American Jewish officials who preferred not to be quoted by name.

13: Rise of the Radicals – The history of the religious right's thinking was based in part on *Haketz Hameguleh Umidinat Hayehudim* by Aviezer Ravitsky (Messianism, Zionism and Jewish Religious Radicalism) (Am Oved, 1993), the late Uriel Tal's study *Yesodot Hameshihut Hapolitit Beyisrael* and writings of the Rabbis Kook and their followers. Material on Gush Emunim's development was drawn, among numerous sources, from *Political Violence in Israel* by Ehud Sprinzak (published in Hebrew by the Jerusalem Institute for Israel Studies, 1995) and an interview with him, and *Dear Brothers* by Hagal Segal (Beit-Shamal, 1988). *Nekudah* the monthly settlers' journal, was a valuable source. Material on Kahanism came from Meir Kahane's own writings, news reports at the time of the Hebron massacre of 1994, an interview then with Ehud Sprinzak, and additional sources. For the development of opposition to the Oslo process, interviews with Yisrael Harel, chairman of the Council of Settlements in Judaea, Samaria and the Gaza District, were very helpful, along with reports from Hebrew newspapers. Material was also taken from *The Report*'s own coverage of settlement activity, the Kahanist movement, and the rabbis' ruling against evacuating settlements.

14: God's Assassin – Biographical material on Yigal Amir and his family was compiled from interviews carried out by *Jerusalem Report* staff, especially Yuval Lion, and from newspaper accounts and interviews in the first weeks after the assassination. The authors interviewed Rabbi Mordechai Greenberg at Kerem B'Yavneh yeshivah, and teaching staff and fellow pupils at Bar-Ilan University.

Reference was also made of the published indictments of Yigal and Hagai Amir and Dror Adani, and to Yigal Amir's statements in court.

15: A Complete Collapse of Security – For previous examples of violence by Jews against Jews, the authors were assisted by *A History of Israel*, vol. II; *From the Aftermath of the Yom Kippur War* by Howard M. Sacher (Oxford University Press, 1987), and the American Jewish Committee's American Jewish Year Books of 1995 and 1996. The authors also drew extensively on newspaper and television coverage of the security failures leading up to the rally and on the night itself, and on testimony to the Shamgar Commission of Inquiry. Other information on the security lapses and on conspiracy theories was provided by sources who wished to remain anonymous.

16: From Man to Myth – *The Jerusalem Report*'s own coverage of the impact on the Israeli public of Rabin's death – and especially the issues of 30 November and 14 December 1995 – provided the basis for much of this chapter. *The Report*'s own staff provided coverage of the funeral and of the various soul-searching gatherings and memorial services that followed. The authors also interviewed right-wing activists Ya'akov Novick and Nadia Matar, and other material was drawn from the Hebrew press.

17: An Unfinished Mission – Much of the material for this chapter was provided by sources who spoke on condition of anonymity. On the record, the authors interviewed Uri Dromi, director of the Government Press Office under Rabin. Additionally *The Report*'s interviews with Rabin were helpful, and its cover story on the West Bank redeployment, "Trusting Arafat" in the issue of 2 November 1995. Rabin's speech presenting the Oslo II accords in the Knesset on 5 October 1995, also served as a reference.

Afterword: Echoes of the Past – Among the sources that proved valuable were *The Hanukkah Anthology*, edited by Philip Goodman (Jewish Publication Society); *A History of the Jewish People* edited by H. H. Ben-Sasson (Harvard University Press); *A History of the Jews* by Paul Johnson (Harper & Row); *A History of the Jews in Christian Spain*, vol. 1, by Yitzhak Baer (Jewish Publication Society); Avi Katzman's piece "An Everyday Affair, Killing the Informers" (*Ha'aretz*, 7 December 1995); *Mystics and Missionaries: The Jews in Palestine, 1799–1840*, by Sherman Lieber (University of Utah Press); *Eliezer Ben-Yehuda in Prison*, edited by Yehoshua Kaniel (Yad Izhak Ben-Zvi), *A History of Israel*, vol. I: *From the Rise of Zionism to Our Time*, by Howard M. Sacher (Alfred A. Knopf); Amos Elon's piece "No Hero, But Also No Traitor" (*Ha'aretz*, book supplement, 8 November 1995); a lecture by David Hartman at the Shalom Hartman Institute, Jerusalem, December 1995; Amin Maalouf's *The Crusades Through Arab Eyes* (Schocken); Gidon Elad's "Learning to Speak Jewish" (*Ha'aretz*, 6 December 1995).

About the authors

David Horovitz, the book's editor and co-writer, is the managing editor of *The Jerusalem Report*. Horovitz is the author of several of the magazine's main articles on the assassination of Rabin and its impact on Israeli society and has also written extensively on the logistics and impact of the peace process. Holder of the 1995 Bnai Brith international award for journalism (for an article on the aftermath of the 1994 Buenos Aires Jewish community centre bombing), he writes many of the magazine's cover stories, and has also written from Israel for newspapers all over the world, including *The Irish Times, The Independent, The Financial Times* and *The Guardian*.

Hirsh Goodman, editor-in-chief of *The Jerusalem Report*, wrote the prologue to the book. Before founding *The Report* in 1990, he was the strategic fellow at the Washington Institute, the defence correspondent of *The Jerusalem Post*, a contributing editor to *US News and World Report*, the Israel correspondent for *The Sunday Times* and a regular columnist for the *New Republic*. He has written two books on strategic issues (*The Future Battlefield and the Arab-Israel Conflict* was published by Transaction) and about a dozen documentary films. He lectures around the world, has appeared on Nightline, the McNeil-Lehrer News Hour, and appears regularly on CNN and CBS, as well as the BBC.

The other co-authors of the book are:

Calev Ben-David, the senior editor for arts at *The Report*, is a former Israeli correspondent for *Variety*, and former arts and film critic of *The Jerusalem Post*. He has also written extensively on Israel-Diaspora relations.

Gershom Gorenberg, senior editor (Op-ed) at *The Report*, has written extensively on religion and Israeli politics, and on the radical right, for *The Report* and American newspapers and magazines.

David B. Green, literary editor of *The Report*, writes on a variety of subjects for the magazine. Before moving to Israel, he was for a long time on the staff of *The New Yorker*, and his writing has appeared there, as well as *The New York Times* and other journals.

Peter Hirschberg, a senior writer at *The Report*, has been with the magazine since its founding five years ago, and has written particularly about right-wing and settler opposition to the peace process, and on the logistics of the unfolding autonomy accords.

Avi Hoffmann, production editor at *The Report*, is a former defence reporter for *The Jerusalem Post*, who covered Rabin's career as Defence Minister in the second half of the 1980s.

Ronnie Hope, chief copy editor of *The Jerusalem Report* joined the magazine at its inception, after 25 years at the *Jerusalem Post*, where he worked as chief news editor. He has also written on military and diplomatic affairs.

Isabel Kershner, senior editor (Middle East), at *The Report*, writes on Palestinian affairs for the magazine, and has written extensively on the impact of the peace process in the West Bank and Gaza. Kershner was the first Israeli journalist to interview Yasser Arafat and Jordan's Crown Prince Hassan.

Margo Lipschitz Sugarman, senior writer at *The Report*, covers economic affairs for the magazine, and wrote extensively on the economic rejuvenation of Israel under Rabin.

Tom Sawicki, a senior writer at *The Report*, has written extensively for the magazine on the domestic aspects of Rabin's premiership, on the strains in Israeli society, and on Rabin's relationship with Diaspora Jewry.

Stuart Schoffman, a *Jerusalem Report* associate editor, writes a regular column for the magazine. He has also worked at *Fortune, Time* and *The Los Angeles Herald Examiner* and worked as a screenwriter in Hollywood and Israel. His most recent film is "The Wordmaker", a drama for Israel Television about Eliezer Ben-Yehuda. In 1993, he was awarded the first Wolf Matsdorf prize of the Bnai Brith World Centre for his columns in *The Jerusalem Report* about Israel-Diaspora relations.

Hanan Sher, a senior editor of *The Report*, has written about Israel and Israeli politics for the past 30 years. Before moving to Israel, Sher wrote for the *St. Petersburg Times*, the *Atlanta Journal* and the *National Tennessean*.

Eric Silver, a senior writer at *The Report*, is a veteran, award winning journalist who has also written for *The Guardian, The Observer, The Jewish Chronicle, The Financial Times* and *The Independent*. His books include a biography of the late Israeli Prime Minister Menachem Begin (*Begin: The Haunted Prophet*, Weidenfeld & Nicolson, 1984) and *The Book of the Just: The Unsung Heroes Who Rescued Jews from Hitler* (Weidenfeld & Nicolson, 1992), which won a Christopher Award in 1993. He too has covered Israeli politics in general, and Rabin's career in particular, for many years.

Leslie Susser, diplomatic correspondent of *The Report*, interviewed Rabin many times over a period of 20 years, and closely followed his entire political career. Susser, who has covered the peace process from its infancy for *The Report*, has a PhD in modern history from Oxford University and is a seasoned public speaker.

Index

INDEX

Goldstein, Dov, vii, 26, 41, 79, 83, 146, 148–9
Gonzalez, Felipe, 210
Goren, Aliza, 13
Goren, Shlomo, 177, 180
Gov, Gidi, 10
Graham, Katherine, 57–8
Greenberg, Mordechai, 184, 217
Grossman, Steven, 160
Gruenwald, Malkiel, 238
Grunzweig, Emil, 195
Gur, Mordechai, 42–3, 70, 72–3, 133
Guri, Haim, 70
Gutman, Motti, 14

Habash, George, 71
Haber, Eitan, vii, 13–15, 147, 149, 213, 221–4, 227–9
Haberman, Clyde, 122
Hacohen, Mordechai Ben-Hillel, 17
Haddad, Wadia, 71
Haetzni, Elyakim, vii
Halevy, Ephraim, 127
Halevy, Shlomo, 198–9
Hamamy, Aharon, 208
Hammer, Zevulun, 70
Haran, Smadar, 122
Harel, Yisrael, vii, 173–4, 179
Harish, Micha, vii, 105
Harkabi, Yehoshafat, 35, 196–7
Harman, Abe, 46, 157
Har-Segor, Michael, 202
Har-Shefi, Margalit, 189
Hartman, David, 239
Hassan, Crown Prince of Jordan, 127–8
Hassan II, King of Morocco, 66–7, 210
Hayek, Amir, vii
Hecht, Abraham, 161
Hermon, Ruhama, vii, 40, 47–8, 156
Herzog, Chaim, 35, 102, 105, 171
Hirschfeld, Yair, 115–7, 119

Hod, Mordechai, 42
Hoffmann, Avi, vii
Holst, Johan Jörgen, 119–21
Holtzman, Navah, 185–6
Humphrey, Hubert, 49
Hussein, King of Jordan, 33, 51, 53–4, 66, 92, 99, 101, 123–5, 127–9, 135, 209, 211–2, 240
Hussein, Saddam, 92, 240
Husseini, Faisal, 100, 117, 120, 188

Ibrahim, Muhsen, 120
Inbar, Avital, vii
Indyk, Martin, 13, 128, 138, 197, 224

Jabotinsky, Vladimir (Ze'ev), 170, 237
Jackson, Henry, 55
Jarring, Gunnar, 52
Jibril, Ahmad, 88–9
Johnson, Lyndon, 39, 41–2, 48–9, 51
Johnson, Paul, 234

Kahalani, Eitan, 203–4
Kahalani, Yehoyada, 203–4
Kahane, Meir, 171–2, 199, 206
Kaner, Yaron, 186–7
Kastner, Rudolph, 238–9
Katz, Aharon, 185
Katzin, Ronnie, 5
Katzir, Ephraim, 77
Katzman, Avi, vii
Katzover, Tzvi, 176
Kempler, Ronni, 190–1, 200–2, 204
Kennedy, John F., 54, 215
Kessar, Yisrael, 105–6
Kigal, Shaike, 207
King, Martin Luther, 215
Kissinger, Henry, 49–52, 54, 63–5, 68–9
Klein, Morton, 160–1
Kook, Avraham Yitzhak, 167–9, 173, 177, 237
Kook, Tzvi Yehudah, 68–70, 167–8, 177, 217